Praise for MONOPOLY:
The World's Most Famous Game—And How It Got That Way

"Game lovers will buy into *Monopoly*." —USA *Today*

"[Orbanes] brings to this book a huge enthusiasm for Monopoly and seemingly everything connected with it." —*Los Angeles Times*

"Orbanes displays not only a deft touch with his pen but an encyclopedic knowledge of his subject." —*New York Post*

"Enough Monopoly trivia to tickle the capitalist impulses of its most fanatic devotees." —*Seattle Post-Intelligencer*

"Brings hope to board game aficionados and edification to anyone interested in how the great game of real estate got its start."
—*Weekly Standard*

"Interesting tidbits of *Monopoly* history will likely be surprising to many." —*Roanoke Times*

"Entertaining . . . The people who developed the game, who study its history, and who collect memorabilia are as interesting as those who play it." —*Richmond Times-Dispatch*

"Goes beyond the game's chronology and brings the familiar board to life." —MSNBC.com

"A wealth of material about the evolution of the Monopoly game, the personalities involved, the historical context, the tournament scene, collectors, and much more."
—*Game & Puzzle Collectors Quarterly*

MONOPOLY®

THE WORLD'S MOST FAMOUS GAME—AND HOW IT GOT THAT WAY

PHILIP E. ORBANES

DA CAPO PRESS
A Member of the Perseus Books Group

Designed by Trish Wilkinson
Set in 11.5-point Goudy by the Perseus Books Group

Cataloging-in-Publication data for this
book is available from the Library of Congress.

First Da Capo Press edition 2006
First Da Capo Press paperback edition 2007
HC: ISBN-13: 978-0-306-81489-1; ISBN-10: 0-306-81489-7
PBK: ISBN-13: 978-0-306-81574-4; ISBN-10: 0-306-81574-5

Published by Da Capo Press
A Member of the Perseus Books Group
http://www.dacapopress.com

Da Capo Press books are available at special discounts for bulk purchases in the U.S. by corporations, institutions, and other organizations. For more information, please contact the Special Markets Department at the Perseus Books Group, 2300 Chestnut Street, Suite 200, Philadelphia, PA 19103, or call (800) 255-1514, or e-mail special.markets@perseusbooks.com.

TRADEMARKS

TRIVIAL PURSUIT is a trademark of Horn Abbot Ltd. used in connection with games distributed and sold in the United States under exclusive license to Hasbro. © 2005 Horn Abbot Ltd. Used without permission.

CRACKER JACK is a trademark of Frito-Lay North America, Inc.

LEXICON is a trademark of Winning Moves International.

NASCAR is a trademark of NASCAR.

PING PONG is a trademark of SOP Services Inc.

THE SIMPSONS is a trademark of Twentieth-Century Fox.

STAR WARS is a trademark of Lucasfilm Ltd.

PICTIONARY is a trademark of Mattel.

TRIBOND is a trademark of TriBond Enterprises.

BANKRUPTCY

A player who is bankrupt, that is, one who owes more than he can pay, must turn over to his Creditor all that he has of value, and retire from the game.

—Excerpt from the rules of MONOPOLY
written by George S. Parker, 1935

I dedicate this book to all who have helped me flourish . . . in the game.

Great engines turn on small pivots.
English Proverb

CONTENTS

ACKNOWLEDGMENTS

The preparation of this book was greatly enhanced by the kind help of the following people.

First and foremost, Chris Williamson, who read every page of the early drafts and contributed significantly to the accuracy of the facts presented, and often to the facts themselves. When not preaching in his church, Chris is an avid student of history, particularly the history of Monopoly. The writing of this manuscript was made far easier by his wit, dedication, and timeliness. My sincere thanks, Chris.

I also express deep appreciation for the help of Randolph Barton and Victor Watson who lived the story at their respective firms—Parker Brothers and John Waddington Ltd. In the 1970s, they founded the Monopoly championships that continue to this day. Matt McNally vividly recalled the 2003–2004 tournaments and provided details of his method. Merwin Goldsmith graciously provided details and photos of his role as Mr. Monopoly, while Heather Campbell of USAopoly kindly provided the photos and list of her firm's games that appear in the appendix.

I am indebted to several collectors and historians for their shared knowledge. Anne Williams graciously provided me with many early trade ads and articles. The Forbes Gallery provided access, information, and permission to reproduce photographs of handmade games in their collection. Albert Veldhuis, who maintains a magnificent website of Monopoly games from around the world, provided knowledge I needed concerning several of the game's European versions. In alphabetical order, Spartaco Albaterelli, Bill Boyd, Adriana Chiari, Jeff Cramer (Curator of Collections of the Thoreau Institute of Walden Woods), Andrew Donaldson (Chair, The Good Life Center), Dan Glimne, Marco Gusmeroli, Michel Matschoss, Thomas Forsyth, Ken Koury, Dave Sadowski, Jennifer Tremblay, Tim Walsh, Bruce Whitehill, Barbara Whitney, and Marc Winters were unsparing in their help. Special thanks to my wife, Anna, for her patience and understanding; my agent, Rob McQuilkin, for his steady guidance; my editor at Da Capo Press, Bob Pigeon, who saw the vision of this book and kept me on course; as well as my copyeditor, Chrisona Schmidt, project editor, Erin Sprague, and book designer, Trish Wilkinson.

I also pay my respects to three who have left us: Robert Barton, former president of Parker Brothers, who shared his memories with me on several occasions in 1987–1988; Sid Sackson, who kindled my interest in the history of Monopoly when we first met in 1969; and Anita Orbanes, my mother, who provided encouragement through so many years.

This historical narrative solely reflects my experiences, observations, and opinions, and may or may not be consistent with those of Hasbro, the owner of the Monopoly game.

INTRODUCTION
PITNEY'S PLAN

The white beach stretched for eight miles, washed clean by dark blue waters, sparkling under a bright sun. The air was balmy, neither humid nor fly infested, as it was on the mainland visible across the bay from atop the dune where Richard Osborne addressed a small group of regional capitalists, trying to persuade them to part with their money.

Windblown sand stung the eyes of these city men, dressed uncomfortably in wool suits and bowler hats—real estate investors; glass, pipe, and iron manufacturers; and a lumber magnate. Their shoes were no match for the sand that infiltrated them during the climb up the dune on the island's only road—a footpath trampled by Lenni Lenape Indians who had named this isle Absecon ("little water") when they summered here long before.

Osborne figured the Indians knew a good thing when they saw it. Now the time had come for Americans everywhere to follow in their footsteps. The capitalists, however, were distracted by reality—the island was virtually deserted. Only seven houses had been built on it. Osborne hurried his pitch. If these fine men would agree to back his scheme, he would transform this virginal isle into a resort city, only sixty miles, as the crow flies, from the noise and smoke of the nation's second largest metropolis, Philadelphia.

Osborne knew the clean Jersey air and warm Atlantic waters would attract thousands here each summer, carried by a railroad he would build. Someone asked how a rail line could be built across the marshland and the bay. Osborne replied, "Leave that to me." The group acquiesced; Osborne's reputation preceded him. Engineer extraordinaire, he had helped build Chicago and linked it by rail to the rest of the nation. More recently, he helped design and start several cities west of the Mississippi. Yes, Richard Osborne had the skill to build a rail line linking Philadelphia to Absecon Island. Yes, he had a knack for building cities. But three questions still nagged his audience on this fine spring day in 1852 . . .

Would the city make money?

Would merchants and laborers be willing to settle here?

And what, by the way, would the city be called?

Osborne said yes in response to the first two questions. To the third he replied, "Atlantic City."

This name, he proclaimed, would create interest in the "minds of men throughout the union." He revealed how his benefactor, a local physician named Jonathan Pitney, had created a plan whereby its streets would be named after the nation's thirty-one states and its north–south avenues after oceans and seas, to envision the entire globe.

Illinois . . . Pennsylvania . . . Vermont . . . Mediterranean . . . Pacific.

The would-be investors liked the proposed name for the place, and they especially liked the imagery evoked by the thoroughfares. One commented that the names had a "rather universal appeal." Osborne shook their hands and promised that Atlantic City would become the great Victorian American resort.

In June 1852, thirty-eight subscribers purchased 10,000 shares of stock in Osborne's railroad company. Two years later, the first train rolled into Atlantic City's freshly painted station on Arkansas Avenue, packed with tourists. Twelve shops and boarding houses greeted them, along with the city's first hotel. Many more would follow.

Richard Osborne and Jonathan Pitney did not endure long enough to see their city become known as the World's Playground. They could not have imagined its subsequent fall from grace when airliners replaced trains and carried vacation travelers to more distant and exotic places, leaving Osborne's brainchild to be reborn as the Las Vegas of the East Coast.

But what would have blown their sandy socks off was the amazing growth of The Game. The one whose game board would bear spaces named after the streets and avenues envisioned by Jonathan Pitney, and would go on to bear the names of cities around the globe, and would be played by hundreds of millions of people.

The Monopoly game.

Monopoly's long journey to fame arguably began on this day in 1852. This American odyssey would make stops in cities like Washington, D.C., New York City, Chicago, and Indianapolis, eventually returning to Atlantic City and Philadelphia before a firm in Salem, Massachusetts, offered it to the American public from coast to coast.

I was born just seven miles from Atlantic City and encountered Monopoly for the first time at age eight. It seemed logical to me that the game's playing spaces were named after the one city I came to know as a child. I played it, and it changed my life. Inspired by it, I became a game inventor and later a game industry executive.

Forty-nine years later, in 2004, I found myself in Tokyo, representing the game to the world.

Thirty-eight nations had sent their champions to compete here, including several once confined behind the Iron Curtain, where the game had been banned. The lavish tournament took place inside a sleek new hotel that moved during a mild earthquake at the tournament's beginning and stood defiant against a raging typhoon at tourney's end.

Antonio Fernandez of Spain was ultimately crowned the new world champion. Reporters from around the globe sprang into action.

After the match, I recalled the many tournaments I had judged during the past twenty-five years—the people, young and old, from many walks of life and many nations, who came together to celebrate this amazing game. But somehow this tournament gripped me more than the others.

I found myself contemplating the enormity of the event, held inside a glittering ballroom decorated with images of the game's famous mascot—Mr. Monopoly—dressed in a kimono sitting cross-legged before a Rising Sun.

The union of disparate cultures at this tournament symbolized, to me, how far the game had come since its predecessor was invented a century ago outside America's capital city, half a world away from where we sat.

Everything I had come to know about the Monopoly game since my childhood flashed through my mind—where it came from, how it intertwined with economic history, how it taught people to navigate real life, and how it has helped bring the world a little closer.

I found myself pondering why it is the quintessential game of American origin and how it had fixed my career path.

This book is the result of what I've learned about the world's most famous game.

1

MAGIE'S MOTHER EARTH

1903–1910

Monopoly had a predecessor that I discovered during my junior year of college when I met Sid Sackson—a civil engineer who lived with his family in a row house in the Bronx. Sid was finalizing the manuscript for his first book, *A Gamut of Games*, and I was in New York City representing my first game company (Gamescience Corporation) at Toy Fair—the industry's national trade show. Sid appeared at my booth in the Statler Hilton Hotel, and I learned that he had invented many of the games my fraternity brothers and I played, including our favorite—a hotel acquisition game named Acquire. I enthusiastically told Sid about Cartel, a business acquisition game I was designing, and mentioned its superiority to Monopoly.

Sid's eyes lit up. He had spent endless hours searching the files of old game patents while doing research for his most recent book and had found one that pertained to a turn-of-the-century financial game. This, he told me, I had to see, and then he invited me to his home for dinner.

Sid maintained a neatly archived collection of games and documents in a spare bedroom that served as his reference library. His bookshelf bespoke an intense interest in the history of games. Sid had even taught

Magie's Mother Earth

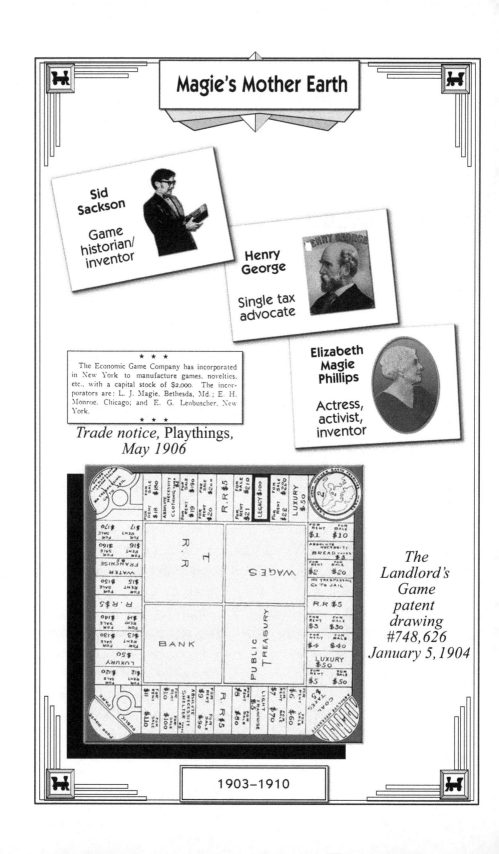

Sid Sackson

Game historian/ inventor

Henry George

Single tax advocate

★ ★ ★

The Economic Game Company has incorporated in New York to manufacture games, novelties, etc., with a capital stock of $2,000. The incorporators are: L. J. Magie, Bethesda, Md.; E. H. Monroe, Chicago; and E. G. Lenbuscher, New York.

★ ★ ★

Trade notice, Playthings, *May 1906*

Elizabeth Magie Phillips

Actress, activist, inventor

The Landlord's Game patent drawing #748,626 January 5, 1904

1903–1910

himself several languages in order to read old game texts from Europe. After allowing me to examine the contents of his private sanctuary, Sid withdrew from a file cabinet a copy of the patent for a business game created in 1903, the Landlord's Game. Sid produced a chart he had compiled comparing its features with those of the famous Monopoly game.

"Every great game has precedents," Sid offered. "Acquire actually began life as a world conquest game based on Lotto" (Lotto being the forerunner of Bingo). "I even used a Lotto checklist and disks for my first version. Eventually I realized that people liked making money more than fighting wars, so I changed its theme."

Having played Sid's game countless times in college, I found it easy to connect the rows and columns of its board spaces and the number/letter identities of its hotels to Bingo. No matter. Sid's application of them worked *great*; Acquire was both fun and compelling. In fact I myself had adopted the idea of rows and columns when laying out the companies on Cartel's game board. For the first time, I realized I was benefiting from a principle in a long-established game.

From Sid I learned that Monopoly was initially published in 1933, three decades after the Landlord's Game was created. As Sackson opined, "That's a lot of time to get it right." We digressed for a moment to lament the modern inventor's plight: pressure to earn a living typically compresses the time span between inspiration for a new game and publication to less than two years.

In my spare time I was studying the history of classic games. I drew a parallel between Monopoly and other perennials—like bridge, rummy, Scrabble, backgammon, Parcheesi—all of which had evolved or benefited from years, even centuries, of play-testing and evolution from similar-playing games.

My thoughts returned to the patent in Sid's hands. I told him I didn't fully grasp what a patent was. Sid carefully explained the meaning of intellectual property—patents, copyrights, and trademarks.

Patents are rights granted by the federal government to the originator of a physical invention or process. A utility patent provides exclusive rights to make, sell, and use the invention for seventeen years. A design patent endures for fourteen years and protects only the appearance of an object.

Copyrights are rights granted by the federal copyright office to protect a particular expression of an idea but not the idea itself. In the case of a game, this pertains to its original graphic elements and its rules. However, modifying a set of rules for use in a similar game without infringing on the original is easy to do.

Trademarks are words and symbols that identify products and services to consumers. The state or federal government can register trademarks. To be valid, a mark must be used in commerce, not just applied to a product for local or personal use. A company improves its rights to a trademark in direct proportion to the geographical scope and duration of its use, as well as the manner of utilization.

I looked again at Sid's photocopy and learned that a woman named Lizzie Magie (pronounced Magee) had filed a patent for the Landlord's Game in 1903. According to the application, she was living in Brentwood, Maryland (a mile north of Washington, D.C.).

Who was she?

Sid obtained one reference to her (courtesy of a friend)—a 1936 press release issued by Parker Brothers, the nation's best-known game company. The release acknowledged her contribution to the Monopoly game and described her as "possessed with an inventive genius for games." The release further explained that Mrs. Elizabeth M[agie] Phillips since childhood had been a devotee of the so-called single tax because her father was a disciple of Henry George, the great single taxer. Mrs. Phillips believed that "a game touching the principles of the single tax" would be an admirable amusement. It related how she tried to patent her idea and how Parker Brothers came to acquire it.

Sid was perplexed. Parker Brothers first published Monopoly in 1935, a full fourteen years after the claims in this patent would have passed by law into the public domain. The press release resolved Sid's concern (and provoked a new one) by mentioning a 1924 patent that Lizzie had subsequently filed. Busy with his job and his book, Sid lamented a lack of time to search for it. The Parker Brothers release went on to describe Lizzie as "a lady of brilliant accomplishment and an actress of no mean ability." She was acclaimed for the "brightness of her personal characteristics and sense of humor."

Sid and I returned to our business games, but I remained curious about Elizabeth Magie Phillips. If she was a mystery, perhaps the man who inspired her wasn't. I turned to my college library in hopes of learning more about this man, Henry George.

George was born in 1839 to a working-class family in Philadelphia. He left school early and made his way around the world to Australia, whose productive cities and peoples made a positive, uplifting impression on him. He then traveled to India, only to become unnerved by the country's urban blight. Cities like Calcutta were decaying, over-populated, and besieged by poverty. The contrast between the two nations influenced his later theories.

After returning to the States at age nineteen, George got caught up in the California gold rush, married, and endured poverty for several years. He tried his hand at prospecting, compositing, and finally journalism. He became a reporter for the *San Francisco Post*, where he found his knack for writing. He wrote an article exposing the poor treatment of Chinese laborers imported to build the new railroads. He also exposed the seizure of land by the railroad monopolists intent on profiting to the fullest from the economic expansion they were engineering.

In the 1860s and 1870s, George wrote about the paradox of nineteenth-century America: modern society and its great progress had also created great poverty. Why?

Henry George concluded that the cause—and the solution—lay with the monopolists who controlled industry and the landlords who owned the nation's real estate. Those who owned the deeds controlled the game to the detriment of everyone else. These new business leaders were referred to as moguls, barons, and trust makers. Collectively they were *monopolists*. The word *monopoly,* of Greek origin, means "exclusive seller." Their goal was to set prices and rents arbitrarily by eliminating competition through economy of scale, thereby controlling an entire industry or gaining a stranglehold on the land.

In 1879 George compiled his theories into a book, *Progress and Poverty*. It was a best-seller for many years, trailing only the Bible and Mark Twain's most popular works. In it Henry outlined his theory of how land, labor, and capital produce wealth. Land ownership yields rent, labor produces wages, and capital earns interest. Taxation is the government's means of collecting a percentage of its citizens' wealth. How much the government collects, from where, and how it spends the proceeds determine the health of the economic system the government sponsors.

Henry George concluded that the only worthy tax is a levy on landowners because they unjustly profit from the increasing value of their holdings by charging higher and higher rents. Thus was born his idea for a "single tax."

Thanks to the disparities of the Industrial Age, George's ideas began to find favor with readers and scholars. In 1880 he moved his family east to New York City. Six years later, he ran for mayor as the candidate of the United Labor Party. He came in second against a Democrat named Abram S. Hewitt, but easily outpaced a little-known Republican named Theodore Roosevelt who came in third.

Despite his loss, George's campaign triggered a national network of single tax clubs, with the New York *Standard* as their mouthpiece. George devoted himself to promoting the single tax within its pages and through speeches across the country. He kept up a tireless pace even after suffering a mild stroke in 1890.

At age fifty-eight and in poor health, George agreed to run again for New York City mayor. As the campaign wound down, he suffered a severe stroke and died on October 20, 1897. His funeral attracted 100,000 mourners. Most of them were middle-class Progressives devoted to his ideals.

Among these may have been the diminutive Elizabeth Magie, whose father (a progressive newspaper publisher) had indoctrinated her in the merits of the single tax. Like her fellow Georgists, Lizzie carried on George's cause after his death. The single tax continued to gain adherents during the Progressive Era because the average man and woman began to feel that "fairness" and reform would become law. There was hope for a better code of conduct to be obeyed by society, business, and government.

The first of these measures was the Sherman Antitrust Act of 1890. In order to blunt business monopolies, it authorized federal action against any interstate "combination in the form of a trust or otherwise, or conspiracy, in restraint of trade." But this language ran smack into the ideals of free enterprise. Given the strength of its support—which dated from the nation's founders through the presidents preceding Theodore Roosevelt—a battle over the definition of trusts, combinations, and restraint of trade hit the courts that took five years to resolve. Finally in 1895 the Sherman Antitrust Act was unleashed. An attempt to break up the sugar monopoly was its first test. It failed. The Supreme Court ruled eight to one that while American Sugar Refining did control 98 percent of the nation's sugar refineries, its manufacturing was local—not interstate—and therefore not subject to congressional regulation. The fact that its goods were sold across state lines didn't seem relevant to the court. Manufacturers were jubilant over their apparent immunity to antitrust breakup. Their joy disappeared, however, when they came to grips with Teddy Roosevelt's determination.

Roosevelt's resolve for reform began before he was nominated to be William McKinley's vice president. New York's political bosses had secured this position for Roosevelt to get him out of their state because he was too intrusive for their taste, too inclined to challenge the status quo. To their dismay, fate handed Roosevelt the trump card. As president, he

President Roosevelt used a "big stick" to break up emerging monopolies in the early twentieth century.

restored order and confidence in the federal government and then launched a series of actions that shifted the Progressive movement into high gear. He set out to establish the authority of the Department of Commerce and Labor to regulate interstate commerce and monitor labor relations. He reaffirmed his belief in the Sherman Act by encouraging antitrust suits against the worst of the monopolists, including James Duke—who held a tobacco monopoly—as well as oil baron John Rockefeller, steel magnate Andrew Carnegie, and banker J. P. Morgan—who financed and assembled many powerful trusts, including U.S. Steel, which was formed after Morgan convinced Carnegie to sell his company to a consortium.

Morgan deserves special attention because he helped create many of the giant monopolies that dominated late-nineteenth-century business, including International Harvester, General Electric, and especially U.S. Steel. In an era when the federal government had no central bank, Morgan—with his powerful financial connections—bailed out the nation's economy whenever panic struck, most notably in 1893. Morgan typified much that was wrong (and right) about this freewheeling era. And his imposing appearance—accentuated by a white handlebar mustache, top hat, cane, and tuxedo—became an enduring icon for wealth and power.

One of Morgan's trusts was the Northern Securities Company, a railroad octopus that became Roosevelt's prime target. This time the Supreme Court narrowly sided with the government, upheld the Sherman Act, and ordered the breakup of Morgan's creation. Monopolies were dealt a telling blow. Roosevelt's soaring popularity inspired him onward. By 1903 trust-busting, monopolies, and the single tax were hot topics. All three came together to inspire a creative woman to design a unique game.

Born outside of Macomb, Illinois, in 1866, Elizabeth J. Magie divided her life between Washington, D.C., and Chicago, where in 1910 she married Albert Phillips. Lizzie worked as a public stenographer and had a knack for the written word. Her inventive genius manifested itself in the creation of the automatic carriage return for typewriters. In the process, she learned about patents and their importance in protecting ideas.

She had a gift for acting and, being wiry, could impersonate boys in so-called trouser roles. (At the time, children were typically not allowed inside theaters.) After she married Albert Phillips, she sometimes came to their door dressed as a lad and carried on a masquerade that lasted several minutes before he caught on.

In 1903 she set forth her idea for a game that replicated the causes and effects of the single tax. She hired John Ataul, an attorney, to draw it up and file the claims for her Landlord's Game at the U.S. Patent Office.

Her invention was strikingly different from popular games of this era, and her patent claims explained its educational merit. A patent application must make clear how its invention will be used and which of its features are unique and worthy of exclusive ownership. Lizzie Magie did so by supplying the rules to her game and providing an illustration of its board and pieces. She did not supply a model, which suggests her idea existed only on paper at the time. Lizzie set forth four "claims" for her game and petitioned for their protection. When the patent office granted her request, it became clear that she was the first person in American history to apply them to a board game.

The most significant of Lizzie's claims was the concept of a continuous path game—a board with corner spaces and intervening spaces uniquely identified by denomination, type, and color. In her day, virtually all game boards featured a start and an end space with spaces in between, but not a continuous path of spaces to be traversed time and again. (Today hundreds of games are based on this concept.)

Early in the twentieth century, nearly all commercial games were easy enough for a child to play. They relied on tried-and-true principles dressed up in a theme. Lizzie's game was mind-boggling for its day. Children (and likely most adults) could not be expected to grasp the play of the Landlord's Game because most had no knowledge of the intricacies of real estate, taxes, and finance.

The first corner of Lizzie's game board was identified as Mother Earth, the second as Absolute Necessity/Jail, the third as Public Park, the fourth as No Trespassing/Go to Jail. In between each corner lay spaces including lots, railroads, and utilities, plus a few additional spaces that required payment to the bank for penalties incurred. Players earned wages at Mother Earth by completing a circuit of the board. The game ended after five circuits, and the player with the highest asset total won. The utensils for the game included deeds, dice, money, notes, mortgages, luxury and legacy cards, and a bank.

There is no record of Lizzie's 1904 game being published, although early handmade copies are extant. If it had been produced, chances are it would have sold for one dollar, as did many board games of its era. Because of their importance to the Monopoly game, rules and claims for Lizzie's Landlord's Game are reproduced in the appendix.

Although Lizzie's game went unpublished, a small circle of devotees embraced it and made it their own. They lit the torch that revealed and preserved its existence.

Its journey would prove to be a remarkable adventure.

2

NEARING'S NEIGHBORHOOD
1910–1915

In the early twentieth century an experimental community, Arden, was established in Delaware. Its community charter was developed to prove Henry George's single tax principle. Arden residents had a handmade copy of Lizzie's game provided by the inventor herself (the copy still exists), which became a mainstay of enjoyment in the small but thriving town. Lizzie based it on a linen board she had fabricated after applying for her patent.

Just as Richard Osborne and Jonathan Pitney envisioned Atlantic City as a resort for weary Philadelphians, sculptor Frank Stephens and architect Will Price (Philadelphians themselves) envisioned Arden as a town that would redeem Philadelphians economically and socially. Both men were adherents of Henry George's single tax philosophy and William Morris's ideal of craft production and village life. With the aid of fellow single taxers, Stephens and Price hoped to put their beliefs into action and show others the merits of their economic model.

In 1900 they purchased a large farm and laid out the town of Arden on its soil. The plan, which featured a central communal space with

Nearing's Neighborhood

Scott Nearing

Economic radical

Socialists and single taxers of Arden Village

The Arden Village's 1905 Landlord's Game

The Sherk family's 1916 game board

1910–1915

rental lots around it, was designed to encourage citizens to mingle and exchange ideas.

The lots were leased for ninety-nine years. Renters were free to improve their lot as they chose and were assured that the amount they paid for rent and taxes would not be influenced by improvements. The proceeds collected would go to the town of Arden, not to Stephens or Price or any other individual.

Curious and committed people began to take up residence in Arden—including single taxers, nonconformists popularly known as bohemians, and utopian socialists, who found Arden ideally suited to their beliefs. They favored a classless society, organized labor, and collective control of business.

By contrast, capitalism requires private ownership of production, a marketplace free of governmental control, and individuals who are free to make their own choices. For example, if a worker doesn't like the job he has, he is free to look elsewhere. If a consumer does not like a particular hammer, he can buy a different brand and shop to find the best price. And if an entrepreneur makes a lot of money through his business, he deserves it, as long as he does so within the bounds of the law.

Unfairness abounded in early capitalism. Many decided it had to go, among them socialists like those attracted to Arden. Their political party counted many prominent Americans among its members. There may have been hundreds of thousands of single taxers, but there were far more members of the Socialist Party—enough to elect two of its members to Congress and mayors in over seventy cities around the country.

At Arden, socialists eventually held more leases than did single taxers. This was unforeseen by Stephens and Price, who had to mediate clashes between the two groups. But gradually common cause was found and Arden became a working success and spawned two related colonies—Ardentown and Ardencroft. I remember being taken to one as a boy and being told it was a "utopian place." To this day, the Ardens remain open, single tax communities.

According to early accounts, the renters in Arden were "advanced thinkers." Scott Nearing was a young, strong-willed economics professor at the Wharton School of Finance at the University of Pennsylvania. Nearing learned of Arden from Fred Whiteside, a "professional socialist" who had leased a lot there. Nearing, already a socialist at heart, was instantly attracted to the Arden lifestyle. In 1905, at age twenty-two, after graduating from both Wharton and Temple College, Nearing leased the last lot facing the common. It rented for thirteen dollars a year. He cleared the weeds from it and built a cabin where he spent summers and weekends for the next ten years. His neighbor happened to be author Upton Sinclair, whose novel *The Jungle*—an exposé of human abuse in the Chicago meatpacking industry—shocked the nation. Arden's regular town meetings and fireside discussion groups accelerated Nearing's transition to radical politics, liberalism, and causes supporting the underdog. Soon after he moved in, a forum was organized where he played the Landlord's Game.

At Wharton, the trim, vibrant Nearing became a favorite among the freshmen and sophomores in his economics classes. However, the school's trustees regarded Nearing with concern. While Nearing's students rallied to his favorite progressive causes—unregulated child labor and the unequal distribution of wealth and income in society—his superiors grew increasingly wary of him. Their financial supporters were the very men Nearing was denouncing.

One day Nearing brought a handmade copy of the Landlord's Game into his classroom as a tool to show the evils of rent gouging. Nearing wasn't certain of the game's title, and he referred to it as the Antilandlord Game. His students nicknamed it Business or Monopoly because Nearing's version emphasized acquiring sets of lots. Lizzie is known to have summered in Arden for many years. Her Arden game board grouped the properties into sets. She likely modified her original game in response to suggestions from players. Its main attraction became acquiring groups and charging increasingly higher rents as they were developed.

The importance of Nearing's decision to add the Landlord's Game to his curriculum cannot be overstated. Its academic nature appealed to his students' level of sophistication and social consciousness. At the same time, it brought out their competitive spirit. Some of them became advocates of the game and made their own copies. A few eventually became economics instructors at other schools and established a tradition of introducing their homemade copy of the game to new students. A few copies even reached beyond the college campuses. One of them still exists. It was made in 1908, or thereabouts, by John Heap of Altoona, Pennsylvania, after one of Nearing's students taught him to play.

Let's pause for a moment to dig a bit deeper into the passionate, if limited, appeal of Monopoly's forerunner. First, it was likely the most intricate simulation game of its day. Bold, detailed, and educational, it was far from commercial. While Lizzie may have hoped her game would educate a wider audience, realistically only the few who studied and taught economics and business, as well as those devoted to the single tax theory, were drawn to it. There was another reason for its narrow appeal: most Americans were not homeowners. While the majority had a landlord, he (occasionally she) was an annoying figure at best, not a fun character to base a game on.

For homeowners, terms like *mortgage* and *interest* are onerous reminders of indebtedness. Not exactly a ticket to encourage families to gather round the table for a game. Ironically, Lizzie's game had a positive objective: make money by becoming the most successful landlord. Rent gouging might be evil, according to the Georgists, but her game required gouging to win. Nevertheless, there is evidence that Lizzie's players weren't satisfied with this capitalistic ending. Rather, winning by bankrupting all opponents became the preferred endgame. Scott Nearing's younger brother Guy, who also lived at Arden, was known as the Bankruptcy King due to the many opponents he left destitute.

Beyond Arden, the conflict between the trusts and the progressive reform movement grew more intense. Roosevelt continued to change the rules to advance reform. In 1903 he had convinced Congress to pass the Expedition Act, which gave trust-busting cases top priority in the courts. His Department of Commerce and Labor was taking its first steps at regulation to foster stability in the economy. Its next target was the beef trust, and it scored another victory with the court-ordered breakup. Congress then passed legislation to outlaw rebates on freight rates posted by the railroads, from which John Rockefeller's Standard Oil mightily benefited. Standard Oil was so dominant that the Roosevelt administration asked for and got the authority to launch an investigation into its practices. A momentous antitrust suit followed.

Firms like U.S. Steel and International Harvester saw the writing on the wall. They too dominated their industries but decided to work with the White House to bring about their own reform. Roosevelt distinguished between good trusts and bad ones, especially those organized by J. P. Morgan. Ironically, when another gut-wrenching panic swept Wall Street in 1907, Roosevelt beseeched Morgan to rescue the economy once again. This latest panic began when two respected trusts failed. A domino effect toppled other firms dependent on them, including banks. Stocks nosedived and the economy entered a tailspin. Morgan responded. He applied his influence on strong bankers and urged them to funnel money into weaker banks in order to restore confidence and stem the decline. Within a few weeks, the panic ended.

In the aftermath, fingers pointed both ways. Progressives attacked the banking system as fundamentally flawed. Until it was fixed, they argued, the economy would never be free of setbacks. Business leaders, especially the monopolists, believed Roosevelt's progressive laws had upset the natural order of the economy. They warned that government meddling in business would prove even more disastrous next time.

A decade earlier, the monopolists would have won a similar argument. This time, the reformers won. As a consequence, bankers like Morgan knew that it was only a matter of time before the government would return to the business of banking. The nation's debt reached a record $2.6 billion when Roosevelt left office in 1909. Reform had a price tag but few seemed to mind. More and more voices like Scott Nearing's advocated further change, regardless of cost.

Nevertheless, there was a notable, cost-free benefit of progressivism— the loosening of restraints on the human spirit. The puritanical bias against frivolity gave way to the natural desire to enjoy the fruits of hard work. Throughout society it became acceptable to spend a "sensible" amount of time each week just having fun.

The music publishing business flourished as never before. Hot styles, like ragtime, became the vogue. Thomas Edison's phonograph made it possible to listen to songs at home, alleviating the need to read sheet music and play an instrument (many lamented this change). Also thanks to Edison, people began packing movie theaters nationwide. Edison's electric light company, General Electric, illuminated many homes and the streets of the nation's cities, with the help of financing by J. P. Morgan.

The future also appeared brightly lit for companies that entertained people by making games. This was especially true for a family-owned business in Salem, Massachusetts, whose founder was about to encounter an inventor named Elizabeth Magie Phillips.

3

PARKER AND PROGRESS
1910–1915

In 1910 George Parker was a forty-four-year-old New England entrepreneur. With the aid of his two older brothers, Edward and Charles, the principled, self-educated Parker had built Parker Brothers, the nation's most successful game company. He had launched the firm when he was sixteen, in 1883 (the year Nearing was born). Rising from humble beginnings, the three Parker brothers built their firm into the nation's largest game company. They did this by supplying quality at a time when it was not a buzzword, by delivering easy-to-read rules and excellent game play, and by sharpening a knack for capitalizing on trends before they took off.

Initially George Parker created most of the games published by the firm but went on to apply his talent by editing the ideas of other inventors. In an age when women were disadvantaged in occupational pursuits, Parker shrewdly realized that women were just as capable as men in creating and making games. One of his first big hits, Innocence Abroad, was licensed from a lady named Sophia Shephard. Parker's wife, Grace, helped him invent and test many games. Dozens of women artfully cut the wooden pieces of his Pastime Puzzles based

Parker and Progress

George S. Parker

Founder of Parker Brothers

Parker Brothers factory, Salem, Massachusetts, 1910

MOCK TRIAL

A GREAT FUN MAKER FOR A ROOMFUL OF PLAYERS.

Just the Thing for Jolly Evening Parties.

The Judge, Prisoner and Lawyers are elected by acclamation. The Witnesses are provided with cards bearing their testimony and the laughable nature of the questions and answers, the objections of the attorneys and cross-examinations are of the most ludicrous description. It will put any roomful of players in a continuous state of laughter.

If you wish **merry fun** for from one-half dozen to twenty people you will do well to play Mock Trial.

Price, 50 cents.

THE NEW GAME
MOCK TRIAL
TRADE MARK
FUN and
LAUGHTER
for a
ROOMFULL
PARKER BROTHERS
SALEM, NEW YORK, LONDON

I'M A MILLIONAIRE

I'm A Millionaire
SCREAMINGLY
FUNNY
PARKER BROTHERS
SALEM, MASS, NEW YORK & LONDON

"I'm a Millionaire" is good fun. Consists of a pack of highly enamelled round-cornered cards, of best quality, and about 100 Gilt Discs, representing hard cash.

The object of the game is to become a millionaire. The cards are divided into various society sets. There is the "outer circle," the "inner circle," the "strenuous circle," etc. There is Mrs. "Get-There" from Butte, "Mr. Clymer" of Denver, etc. There is also a "Major Butt-in," a celebrated character in the game, who disturbs the social gatherings by his too frequent introductions.

Price, 50 cents.

Mock Trial—Lizzie Magie's first sale to Parker Brothers. I'm a Millionaire—the money game the firm published rather than her Landlord's Game, that same year. From the 1911 Parker Brothers catalog.

1910–1915

on shapes they created. And in 1909 Parker was impressed by a game submitted by a woman named Elizabeth Magie Phillips.

Parker published her lively card game entitled Mock Trial. But he rejected the Landlord's Game, ever so politely, because he did not see how he could "put over" a game of its complexity and instructive overtones on the American public, especially after Lizzie insisted it remain true to its purpose and not be "made silly." Parker's rejection was based on years of practical experience. He was pleased to see the American public developing a more discerning taste in games, yet rolling a die, drawing cards, and advancing a token from start to finish still summed up the majority of successful games on the market—even those with realistic themes. For example, players traveled across the nation by rolling dice during the play of the United States game or delivering mail around town and getting back to the post office in the Parker game by the same name.

Further, the public's broader interest in play had diversified. Fads sprang up seemingly out of nowhere. Even proper people were tossing wood or metal spools called diabolos into the air and then catching them on a string between two rods. Millions were hunched over tables assembling wooden jigsaw puzzles. Clever cards games, like Pit, Flinch, Rook (all of which endure to this day), and whist (a forerunner of bridge) were enormously popular. The lively card-exchange game Pit was based on the trading in Chicago's commodity pits. Interest in its theme stemmed from the popular Frank Norris novel, *The Pit*. Psychic Edgar Cayce had come up with the basic idea and sold it to George Parker. George added two cards to Cayce's idea and turned a pleasant game into a laugh-filled riot. People from all walks of life purchased millions of copies. Parker once met Teddy Roosevelt on a trip to Washington, and the president told him how much he liked Pit. Parker was awed.

In George's estimation, Pit was about as far as the public could be pushed into the arcane world of business. It exemplified his belief that Americans didn't mind learning something fortuitously while playing a game. But he knew they would rebel if forced to learn in order to play. That's what schools were for. In Parker's mind, the Landlord's Game was not only complex but patently instructional. Worse, it was *politically* instructional. Nonetheless, Lizzie may have persuaded George Parker that the time was ripe for a new moneymaking game. When Mock Trial appeared in 1910, his line did include such a game—a simple card game, not far removed from the simplicity of Pit, entitled I'm a Millionaire.

Ironically, after a quarter century's enjoyment with board games, card games, and puzzles, the nation's new willingness to have fun did not translate into continuing success for Parker Brothers. The public's taste shifted from games to crossword puzzles and innovative toys, like the Erector Set, Lincoln Logs, and toy wagons.

The Landlord's Game that George Parker rejected was not a hand-made prototype. In 1906 the Economic Game Company of New York had published an improved version of Lizzie's brainchild. She was the principal shareholder of this endeavor, having incorporated the firm with two other Georgists—E. H. Monroe of Chicago and E. G. Leubuscher of New York. This version was similar to her 1904 original, except for the addition of property names and a rule permitting a player to charge higher rents upon acquiring multiple railroads. It also added four fields of work.

At least four copies of this version are known to exist. The one pictured in this book has been in the family of photographer Thomas Forsyth since it was purchased in the year of publication. Another handmade game of this era bears a striking resemblance to Lizzie's game. It was made by the Buckwalter family of Pennsylvania and today resides in the Forbes Gallery in New York City.

During the second decade of the new century, many of the original monopolists—especially Carnegie and Morgan—lost their zeal to accumulate wealth and gave away significant portions of their fortunes before they died. Faced with dwindling opposition, Presidents Taft and Wilson enacted many Roosevelt-inspired reforms. Rockefeller's Standard Oil trust was dissolved. The Federal Reserve System was established. The Clayton Act further restricted the abilities of monopolies to form and survive. The Federal Trade Commission became the government's watchdog to enforce its growing body of antitrust laws.

Business flourished, especially the automobile industry led by Henry Ford. By 1916 his Model T was available for just $360. Europe was supplanted as the prime source of global innovation as U.S. exports rose steadily. Fashion and ideas were flowing out of the country as well, including a license for the Landlord's Game.

In 1913 the Newbie Game Company published Lizzie's game in Annan, Scotland. This enterprise was an arm of the Scottish Newbie Liberal Committee, which referred to the game as the Landlord's Game in its initial publicity. Curiously, however, it appeared under the name of Brer Fox and Brer Rabbit, characters in Joel Chandler Harris's book *Uncle Remus and Brer Rabbit* ("brer" meaning brother). The British looked on these tales as quintessential American stories, much as Americans perceived Mark Twain's *Tom Sawyer* and *Huckleberry Finn*.

In Brer Fox and Brer Rabbit, England's top money minister, David Lloyd George (Chancellor of the Exchequer), appeared as Brer Fox because he was attempting to achieve land tax reform and establish a welfare state. Brer Rabbit was the agile landlord, trying to avoid his responsibility. Lloyd George had read books by Henry George and advocated his ideas. Name aside, this game was very similar to Lizzie's Landlord's Game and included the same types of components. Of note, jail was called *gaol*—a Middle English term from which the word *jail* originated. Gaol was derived from the Latin word for cage. Enough said.

The rules of Brer Fox (see Appendix VIII) are worth studying as they include changes that Elizabeth Magie Phillips made to her original game.

The Brer Fox and Brer Rabbit game was launched a year before England entered the Great War (as World War I was referred to at the time). Interest in Lloyd George's reforms waned quickly; the game did not establish itself in the United Kingdom and soon disappeared.

Before America joined the conflict in 1917, fearless University of Pennsylvania professor Scott Nearing was speaking out against war profiteering by American businesses. By now, he was a pacifist as well as an economic radical and socialist. To him, it was not meritorious for American businesses to supply food to a hungry continent. Food fostered the ability to wage war as much as the munitions crossing the Atlantic did. Nearing urged all Americans to stay out of the business of war. This stance put him squarely at odds with his privately funded university. Nearing was tried and cleared under Wilson's Sedition Act. But by the time this happened in 1917, Nearing was already two years removed from his post at Wharton, his dismissal directly linked to his outcry for tough new child labor laws.

Scott Nearing had seen child labor firsthand in the coal mines of his hometown in western Pennsylvania and then in the mills and factories outside Philadelphia. Children as young as thirteen were forced to leave school and go to work (even four-year-olds were seen working in facto-ries). Thirteen cents an hour was a typical child's wage. Nearing sup-ported laws to raise the minimum age to sixteen and limit the number of hours a teen could work. Since the profitability of many businesses depended on cheap child labor and some of these firms had endowed the University of Pennsylvania, Nearing was an embarrassment to the school. Nearing's contract was not renewed when the spring 1915 term ended. Many believed that one of the school's benefactors demanded this, but proof is lacking. Nearing himself did not encourage the charge. He was a thorn, he figured, and he expected to be removed.

Eventually strong child labor laws were enacted, and in June 1919 the Nineteenth Amendment was passed, making it illegal to deny women the right to vote. With these accomplishments, the Progressive Era wound down. Its vision of fairness in American society had been largely fulfilled (although much remained to be done, especially in the fields of civil rights and environmentalism).

Scott Nearing moved on to the University of Toledo after a solid record of achievement at Wharton, including the education of hundreds of promising students, the publication of a dozen books, and the tough stance he adopted in favor of reform. In addition, he kept the Landlord's Game alive.

Some of his students took their own versions home after the school term concluded. Among examples of these hand-fabricated games is one made in 1916 by a Reading, Pennsylvania, man named Paul Sherk. He based his game on one made by a cousin, Thomas Wilson, who was a student of Nearing's at the University of Pennsylvania. Of note, the values found on Sherk's board double the values of prior boards. This change likely occurred to simplify mortgage calculation. Nevertheless, Sherk's game represented 100 percent inflation. The Georgists had warned of this kind of gouging.

Among Nearing's most devoted students, one in particular went on to win great acclaim during the next two decades. His name was Rexford Guy Tugwell, and he began teaching economics at Wharton just weeks after Nearing was let go. Better jobs would lure him away from Wharton and by 1920 Tugwell and his handmade game were ensconced at Columbia University.

The Landlord's Game had arrived in New York City.

4

TUGWELL'S TURN

1916–1924

Rexford Tugwell was twenty-nine when he arrived at Columbia University. Tugwell's fortunes, like his nation's, were on the rise. Within fourteen years his handsome, beguiling face would grace the cover of *Time* magazine. He would remain at Columbia until 1932, when the Democratic presidential candidate, Franklin D. Roosevelt, asked him to formulate his economic policy and assemble a Brains Trust (plural intended; Tugwell would write a book by this title).

Two years after arriving at Columbia, Tugwell was promoted to assistant professor, having secured a doctorate from his alma mater. He was now ready to "Advance to Go" and exert influence. Much like Scott Nearing, Tugwell was restless with the status quo. He didn't care for the "business-friendly" method of teaching economics because he believed that yesterday's techniques were insufficient to keep up with changing times. How could business leaders cope if they weren't challenged to initiate change?

The inequities in capitalist America worried him, while the apparent success of Lenin's 1917 Bolshevik Revolution in Russia aroused his curiosity. He visited the Soviet Union to study its planned economy

Tugwell's Turn

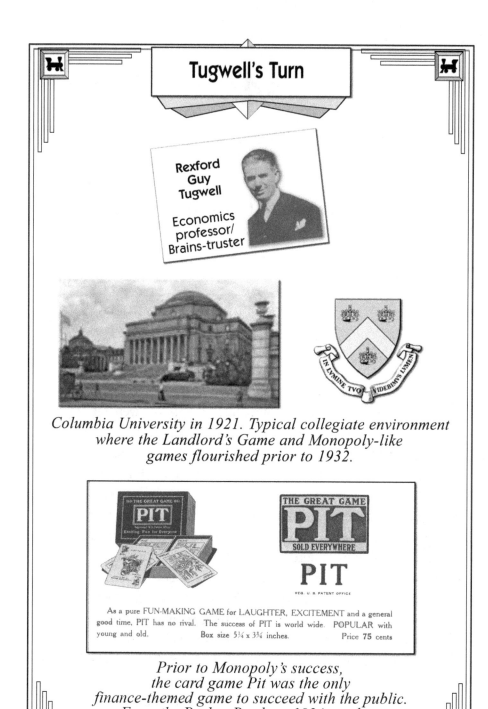

Rexford
Guy
Tugwell

Economics
professor/
Brains-truster

Columbia University in 1921. Typical collegiate environment
where the Landlord's Game and Monopoly-like
games flourished prior to 1932.

THE GREAT GAME
PIT
SOLD EVERYWHERE

PIT
REG. U. S. PATENT OFFICE

As a pure FUN-MAKING GAME for LAUGHTER, EXCITEMENT and a general
good time, PIT has no rival. The success of PIT is world wide. POPULAR with
young and old.   Box size 5¼ x 3¾ inches.   Price **75** cents

Prior to Monopoly's success,
the card game Pit was the only
finance-themed game to succeed with the public.
From the Parker Brothers 1924 catalog.

and applauded the stability and accomplishments achieved by central planning. Meanwhile, Nearing joined a socialist organization in New York, and forecast the failure of capitalism. In 1924 he challenged the English philosopher and future Nobel Prize winner, Bertrand Russell, in a famous debate on Bolshevism and the West. Russell advocated capitalism, Nearing communism.

Karl Marx, who created the ideas behind the Bolshevik Revolution, thought that essential goods should be owned in common and shared. Nearing favored this idea. Americans by and large did not, and the United States refused to recognize Lenin's government. In the great debate, Nearing argued that Western civilization should adopt the Soviet form of government. Russell took exception. The debate was inconclusive, but the question caused many people to wonder if America was behind the curve and needed major changes in its economic system.

Tugwell, unlike his mentor, did not advocate revolution, nor did he confront authority. He knew his peers coddled big business because they were frequently sought out to become corporate economic advisers at high salaries. So be it. He had seen Russia's planned economy humming along. What to learn from it? How to apply its merits here?

Nearing had trained Tugwell to probe and question. This he did. His questioning extended far beyond the methods of teaching economics at Columbia. He felt hindered by the economic equivalent of a military leader's fog of war. A field commander's dilemma is uncertainty about the location and capabilities of his enemy and even his own troops— and the inevitable chaos once orders are issued to engage.

To Tugwell, America's economic leaders were facing a similar quandary. Whether they were aware of it or not, they were coping with the fastest, most vibrant growth in American history. While the 1920s had started off with a sharp recession, once the troops in Europe had returned home and were working, the economy took off. During this expansion, the nation was led by three successive Republican administrations—those of Warren Harding (who died in office), Calvin Coolidge (famous for his quote, "The chief business of the American people is business"), and Herbert Hoover (arguably the brightest of the three). All three favored a hands-off approach to business. Any excess or neglect during the Roaring Twenties would be resolved through the guidance of Wall Street and corporate America, not by government intervention.

Tugwell was no soothsayer, but he knew that past expansions had frequently ended in bust (witness 1893 and 1907). This concern reinforced Tugwell's reliance on the Landlord's Game as a teaching tool. The game he had copied in Nearing's class entered his classroom at Columbia to aid his pedagogic goals.

Tugwell probably did not know who originated it. He was only twelve, growing up miles away in Niagara County, New York, when Elizabeth Magie patented her idea. By the time Tugwell arrived at the University of Pennsylvania, many of Nearing's students assumed their esteemed professor had created it. (Nearing apparently did not mention Lizzie's name to his students.) But the simulation game spoke for itself, and Tugwell became one of its principal evangelists.

Among other enthusiasts was a student at Smith College in Massachusetts, known to us by her married name, Catherine Allphin. In 1921 she learned the game from her Princeton friend Ellen Feda. Allphin introduced it to her brother-in-law, Pinfield Roberts, who was a professor of English and history at MIT in Cambridge, Massachusetts. The Landlord's Game had now reached an elite educational institution in New England, just a few miles away from Parker Brothers.

Catherine's husband-to-be, William Allphin, was a student of Roberts's at MIT. Roberts taught him how to play. William Allphin was perhaps the first player (other than Lizzie) to toy with the idea of manufacturing a version of the game. But before he could get serious he would have to overcome its most glaring weakness: a lack of written rules. The handmade games based on Lizzie's concept were explained by word-of-mouth. Consequently, William Allphin sat down and slowly committed his version of the rules to writing. Nonetheless, he was forced to put aside his work because he failed to secure a backer or publicist. Years later, in 1931, he tried to interest Parker's main rival, the Milton Bradley Company, in publishing it. Bradley declined. (Allphin's role in the history of the game would resume in 1975. Stay tuned.)

Students like Allphin continued to be the prime experimenters of Lizzie's invention. After Scott Nearing promulgated her game, Lizzie lost control of its development. With her 1904 patent expired, she decided in 1923 to regain control by revising her game and considered applying for a new patent.

While Tugwell wondered about the impact of events driving the 1920s economy, several unrelated events in society came together that would lead to the publication and acceptance of the Monopoly game in the following decade.

The first was the electrification of the nation's urban areas and the spread of telephone systems from coast to coast. This compelled the legalization of "regulated monopolies" to untangle the maze of competing wires. (If you've ever seen photos of Lower Manhattan and Wall Street overrun by wires prior to this decision, you know the need for so doing.) Each state-regulated utility monopoly was immune from competition within its territory, but its rates were subject to government approval. Trolley lines, interurbans, and railroads also become government-regulated monopolies for similar reasons. In the case of the 1913 federally blessed telephone monopoly, American Telephone and Telegraph (AT&T)—the mother of all monopolies—the entire country was its territory.

Telephones, telegraphs, and electricity vastly shortened the reaction time between a store's need for a product and the manufacturer's processing of the order. This enabled "hot" products to stay hot.

All forms of entertainment were hot—the second condition of importance in creating a demand for Monopoly. With World War I concluded, a semblance of automation in the home, and the economy on the move, the pursuit of leisure became big business. Radio was now the communications medium of choice; the Radio Corporation of America (RCA) held a monopolistic grip on this new rage. General Electric, AT&T, Westinghouse, and other firms had created RCA in 1919 to exploit the radio patents they owned. In 1926 RCA became the dominant owner of the National Broadcasting System (NBC). NBC blanketed the nation with powerful signals from stations whose programming was paid for by sponsor advertising (a first). Scott Nearing railed against the "new media monopolies," AT&T and RCA, but few bought into his concern about information being controlled by the few; that worry was the province of nations in Europe threatened by a new wave of dictators.

Advancements in motion picture technology, including sound, made Hollywood films immensely popular. In clubs, jazz was *the* style of music and its many Afro-American musicians enjoyed breakthrough acceptance. The Charleston (and short skirts) dominated the dance scene.

The demand for new forms of entertainment rejuvenated the game industry, as three games—Mah Jongg, contract bridge, and backgammon—successively swept the country. The third event, therefore, was the mass acceptance of certain games across America. Elusively, there was no secret formula to determine in advance if a new game would take the public by storm. George Parker would attest to that. But common ingredients of success seemed to be familiarity and a twist—a small but clever improvement that enhanced a previously known game or accepted method of game play.

George Parker could have owned the Mah Jongg craze lock, stock, and barrel. The fact that he let it slip through his fingers changed his life (and the fate of the Monopoly game). Mah Jongg was rummy played with lovely tiles bearing Chinese characters and artwork. Parker wasn't sure Americans would take to it.

An American engineer named Joseph Babcock joined the Standard Oil Company in the year of its breakup (1911) and was sent to China as Standard's representative. There he discovered and Americanized this addictive tile game and named it Mah Jongg. His American agent headed straight for Parker Brothers and tried to interest George Parker in acquiring exclusive marketing rights. But Parker, smarting from a decade of lackluster games that had not connected with the public, decided to pass. After all, Mah Jongg was much like the card game rummy, which was essentially free. All one needed to play it was a deck of playing cards or Parker's Rook game. Parker was convinced consumers would not spend five or ten dollars ($100 to $200 today) for a set of Chinese tiles just to enjoy the same experience, especially after a market test in Macy's Department Store on 33rd Street in New York yielded desultory results.

No sooner had Parker declined than rival importers began selling thousands of Mah Jongg sets (under slightly different names) on the West Coast. By the time George Parker reacted, the country had gone crazy for this expensive game. Apparently the aura and visual appeal of its Chinese theme and tiles, coupled with a familiar play principle, compelled consumers to open their pocketbooks. Eventually Parker licensed the trademark and rights to distribute the official Mah Jongg line from Babcock. But Parker could satisfy only a fraction of the public's enormous appetite for this game. The effort to stop infringers in court would have cost a small fortune and taken years to prosecute. So Parker watched in dismay as Mah Jongg effectively fell into the public domain. He vowed never to make that mistake again.

At about the same time, Elizabeth Magie Phillips came calling to show Parker her 1923 version of the Landlord's Game. Parker liked it even less than her older version because its political/educational overtones were now out of fashion. What he sought was a light-hearted fad, not a heavy-handed brainwasher of a game. He again let her down gently, by suggesting she obtain a new patent. She did so. (It became the one Sid Sackson wondered about, forty-five years later.)

In her 1924 patent she formally claimed her monopoly rule, which doubled the rents charged by a player who owned all the railroads or utilities. But it was too little, too late.

The most obvious change in Lizzie's revision was her decision to shift her game board's layout so that its three railroads occupied three of its corner spaces. The fourth corner, once "Mother Earth," was now entitled "Wages." Overall, her new patent (see Appendix IX) made five important claims.

There is no evidence that this game was published during the 1920s.

As the Roaring Twenties wore on, Mah Jongg's popularity began to wane, in large part because of the many competing versions played by different rules. There being no standard, disputes were common and players lost interest. A hastily formed Mah Jongg association adopted a unified set of rules, but it came too late. Nevertheless, Mah Jongg had whetted the public's appetite for social games. A new one soon appeared, with the impact of an asteroid crashing to earth.

Contract bridge was fashioned by three New York socialites— Harold Vanderbilt (a yachtsman and grandson of William Henry Vanderbilt), Ely Culbertson (an American who had grown up in Russia and made a living by playing and writing about card games), and Waldemar von Zedtwitz (heir to the Breckinridge lighting fortune, whose father died in an accident onboard the German kaiser's yacht when Waldemar was six months old).

Vanderbilt conceived the ideas that transformed ordinary auction bridge (successor to whist) into spine-tingling contract bridge. His revisions changed bridge from a game in which you scored what you *won*, to a game where you scored what you *bid*. This seemingly modest change made a huge impact on the "scientific" nature of bridge. Culbertson was instantly taken by the improvement. He had the marketing savvy to popularize it, especially through books and lectures. Serious-minded socialite von Zedtwitz possessed the skill and means to organize and legitimize the game through tournaments and a contract bridge league.

To this day, contract bridge is arguably the greatest intellectual card game of all time.

At this point, the Landlord's Game and I become woven into the story of bridge. Early in my career, I worked for a game company named Gamut of Games that was financed by Waldemar von Zedtwitz because he liked its initial product—a two-handed bridge game entitled Brid-gette. "Waldy" (he always preferred this informal nickname) was in his late seventies at the time, the last survivor of the bridge threesome. His mind was still sharp and his tall, thin frame and erect bearing made him appear younger than his years. Periodically I would be invited to his two-story penthouse apartment at 812 Park Avenue in New York to deliver a business update. Waldy also had a more personal interest in my visits. He wanted to play a game of chess or backgammon.

The setting was his majestic library, which featured his most valuable work of art—a large painting worth millions of an unattractive woman (at least to me, the uninitiated). It was painted by sixteenth-century artist Lucas Cranach the Elder. A bachelor, von Zedtwitz was the wealthiest person I knew, the beneficiary of his mother's wealth. Her ancestors, the Breckinridge family of Kentucky, were noteworthy for several reasons. John C. Breckinridge was a U.S. Representative, Senator, served as Vice President, and was the Democratic candidate for President in 1860. He ran against Abraham Lincoln and others (he came in second); his son lit many of America's streets with Thomas Edison's lightbulb.

Waldy found business tedious. Once I concluded my report, we moved to his large game table, which stood on a riser, for chess or backgammon. I'd make a move that temporarily vexed Waldy; he'd rake his white hair with his fingers and then figure out a perfect coun-termove. He was nearly impossible to beat.

I learned that Waldy had met Rexford Tugwell and had played the Landlord's Game years before Monopoly was published.

During the mid-1920s, Waldy was living at the Plaza Hotel. At an event held there to popularize contract bridge, he was introduced to one of the guests: Rexford Tugwell. Tugwell was then an associate pro-fessor of economics at Columbia and enjoyed an expanding circle of friends and admirers. The topic turned to games in general, and Tugwell asked Waldy if he had played Landlord. Waldy hadn't heard of it but was intrigued by its subject and apparent intricacy. Tugwell arranged for Waldy to join in a game shortly thereafter. As Waldy explained to me that evening in his library, he didn't much care for Tugwell's game, however novel it appeared, because "luck played a more predominate role" than in backgammon. Waldy scoffed at games that had luck determine the outcome.

Waldy loved backgammon because the element of luck could be managed. This ancient game (it was a favorite of the Romans) became the third rage of the 1920s after an unknown gambler added the "doubling cube" to its play. The object of backgammon (a two-player game) is to be first to move all fifteen of your pieces successfully through those of your opponent (moving in the opposite direction) into your home area and then off the board. Money is often at stake. The cube enables a player to double the stakes. If his opponent refuses to accept the double, the game ends immediately and the doubler wins the original bet. If accepted, the game continues. The stakes rise exponentially each time a double is accepted: a $1 bet could result in a loss or gain of $64. Despite the luck of the dice in backgammon, mathematical analysis makes it possible to learn the best move for each throw. Waldy liked this. He called it "organized chaos," unlike the "random chaos" he'd encountered in Tugwell's Landlord Game.

There was a second reason. Money had never been lacking in Waldy's life, and the thrill of accumulating play money did not stir his heart. Undeterred, I probed Waldy's memory because it seemed to somehow tie into Sid Sackson's discovery of Lizzie's Landlord patent. As fate would have it, what Waldy recalled meshed perfectly with the design of a handmade game I would purchase three decades later. This game was made by one of Tugwell's most famous students, and then passed down to his daughter and granddaughters.

This man's name was Roy Stryker who, like Tugwell, was destined for a measure of greatness in years to come.

5

STRYKER'S STYLE

1925–1932

R oy Emerson Stryker was a patriot who served his country during the Great War, fighting in France alongside his fellow infantrymen. Roy's populist father had instilled in him a love of country and duty. Stryker volunteered for service even though he was overage at the time. He returned home in 1918, a mature twenty-five-year-old. He married Alice Fraiser, worked to scrape together money for college, and entered Columbia in 1921. Because he chose to study economics, his path intersected that of Rexford Tugwell. The two became friends and confidants. Eventually they would collaborate on a book titled *American Economic Life*, with illustrations drawn by Roy Stryker—an innovation among economics textbooks of the day.

During his undergraduate years, Stryker—like many of Tugwell's students—learned to play Landlord in the classroom. After Stryker graduated in 1924, Tugwell urged him to remain at Columbia and teach economics under him. Stryker agreed. He also perpetuated the Landlord game by making his own copy.

Roy Stryker carefully planned and rendered this new set with the help of his wife, Alice. It remained in use until 1935, when Stryker was

Stryker's Style

Roy Emerson Stryker

Economics professor, New Dealer

The handmade
Stryker Landlord game
below,
circa 1925

Color
chart
for
property
spaces

Game board planning sheet

*Oilcloth
game board,
sample cards
on the board,
paper houses,
key tag money,
and
1927
wooden
houses*

1925–1932

asked once more to serve his country—this time in Washington, D.C., at the behest of Tugwell, who had become President Roosevelt's assistant secretary for agriculture. Alice and Roy carefully packed their game in a box, together with their planning documents, and there it remained for the next sixty-seven years. All of these survived the passage of time.

Their Landlord game bears study because it provides a unique snapshot of the evolution of Elizabeth Magie Phillips's Arden game, as customized by third-generation admirers.

The Strykers purchased paper, unlined index cards, paint and ink, and a thirty-six- by forty-inch sheet of white oilcloth. Originally used for sailors' wear and coach robes, by the 1920s oilcloth was primarily used for waterproof coverings. The Strykers purchased a thirty-six- by forty-inch plain white oilcloth from a home furnishings store and set about to design their game board.

Roy Stryker's profession required precise planning and documentation, at which he excelled. He began this project with a small plan of the game board sketched in ink. Next came the choice of color scheme for the spaces, most importantly the use of a single color of paint for each set of properties.

Then Roy Stryker inked a grid of spaces on the oilcloth and, together with his wife, applied the paint. Roy added original line art on the corner spaces. Then he drew little houses on index card stock and the Strykers carefully cut them out. For play money, colored door key tags were enumerated. Finally deeds for each of the twenty-eight properties and a few Chance cards were typed onto index cards.

Alice also typed several copies of the rules on carbon paper in abbreviated form. Just one page in length, they were intended as ready reference for players who already understood the game.

LANDLORD

Each player starts the game with title to certain pieces of property and $300 in cash.

The dice are thrown and the player moves according to total number of spots. Rent is collected by the owner of the property upon which he stops. If a property is not owned at that time, it is sold immediately at public auction to the highest bidder, but no rent can be collected from the "squatter."

A house on a property doubles the rent. Houses may be purchased from the bank for $100 each.

Each time a player goes through "home" he collects $100 from the bank.

If he should have to go to jail, throwing a double will let him out free—he can't stay in more than 3 turns.

In order to obtain higher rents, one or more persons may combine certain properties, which correspond in color and letter. (Notification must be given all players that this monopoly has been formed.) A monopoly doubles the rent on each property, a house on a property in the monopoly doubles the rent again, a row of houses (one on each property) doubles it again, a second house doubles it again and a second row of houses doubles it again.

For example—No. 17. The Bowery

Rent $10; monopoly $20; house $40; row of houses $80; second house $160; second row of houses $320.

It is to your advantage to buy properties which will help form a monopoly.

Individuals may buy and sell properties among themselves or may loan and borrow money.

Everyone must be honest with the bank.

The Strykers found a suitable box from the Arrow Department Store, wrote "Landlord" in big letters on its cover, and their game was complete. In time they made improvements, adding triangle-shaped pieces of colored wood to serve as houses (the paper houses proved too fragile).

Years later their daughter Phyllis recalled how she'd greet friends of her parents who came to play the game. Shortly after she became old enough to play, the game was stored away. When her parents passed away, Phyllis inherited the game. It passed to her daughters upon her death.

The Stryker game represents the care and pride the game's early torchbearers invested in their handiwork. It is interesting to note how the names on their spaces compare to the Arden board. On both boards the spaces were sequentially numbered, except the corner spaces.

A parallel comparison shows that most spaces on each board are identical in value and nature, except for their names. Clearly each designer had fun naming the spaces. Likely the Strykers named many after hometowns of students and favorite places. Lizzie Phillips named some of the Arden board's streets after famous Georgists (George himself, Maguire, and Johnson) and Georgist colonies, like Fairhope, Alabama. After twenty years of play, Lizzie's board arrangement remained virtually intact.

The Strykers were not the only ones making the game in the late 1920s. At Williams College in Williamstown, Massachusetts, the Thun twins, Ferdinand and Louis, encountered the game in their hometown— Reading, Pennsylvania (from which the Reading Railroad got its name). Reading lies north of Philadelphia, not far from the University of Pennsylvania. The Thun family had emigrated from Germany, a country with a long tradition of playing serious-minded games. Because wood was used in German games, the Thuns made their board out of wood and fabricated a wooden chest to hold their copy. As second-generation Americans, they still had contacts in Germany who found a German source to make their little house pieces.

The Thuns came by the game indirectly, thanks to a student of Scott Nearing's from Reading named Thomas Wilson. It seems that Wilson's cousin Charles Muhlenberg had married their older sister who in turn taught it to her brothers. In 1926 Louis and Ferdinand Thun made a few copies of their game and sold them for $25 a piece (about $350 in today's dollars). They had the use of the small printing press and woodworking equipment in the family's factory, the Berkshire Mill. Since the brothers were being groomed to manage this business, they did not have the need or the incentive to further commercialize their game.

#	Stryker—Mid 1920s	Arden, 1906
Start	Home, Collect $100	Mother Earth Collect $100
1	Peoria, Ill. (cost) $25/$1 (rent)	Wayback $25/0
2	Alameda, Cal. $25/2	Absolute Necessity Fuel $10
3	Absolute Necessity Fuel $10	Lonely Lane $25/2
4	No Trespassing, Go To Jail	No Trespassing, Go To Jail
5	Jazzmania & Wt. R.R. $50/5	Royal Rusher R.R. $50/5
6	Winnepesaukee, N.H. $25/4	The Pike $25/4
7	Pottawottamie, Mich. $25/4	The Farm $25/4
8	Speculation $50, Ante $10	Speculation $50, Ante $10
9	Kabinogagami, Ont. $25/6	Rubeville $25/6
Jail	Jail, $50 fine/War Tax* $10	Jail $50/Abs. Nec. Shelter $10
11	Ann Arbor, Mich. $50/6	Boomtown $50/8
12	Nescopeck, Pa. $50/5	Goat Alley $50/8
13	The Public Serves Us Gas & Light Co. $50/5	Soakum Lighting System $50/5
14	Aldene, N.J. $50/8	Beggerman's Court $50/8
15	The Erie R.R. $50/5	Shooting Starr RR $50/5
16	Washington Heights $50/10	Rickety Row $50/10
17	The Bowery $50/10	Absolute Necessity, Food $10
18	Necessity, Doctor pay $25	Market Place $50/10
19	Jackson Heights $75/12	Cottage Terrace $50/12

*Even though the Great War was long over, many of the tax increases in the War Revenue Act of 1917 had not been repealed, so the Strykers perpetuated Tugwell's use of this tax on their board.

#	Stryker—Mid 1920s	Arden, 1906
Park	Central Park, Free	Poorhouse/Central Park, Free
21	Hohokus, N.J. $75/12	Easy Street $75/12
22	Hoboken, N.J. $75/12	CHANCE
23	CHANCE	George Street $75/14
24	Weehauken, N.J. $75/14	Maguire Flats $75/14
25	New York, New Haven, and Death Railroad $50/5	Gee Whiz RR $50/$5
26	Mosquito Terrace $75/16	Fairhope Avenue $75/16
27	Crimson Rambler Apt. $75/15	Slambang Trolley $50/5
28	Toonerville Trolley Co. $50/5	Johnson Circle $75/16
29	Huletts Landing $75/18	The Bowery $75/18
Go To Jail	Keep Off, Go To Jail	Go To Jail, Lord Blueb's Estate
31	Newport News $100/20	Broadway $100/18
32	Hylan-Hurst $100/20	Absolute Nec. Clothing pay $10
33	Absolute Necessity pay $10	Madison Square $100/20
34	Westchester Cty. Club $100/20	Fifth Avenue $100/20
35	Pacific Phila. RR Co. $50/5	P.D.Q. RR $50/5
36	Fifth Avenue $100/22	Grand Blvd. $100/22
37	CHANCE (oil stocks)	CHANCE
38	Wall Street $100/22	Wall Street $100/22
39	Luxury Tax pay $75	Luxury Tax pay $75

But one of their Delta Kappa Epsilon fraternity bothers at Williams College did. He hailed from Indianapolis and his name was Daniel W. Layman.

Layman and other Dekes enjoyed competing with the Thuns over their game board. Layman made a nearly identical version out of wood and began to ponder commercializing the game and what it might be called: Finance, Business, or Monopoly.

The bigger question was, When?

Back in New York City, Rexford Tugwell and Roy Stryker were asking a similar question. But their uncertainty pertained to the longevity of the current economic boom, when it would end, and how hard it would fall. Economic excess sparked their worries. Presidents Harding, Coolidge, and Hoover all took a laissez-faire attitude toward the nation's economy, which was sailing blissfully into uncharted waters.

During the war, with the advent of the tractor and orders from Europe to feed its population, farmers had tilled more land than ever before. And they no longer needed to set aside acreage to feed horses or mules because the tractor consumed gasoline, which cost pennies a gallon. Throughout the 1920s supply increased and demand diminished. Overproduction and falling prices soon crushed the nation's 10 million farmers.

Productivity gains in industry meant that a typical laborer in 1930 performed 30 percent more work per hour than his 1920 counterpart. Factory output soared. Not only did power and machinery yield more output, but they led to the manufacture of more conveniences and luxury goods. New appliances and gadgets appeared monthly. This new consumerism had a jolting impact on society. Firms began to use catchy, repetitive advertising to persuade consumers to buy their brands rather than those of competitors. ("Ivory Soap: It's ninety-nine and forty-four one hundredths percent pure!" "Parker Games: The difference is the excellence of their playing qualities.") Radio carried these messages to every corner of the nation.

Tugwell studied this consumer-led revolution and realized that increasing numbers of people needed to purchase these products if the economy was to keep growing. Goods made quickly and economically were worthless if they could not be purchased by the workers who made them or the farmers who grew the crops. (Automobile king Henry Ford knew this. He paid his workers wages high enough to enable them to buy his cars.)

Herbert Hoover had been secretary of commerce during the Coolidge administration and believed the nation was on the verge of eliminating poverty. But a year after he moved into the White House, the nation's citizens faced despair and empty bank accounts. The stock market crash of October 1929 wiped out the savings of millions who had used borrowed money to buy shares. Most believed this "leverage" would make them rich because the market always seemed to hit new highs. Few realized that a sudden drop of 10 percent would destroy their equity. It was as if everyone had simultaneously landed on a space in the Landlord's Game that demanded rent they could not pay. If this blow weren't enough, restrictive measures on foreign trade and the Federal Reserve's ill-advised tightening of the money supply clinched the demise of the economy.

By 1933, unemployment afflicted a staggering 25 percent of the workforce.

Dan Layman graduated from Williams College in 1929 a few months before the Crash. He found employment with the Young & Rubican advertising firm, but he couldn't make ends meet on his low salary in expensive New York City. So he joined a shaving cream company named Barbasol back in Indianapolis. There he decided to publish his version of the Landlord's Game. His work hours of 7:00 a.m. to 2:00 p.m. left time each afternoon to work on the rules for his game. It took him a few months to get them right. Then in 1932, with the help of a friend who owned a small battery business named Electronic Laboratories, he began to print and assemble copies of the game under the name Finance.

Layman's utilitarian game featured a plain box containing small wooden playing pieces and little cards (including money cards) plus a separate, bound game board fabricated like a book jacket. Layman used the same names and spaces employed by the Thuns, including the Community Chest, the name of a Reading charitable institution. In fact the name had been coined in Rochester, New York, back in 1913 to represent a cooperative organization of citizens and social welfare agencies in that city. The Community Chest eventually became known as the United Fund.

Layman's initial sales efforts were met with trade skepticism. His game, however clear its rules, was deemed too complicated and its design too plain and abstract. Eventually Layman moved to California. There he needed $200 to "Pass Go" and marry his fiancée. He accepted an offer of this amount and sold his rights to Electronic Laboratories. Electronic Labs in turn licensed Finance to Knapp Electric, another Indianapolis-based company that made electric learning games and maintained a sales office in New York's Flatiron building.

Layman's Finance game was eventually acquired by Parker Brothers and endured on the market for over fifty years. Daniel Layman is recognized as the first person to publish a nonpolitical version of the Landlord's Game, with complete, precise rules (see Appendix X).

At about the same time, Elizabeth Magie Phillips found a publisher for her latest endeavor, which combined her 1923 game with a new version entitled Prosperity. The Adgame Company, a previously unknown firm, issued the Landlord's Game and Prosperity. Unfortunately it appeared during the depths of the Depression. Lizzie tried to turn this timing into an advantage by trumpeting her game's educational nature. She proclaimed that her Landlord's Game revealed why the nation had gotten into an economic mess, while her Prosperity game pointed the way to recovery. Game play began according to the Landlord's rules and shifted gears after at least one player accumulated $2,000. The others could then enforce the rules for Prosperity. Prosperity was a true single tax game: benefits from land improvements went toward the public good and not into the landlord's pockets. However noble its intent, the game landed like a lead balloon on the cash-starved landscape of 1932.

In Salem, Massachusetts, George Parker was struggling to keep his game company afloat. The ill tide had swept away the heady game sales his firm had enjoyed in 1929. People just didn't have money to spend on entertainment anymore.

As losses mounted, Parker began to wonder if his firm could survive. Then something happened.

6

DARROW'S DEPRESSION

1932–1934

On a cold winter evening in early 1935 George Parker's daughter received a phone call from an old school chum living in Philadelphia. Helen Coolidge wanted to make sure Sally Parker Barton knew that a game called Monopoly was a big seller locally. "Have you heard of it?" Helen asked, adding that it was a great game to play.

Sally had not but her husband had. His name was Robert Barton. At age thirty-two, he was the new president of Parker Brothers. Barton remembered a game by this name being submitted—and rejected—by his father-in-law months ago. George Parker felt the game had three fundamental errors (not fifty-two as legend would have it). It was too complex, took too long to play, and was based on concepts unfamiliar to most game players. Case closed.

Given the poor state of his firm's business during the ongoing Depression, Barton pushed aside his father-in-law's concerns and made a deal to license the Monopoly game from its maker.

Within eighteen months, over 2 million copies were sold, and the fortunes of the Parker Brothers company and its employees soared

Darrow's Depression

Caricature of Charles Darrow from his box lid

Monopoly maker

Monopoly

A new adult game that is geared to the tempo of the present day has been introduced by Charles Brace Darrow, 40 Westview St., Philadelphia. This game, called Monopoly, has been displayed in New York and Philadelphia during the last few months and is reported to have enjoyed a heavy sale. Now that its success has been established production is being increased and Monopoly will be available all over the country. As the name of the game suggests, the players deal in real estate, railroads and public utilities in an endeavor to obtain a monopoly on a piece of property so as to obtain rent from the other players. Excitement runs high when such familiar problems are encountered as mortgages, taxes, a Community Chest, options, rentals, interest money, undeveloped real estate, hotels, apartment houses, power companies and other transactions, for which scrip money is supplied.

Darrow's first manufactured White Box edition

Trade announcement, April 1934

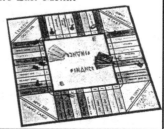

The New Knapp Game That Was A Sell-Out Everywhere Last Month

Finance has earned a place at the top of the list of best game sellers strictly on its own merits as a game of exceptional appeal. Teaches older children the wise use of money and offers adults plenty of opportunity to display their wits. Just the thing for the winter party season and just the thing to display *now* and all the year for steady sales. $2.00 retail. Order a trial dozen today.

KNAPP ELECTRIC,Inc.
414 SO. MISSOURI ST.   INDIANAPOLIS, IND.

Trade ad, December 1934

1932–1934

once more. How this happened is a rags-to-riches American success story, filled with unexpected twists, turns, surprises, disappointments, and triumph.

Ironically, the highly educated professors and students who kept the Landlord's Game alive did not bridge the gap between collegiate endeavor and nationwide fad. Rather, it took an unemployed repairman to transfer the game made by Dan Layman, which made an important stop in Atlantic City, New Jersey, into the game Parker Brothers finally acquired and published.

Two months after the 1929 stock market crash, a young teacher named Ruth Hoskins returned to Indianapolis to spend Christmas with her family. Ruth had just graduated from nearby Earlham College and was appointed teacher/principal at the Friends School (a Quaker institution) in faraway Atlantic City, New Jersey. During the holidays, she met up with old friends, including former neighbor Pete Daggett, and was invited to play a copy of a game made by Dan Layman (also an acquaintance). Ruth loved the game and asked to take it back to Atlantic City.

Hoskins introduced it to her fellow Quakers. They too liked it but felt no connection to the names of its spaces. It was suggested they make a board with new names. Ruth recommended using names of Atlantic City streets. Hadn't they been named for the states of the union and seas of the world? What could be grander? The group agreed. Atlantic City's streets had remained largely unchanged since 1852, except for the addition of a few alleys, like St. James Place, which subdivided blocks to make room for more housing.

Pitney's plan was about to be united with The Game.

Dorothy and Cyril Harvey helped lay out the grid for the new board, and Ruth added some graphic flourishes. The new board foreshortened the spaces into small rectangles and corner squares (doing away with the elongated spaces on Lizzie's and Dan Layman's board). Another Quaker, Jesse Raiford, was familiar with the values of Atlantic City real estate. He recommended street names that matched the slums-to-riches progression around the board and modified the property prices and rents accordingly. Some of these street names held personal significance for this group of Friends. Of special note, instead of the Short Line railroad there was Shore Fast Line, and Marvin Gardens was correctly spelled as "Marven" Gardens (the name of an attractive suburb whose name is a contraction of two neighboring towns: Margate and Ventnor). Because teachers at the Friends school were often boarded in Atlantic City's famous hotels, the group decided to convert the fifth house on each property to a hotel piece.

Lizzie's rule of buying an unowned property at a fixed price had been replaced by a rule requiring an auction to be held whenever an unowned property was landed on. Hoskins and her group did not favor this because auctions were noisy and considered deceitful according to their religion. So, while their board had no prices on its spaces, they (unwittingly) reverted to Lizzie's "buy it for the price on its deed if you land on it" rule. This turned out to be a good change because many players, especially children, are unskilled in auction strategy. Within days of Ruth's return from Indianapolis, the Atlantic City version of Dan Layman's game was basically complete. Several handmade copies were eventually made and began to circulate. (My mother remembered being introduced to one by Riva Klein, one of her teachers at Woodbine High School, twenty miles from Atlantic City.)

Three years later, another one of these copies entered the life of the unemployed plumbing repairman.

Jesse Raiford's brother, Gene, and his wife, Ruth, lived in Philadelphia. Being teachers and Quakers, they were invited into the Atlantic City circle and taught the game. Like many others, they made a copy. Among their friends were Charles and Olive Todd. The Raifords taught the Todds how to play. The Todds had taken up residence in Germantown (which had become part of Philadelphia a century earlier) because Charles renovated hotels, and his latest project happened to be in Germantown. Years earlier, Jesse, Gene, Charles, and Ruth had attended the Westtown Quaker Boarding School, where Gene taught chemistry. Among their classmates was a girl named Esther Jones.

During a walk on an evening in late 1932, Charles and Olive Todd bumped into Esther Jones and her husband. Charles Todd, short and sturdy, was delighted to see his pretty red-haired schoolmate for the first time in twenty years. Esther introduced him to her spouse, who was also named Charles—a pleasant man with thinning hair and a thickening waistline. Olive Todd extended a dinner invitation and the Darrows happily accepted. On a return engagement at their hotel, the Todds brought out their blue oilcloth game and taught the Darrows to play. Todd's board was an exact copy of the Atlantic City board, with three notable exceptions. He had changed Arctic Avenue to Mediterranean Avenue because they often played on cold winter nights and Mediterranean had a warmer association. Todd also changed the longish Shore Fast Line to the briefer Short Line. And he misspelled Marven Gardens as "Marvin Gardens."

The Darrows had an enjoyable time. Esther's husband, Charles, was taken by the game. Being unemployed, he had time to play it often in the ensuing days. The Raifords joined in on occasion. During these sessions, Darrow learned that the game had come up from Atlantic City (a place of fond memories for him and his wife). He also learned that it was based on a game that had been published in Indianapolis.

Eventually Charles Darrow informed Todd that he'd like to make his own version. Todd encouraged him to do so. Darrow then asked Todd for twelve copies of the game's rules. Todd found the request curious but had his secretary carry out the task.

Charles Darrow laid out his first board on a circular oilcloth that had likely served as a covering for Esther's dining table. Neither the narrow rectangles of Layman's game nor the small rectangles of Todd's board fit, so Darrow created larger rectangles with colored bands at their tops and added graphic icons to many of the spaces. By doing so, he added a look and feel to his board that would prove immensely appealing. Instinct drove him, as he would later explain, because the boards used by Todd and Raiford were so dull. In that moment, Charles Darrow, an "ordinary laborer," created the small but vital magic that transformed the game for academics that Lizzie had invented into a game that would resound with working-class people everywhere.

It was the pivot point—a "tipping point" as author Malcolm Gladwell defined in his book *The Tipping Point: How Little Things Can Make a Big Difference* (2000).

To complete his game, Darrow purchased dice and play money at a nearby dime store, methodically typed and painted title deed cards on laundry cardboard, typed the Chance and Community Chest decks on index cards, and topped off his game with wood moldings, sliced on his jigsaw, to represent houses and hotels (which he left unpainted). Once complete, the game went into service in the Darrow household and later circulated among relatives. (This seminal Darrow game, along with the Todds' game and a second Darrow square oilcloth version, survived several dangers and is now on display in the Monopoly room at the Forbes Gallery in New York City.)

Unlike earlier players, Darrow did not stop there. When friends and relatives asked for copies, Darrow agreed to make them for a price. Each included a square piece of oilcloth on which Darrow transferred his newly created design. He recalled this experience in a letter.

> During [this] period of time, when I was selling to friends and friends of friends, there was a tremendous thrill in every sale. One game a day was our objective and when we reached it, there was rejoicing. . . . I drew each figure on [square] oilcloth with a drafting pen and a sketching pen in India ink. Colored each plot of ground with odds and ends of oil paint. Put in the lettering by hand, cut houses and hotels out of scraps of wood and painted them and then typed all of the paper work. It was a big eight hour job, for four dollars.

Emboldened, Darrow posted a notice at a local bank where he demonstrated the game to customers and took orders. In a moment of persuasive salesmanship, he accepted credit as its inventor. Sales were modest but steady and the Monopoly game began to provide a living for Darrow. Fabricating each game by hand, however, grew old fast. What to do? Darrow made friends with Lytton Patterson Jr. of Patterson and White printers. Patterson agreed to help Darrow automate the process by printing the black lines and words on large squares of oilcloth. This proved difficult but Patterson finally figured out a reliable but slow way of doing it. When demand persisted, Patterson began to print the game's cards and a small label that Darrow pressed on any kind of gift box he could lay his hands on, for example, discarded necktie boxes from department stores. Darrow scrounged for scraps of moldings to use as material for the houses and hotels.

How many sets he actually made is unknown—perhaps as many as two hundred, probably less.

In the spring of 1934 Darrow took a deep breath and commissioned Lytton Patterson to make five hundred fully packaged, fully printed Monopoly games. They hired an artist (possibly Patterson himself) to design an original graphic for its cover and crisp designs for the board's icons (many of which, like the train and chance question mark, Darrow had previously drawn with the aid of stencils). With his savings tied up in this inventory, Darrow convinced a toy industry journal to post an announcement. When orders outside his local area did not materialize, he submitted copies of the game to both Milton Bradley and Parker Brothers. Both deliberated and then rejected the opportunity to license it.

Darrow was left with one ace up his sleeve. He called on the buyer at the prestigious John Wanamaker Department Store in central Philadelphia. Based on reports he had gotten, the buyer agreed to stock Darrow's game for the Christmas season.

Darrow was poised on the edge of history, destined either to fall into obscurity (as had those who tried to commercialize the game before him) or rise into the precious light of success and be carried off by it.

Who was this man, Charles Brace Darrow?

What drove him to make and sell the Monopoly game?

By 1927, when Charles Brace Darrow and his wife, Esther, moved from Pittsburgh to Germantown, he was thirty-eight years old. Germantown was a onetime suburb that had been absorbed into the city and now formed its western, protruding rectangle. (It was named for the German immigrants who settled there during the Revolutionary War period.) Darrow was a man of the steam trade, having been a plumber, a radiator repairman, and a steam engineer. He had come east for work, but after the Depression struck, he lost his job at a steam boiler company. The hard times weighed especially heavily on Darrow. Somehow he had to provide for his family, which included a son, William, and a baby on the way. A good wife, Esther tried to help make ends meet by selling needlepoint whenever possible. Her resolve drove her husband on.

With no prospect of returning to his trade, Darrow looked elsewhere to earn a living. While he lacked a college education, he had the knack of a practical man. Darrow was not a dreamer; he did things. He accepted whatever odd jobs he could to preserve their home at 40 Westview Avenue, be it repairing electric irons, patching sidewalks, or peddling anything he could sell. While many people are uncomfortable selling, Darrow discovered that he had moxie—a salesman's bravado. He could take rejection and keep on plugging. How to apply it? Contract bridge was here to stay, he figured, so why not improve its scoring pad? Good idea, perhaps, but few takers were found. How about wooden toys and puzzles? They were perennially popular. Darrow bought a jigsaw and hand cut plywood to make some. No luck, once again. Then, just as he was about to sell his jigsaw, he and Esther bumped into the Todds on that fateful evening in 1932.

Thereafter necessity drove his actions. The Monopoly game was not available commercially. It was a great game. Why not make and promote it? People seemed to really go for it. Hadn't some fellow published a similar game in Indianapolis?

Across the country, need and responsibility were driving people to do whatever it took to keep a roof over their heads until better times returned; when was anyone's guess. No one was really sure what the new president would accomplish, but many thought Franklin Roosevelt had good ideas. His election offered hope to the downtrodden, but his inauguration was months away. Meanwhile, despondency, poverty, and fear lurked on every corner. Some feared the nation wouldn't last until he took office in March 1933.

In this atmosphere of hope and gloom, Darrow banked everything on Monopoly.

In Washington, Rexford Tugwell was among those working hard to find a cure for the nation's economic ills. The prior month, he and his fellow Brains Trust members had guided Franklin Delano Roosevelt into the presidency, sweeping aside Herbert Hoover and sixty-eight years of Republican dominance in Congress. The nation now looked to the polio-stricken governor of New York State to save them from what many believed could be a violent revolution.

Around the country, fascists were gaining strength and communists manipulated workers and students in an attempt to instigate revolt. Their party would gain real credibility after Roosevelt recognized Stalin's government. Roosevelt's aim, encouraged by Tugwell, was practical: promote trade with the Soviet Union to bolster business (it proved to be a pipedream).

Some individuals held views that were even more extreme: two years earlier, the Communist Party of America asked for and got Scott Nearing's resignation. Nearing wasn't fazed. He believed that radicals were about to witness the realization of their prophecies. "I saw the Great Depression not as an accident but as a logical outcome of the private enterprise economy," Nearing wrote in his autobiography. He foresaw the end one evening when he was the only paying passenger on an express train from Cleveland to Cincinnati. Unregulated capitalism, he and fellow radicals proclaimed, fostered greed, hoarding, and monopolistic practices. The Founding Fathers had got it wrong with free enterprise. The body of America now lay prone, and stiff medicine was required to help it stand again: central economic planning and suspension of liberties.

Few people knew how closely Roosevelt and his advisers were in harmony with the radicals' conclusions. However, they believed that strong government intervention and control could be achieved by letter of law within the capitalist system and without a revolution.

Tugwell was the least submissive of Roosevelt's advisers. He doggedly persuaded Roosevelt that government could right the economy if the new president would put politics aside and push several objective measures through Congress. Roosevelt had taken many business courses as a student at Harvard, but Tugwell knew that during the intervening quarter century, many of the president's beliefs had become outdated. In 1927 he wrote a book entitled *Industry's Coming of Age*. In it, he spoke of not only the benefits of industrial efficiency but also the need for government to take over the planning of industry. He convinced Franklin Roosevelt to read it. Roosevelt thought its ideas might work, if he could overcome opposition. After all, free enterprise and central planning were polar opposites—oil and water.

Things continued to get worse before that bone-chilling day in March 1933 when Franklin Roosevelt took office. By then the nation was ready to try anything. Banks throughout the country had closed their doors after running out of money like so many failed Monopoly players. Workers couldn't cash their paychecks, savings were impounded, and businesses couldn't pay their bills. Firms like Parker Brothers that had printing capability improvised by issuing scrip. In Salem, Massachusetts, most shops honored the scrip presented by Parker employees. What was the alternative?

With the nation on the verge of collapse, Roosevelt decided that under the circumstances oil and water might mix quite nicely. Without the luxury of a transitional honeymoon, Tugwell and Roosevelt's other advisers engineered a lightning campaign that became known as the Hundred Days.

In Philadelphia, Darrow was relieved when his local bank reopened. Roosevelt had seen to this. To Darrow, FDR seemed precisely the kind of man the nation needed—a man of action. Darrow's faith was renewed. So were the hopes of 14 million unemployed workers (nearly 30 percent of the labor force). As the Depression emptied pocketbooks, one factory after another closed, like a line of toppling dominoes. Farmer after farmer was evicted from his land for failing to pay the mortgage and many headed west to an uncertain future. Clusters of ships lay at anchor with nothing to transport. Six out of seven steel mills extinguished their furnaces. Mines shut down. Miles of freight cars sat empty on sidings. In many heartland states, prolonged drought and crop failure created the Dust Bowl, adding to the misery.

There were no federally sponsored programs to help the victims of this disaster, only state and local relief agencies and charities like the Community Chest.

Roosevelt's team knew the emergency was too urgent to wait out. Confidence must return quickly or fear would rule—thus the Hundred Days, a period of fevered activity. Tugwell believed that salvation lay in sparking demand, which would raise prices, jump-start businesses, and rehire workers. He advocated a full state-administered economy, but other members of the Brains Trust thought this too drastic, at least at first. So they settled on a plan that emphasized public works projects, coupled with more direct government aid than at any time in human history.

Banks were supplied with newly printed Federal Reserve notes. Roosevelt used radio to broadcast his reassuring fireside chats and inspire confidence. He took the nation off the gold standard (making it easier to issue money) and obliged everyone to sell their gold coins to the government. ("We're off the Gold Standard" was a message on an early Community Chest card.) Millions gained work through new government initiatives such as the WPA—the Works Progress Administration (one of many alphabet soup agencies created during Roosevelt's New Deal era). Prohibition, begun during Wilson's term, was repealed. "Happy days are here again," were the opening words of a newly popular song. It became Roosevelt's theme.

Tugwell now reached into Columbia University to bring more talent to Washington; among those who heeded his call was Roy Stryker. Capitalizing on Stryker's knack for illustrating, Tugwell asked him to photograph the face of the Depression. Eventually Stryker's team of photographers recorded over 100,000 images of people in all walks of life coping with poverty and misery, their spirit largely unbroken thanks to their faith in Roosevelt.

By the time Charles Darrow ordered his first five hundred production copies of Monopoly, about 20 percent of the nation's workers lacked steady jobs. A small improvement. The average family's income had risen slightly to thirty dollars a week. Gasoline steadied at ten cents a gallon; eggs, seventeen cents a dozen; milk, forty-seven cents a gallon; bread, eight cents a loaf. Landlords charged an average rent of twenty-two dollars per month. Nevertheless, Darrow's game was expensive—three dollars versus the more typical dollar or two. Today's Consumer Price Index is about fifteen times higher than in 1935, so a dollar game then would equate to a fifteen dollar game now. Darrow's Monopoly would be the equivalent of forty-five dollars (games were relatively more expensive seventy years ago).

Darrow's White Box edition was packaged in a large box, which contained a game board of black-bound cardboard, printed Chance and Community Chest cards (without illustrations), large deeds printed on colored cardboard, play money, and two dice. Its houses and hotels were cut from wooden moldings, stained green and red, respectively. There were no tokens; in Darrow's brief rules (printed on the platform in the bottom of the box) he advocated using small objects found around the home.

Most games were purchased in the last four months of the year, just as today, for use as holiday gifts. The buyer for Wanamaker's Department Store counted on this seasonal demand to move Monopoly off his shelves. His name was MacDonald and his Philadelphia store was a destination for most area shoppers (as my mother's long trips there by bus to shop attest. I will forever remember the sight of the massive pipe organ in its lobby.) Wanamaker's was a sterling example of retailing in 1930s America. A shopper then had fewer choices to contemplate. There were small merchants who typically specialized in a type of goods such as food, shoes, or toys; five-and-dime stores like Woolworths that sold low-price closeout merchandise; and department stores that offered quality household goods and fashion. (Shopping malls and discount chains were decades away.)

Many department stores had entertainment areas and food courts. Wanamaker's was the first department store in America to open a public restaurant (1876). It also originated store elevators (1882), foreign motion picture showings (1910), Christmas carolers (1918), and broadcasting music (via its pipe organ) over the radio (1922).

Gimbel's, Macy's, Marshall Field's, and Wanamaker's were among the leading retailers that carried games by Parker Brothers and other major game makers. For Charles Darrow to get a listing in such a store was a significant achievement. MacDonald gave him a purchase order because Darrow had not cut corners on quality (aside from the lack of tokens). While MacDonald complained that Darrow's box was too large, he liked its eye-catching design. Monopoly no longer looked like a collegiate game.

Darrow next convinced FAO Schwarz, the leading toy merchant, to stock his Monopoly game. By October 1934, both stores were reporting good sales and placed reorders. Darrow instructed Patterson and White to make a second run of five hundred games.

While the new orders promised a happy Christmas in the Darrow household (he hoped to clear a dollar a game profit), Darrow was coming to grips with the demands of running a small business capable of satisfying professional retailers. He had to worry about purchasing materials, having gameboards and boxes fabricated, arranging for trucks to deliver his goods, typing invoices, arguing over terms of payment and packing requirements, collecting his money, and paying taxes.

Before the 1934 holidays arrived, Gimbel's Department Store—Wanamaker's chief rival—placed an order, as did a few smaller stores. By New Year's Day, a buzz permeated the Philadelphia air. Monopoly was engendering good word of mouth. MacDonald of Wanamaker's had become, according to Darrow, "a splendid friend . . . A brutal critic but a fine friend." MacDonald now persuaded Darrow to down-size his package, in order to fit more games on the shelf and lower the "stiff" three dollar price. After all, money was still in short supply among his shoppers.

MacDonald pointed to Parker games as examples. It was common practice for the big game maker to offer its leading games in small boxes containing the playing pieces, along with a separate game board. (This is how Electronic Laboratories and Knapp Electric offered Daniel Layman's Finance game.) Parker Brothers published its most popular games in two versions: the standard version with small utensil box and separate board, and a deluxe edition with a box large enough to house the board inside. Unwittingly, Darrow had created a deluxe edition for his initial production. Now he was being asked to make a standard edition. These were typically displayed in a glass case overseen by a store clerk, while their game boards were stacked on a shelf behind.

Perhaps inspired by MacDonald's vision of bigger sales and likely needing a substantial production run to satisfy his two dollar price de-mand, Darrow ordered 7,500 copies of his new Black Box edition. Its utensil box was barely big enough to store the rules, money, deeds, cards, buildings, and dice (tokens were still supplied by the purchaser).

In early 1935, shortly after Darrow began to ship orders from this enormous inventory (whose storage provided another headache), word arrived from the president of Parker Brothers, Robert Barton. It seemed that his firm had recently learned of Monopoly's success in Philadel-phia. Darrow was invited to the Parker showroom in New York for a conference and a deal offer.

His appealing design had caused the firm to change its answer from no to yes.

7

BARTON'S BURDEN
1935–1940

After graduating from Harvard Law School in 1926, Robert B. M. Barton could not imagine he would one day join a game company. His career seemed preordained: he would return to Baltimore and join his father's practice. The Barton family had settled in Baltimore after the Civil War when Robert Barton's grandfather Randolph Barton—who had served on Stonewall Jackson's staff— came north to practice law. For eight generations, a Barton had been an attorney—a tradition that began with distant relative John Marshall, the nation's first chief justice.

Robert Barton's journey from law into the game business began in 1931, when he married George Parker's only surviving child, Sally. Their first child, Randolph, was born the following year. Then Barton had a falling out with his father over legal ethics. At Harvard, Barton had developed an appreciation for the plight of the common man, and he disliked some of his father's wealthy clients, who exploited the "little guy."

In Salem, Massachusetts, George Parker was desperate to find a successor to head up his firm. This need became acute when his older brother Charles resigned because of illness. Charles had guided his

Barton's Burden

Robert B. M. Barton

President of Parker Brothers, 1934–1968

• Parker Bros. Acquire Rights to Game "Monopoly"

As Parker Brothers of Salem, Mass., have recently acquired the rights to the popular game, "Monopoly," all orders for the game should be sent to them instead of to the former publishers. "Monopoly" is an outstanding game hit—the game that tests your business skill in managing real estate and property. Your fortune rises and falls just like it does in real life! It has been reported that the demand for this game is tremendous.

Trade announcement
May, 1935

The PARKER GAMES

You inherit $97.

MONOPOLY
A PARKER TRADING GAME

WORLD WIDE GAME CRAZE

The improved White Box Set with removable Bank (compartment tray), double supply special "Slip" Money and gold stamped Grand Hotels is the favorite medium priced set. 3 to 10 players. Price $3.50. Monopoly from $2 upwards. Beautiful New $10 and $25 Sets. **Rules include Two Forms of "Short" Monopoly for a Quick game.** Sold everywhere!

Ads: 1936 above:
1939 below

CAUTION
IMPORTANT LEGAL NOTICE!
"MONOPOLY"

The name "MONOPOLY" is protected by a registered United States trade-mark.

The game "MONOPOLY" is protected by copyright and by United States Patents No. 1,509,312 and No. 2,026,082.

Any infringement of these rights will be prosecuted to the full extent of the law.

PARKER BROTHERS, INC.
SALEM, MASS.   NEW YORK   LONDON

MONOPOLY
MOST POPULAR of the World's Great Standard Games
Sets, $2 to $15

Trade ad,
February 1936

1935–1940

business for fifty years along with eldest brother, Edward, until his death in 1915. Tragically, George had lost both of his sons—one during the great influenza epidemic of 1918 and the other in an airliner crash in Paris in 1922. Consequently Parker turned his attention to his daughter's young husband. He was impressed by his son-in-law's serious, principled nature. Initially Barton declined Parker's offer to join Parker Brothers, but Parker's persistence and Barton's impasse with his own father altered his stance.

And so it came to be that in 1932, to the shock of Parker's veteran workers, a young attorney with no direct business experience and no knowledge of the game industry arrived and became the heir apparent. The following year he became president. George Parker took the title of chairman and only retained control over new product development. The burden of running the remainder of the business—factory, workers, sales, and finance—would rest squarely on Barton's young shoulders.

The ascent of the tall, bespectacled Barton could not have been more ill timed. After forty-six prosperous years, Parker Brothers was wavering under the blows wrought by the Depression. Sales had dropped steadily since 1929. While the firm manufactured mainstays like backgammon sets and bridge supplies, there was little profit in them because of severe competition. Sales of proprietary games were off by 50 percent. In March 1934, Barton fired everyone at Parker Brothers and then rehired only the best—at lower wages. George Parker did not have the stomach for such an extreme measure, but Barton kept the firm alive long enough for Monopoly to arrive. From that day forward, there was no doubt who the leader of Parker Brothers was.

George Parker's touch for finding hit products faded during the 1930s, and Barton gradually took matters into his own hands. He began by licensing Sorry!, a popular Parcheesi-like game from England, over George Parker's objections (the firm already had similar games, including a staple named Pollyanna). But Sorry!, however familiar its play pattern, possessed a significant improvement—a deck of cards to regulate the movement of playing pieces. This sped up its "race around the board to home" play with added suspense along the way.

Sales of Sorry! helped, but Barton needed a more substantial hit. In a move with far-reaching significance, he established a relationship with John Waddington Ltd., a major printing firm in Leeds, England, a recent and successful entry into the game business. Its general manager, Victor Watson Sr., had stumbled on a card word game named Lexicon and decided to give it a try. His firm, like so many others, needed to boost sales and had obtained the required production savvy from its manufacture of playing cards. Recovering from Lexicon's initial failure, Watson revised its packaging and turned it into England's most popular game. Robert Barton liked Lexicon's potential for America, even though anagram-style games had been a mainstay throughout Parker's history. Lexicon's deck of letter cards was not terribly original, but it had game play twists that made it more appealing than its predecessors. In addition, Barton foresaw more games coming to Parker Brothers from Waddington. He promptly licensed Lexicon, and soon Americans were having as much fun playing it as the British.

Barton had accepted the need to learn the game business from the ground up. To do so, he decided to surround himself with competent department heads and elevate them to vice presidents. George Parker had long resisted the notion of vice presidents but acquiesced once more. One of these, Roy Howard, served Parker as the firm's game editor and was its only R&D employee. Howard would continue to report to Parker. Nevertheless, Barton's staff and the firm's few salesmen would continue to augment Howard by play-testing new game ideas. Employees were invited to join in every Friday afternoon.

By the beginning of 1935, Barton had stabilized the firm, empowered his staff, and held the reins of command firmly in hand. And thus on March 18, 1935, it was he, not George Parker, who journeyed to New York City to do business with Charles Darrow. Thirty-two-year-old Robert Barton met forty-six-year-old Charles Darrow inside Parker's New York showroom at the Flatiron Building on the corner of Fifth Avenue and 23rd Street. The no-frills showroom looked as austere as Barton, with his razor-cut hair, pursed lips, and wire rims. By contrast Darrow wore a loud tie, his thinning hair was combed straight back, and he sported a nervous smile. Barton decided to soften his businesslike tone and put Darrow at ease, "You made us stand up and take notice. I admire your courage." Darrow relaxed. This brief exchange marked the beginning of an improbable relationship: an odd couple come together. By the time the deal was completed the following day, as Barton later recalled, he felt a special liking for Charles Darrow. "I regarded Darrow as a common man, assaulted by the economy, but not beaten. The kind of man I had come to root for in college." The kind of man whose plight inspired him to part ways with his father's law firm.

Darrow confessed that he disliked the weight of running a one-man business with just one product—a common lament among entrepreneurs by chance. However, the negotiations were threatened by the issue of how to dispose of Darrow's remaining 5,900 units of inventory. Barton didn't want them; he wanted to start fresh with boxes and boards bearing his own firm's name. But his legal experience had taught him that significant compromise is often the key to striking a deal. When evaluating the need for give and take, Barton employed a simple criterion: will the concession undermine the desired goal of the deal? In this instance, Barton decided it would not. He agreed to buy the games at a slight profit to Darrow. With this issue out of the way, Barton dictated an otherwise standard inventor's contract and both parties signed it on March 19. Included was language affirming that Darrow was indeed the inventor of the product he was selling to Parker Brothers. Perhaps driven by his sense of accomplishment during the prior two years, his boast at his local bank, and his salesman's confidence, Darrow signed without hesitation.

George Parker felt hopeful about Monopoly's prospects. Memory of misjudging Mah Jongg's improbable appeal led him to put aside the reasons he had rejected Darrow's submission the prior year. His concerns were now centered on making Monopoly comprehensible to a wide audience and devising a way to make the game play quicker. He shuttered himself away and emerged with finely crafted rules, clear and comprehensive, plus instructions for two shortened versions of play. Practicality also guided his devotion: Parker Brothers assured its consumers that every question submitted by mail about its games would be answered (if a stamp for the reply was included). No sense adding to the burden.

Even before the new rules were finalized, Parker shipped some hybrid games to impatient customers, like Wanamaker's. These came from the Darrow inventory, to which was added an interim set of rules and wooden tokens from Parker's stock. A Parker Brothers Monopoly label was applied to the back of the accompanying Darrow game boards. The remaining Darrow games were then stripped of reusable components and dumped (after some were given to employees).

As the first Parker version neared production, a decision was made to include metal tokens in the game. It seemed that Darrow's eleven-year-old niece and her friends liked to use, as playing pieces, charms from bracelets (very popular at the time) or straight out of the boxes of Cracker Jack treats (which always included a prize). This idea sat well with Barton for two reasons: it was novel and Parker Brothers already had a relationship with the Chicago die-casting vendor who made these charms—Dowst Manufacturing. Dowst innovated the popular metal Tootsietoys and marketed an unusual Favor Cake Mix fortune-telling set for girls. It featured fifteen metal charms, four of which would eventually be purchased by Parker Brothers for use in its Monopoly game. (The kit's idea was to wrap these tokens in the sheets of paper provided and bake in a cake. The recipient of each piece would be surprised by a token, whose fortune would then be read on a printed piece of paper, supplied with the kit.) The thimble token bore the curious inscription FOR A GOOD GIRL. It was based on a child-size thimble, often given as a gift (thus "for a good girl"). The original dated back to the century's early years. Parker Brothers elected to include it in Monopoly sets until a new design could be created.

The first Parker Bothers edition included eight metal tokens packed inside a small box, along with dice, $15,140 of play money of Darrow's generic design, and cards that used Darrow's art and type. A separate game board, which retained Darrow's design, accompanied this box of utensils. It was enhanced by a larger Monopoly logo above the word *trademark*. It retailed for two dollars and utilized Darrow's artwork on its cover: two locomotives and the caricature of a smiling man, money in hand. Ironically, this was an exaggerated portrait of Darrow, as rendered by his artist. This cartoon would appear on millions of Monopoly games during the next few decades.

George and Grace Parker returned from their annual trip to Europe to find Parker's Monopoly game ready to ship. Longtime ace salesman Albert "Rich" Richardson hit the rails and tirelessly placed the game in stores west of New England. The Monopoly game now enjoyed national exposure.

And it sold, steadily and increasingly.

When initial sales reports reached George Parker, he knew from experience that sales would mushroom come fall. He urged Barton to add a deluxe version to satisfy the demands of more discerning game players. For its package, Darrow's White Box artwork was resurrected and the Parker Brothers script logo applied (George himself had penned this signature logo).

George Parker was ever mindful of past hits whose exclusivity had been lost. He had discovered Ping Pong in London at the turn of the century and brought it to America. Despite owning the game's trademark, he could not protect its play. Dozens of savvy competitors launched generic table tennis games that dug into his market share. More recently his hesitancy to license Mah Jongg lost what could have been a bonanza for Parker Brothers. Worse, the competitors who sold sets of these Chinese tiles under their own brand names fiddled with the rules to avoid copyright infringement. This led to confusion among the game's millions of fans, which ended the Mah Jongg fad.

To Parker, it was inevitable that Monopoly's success would inspire knockoffs in desperate times. But the toy industry was notorious for copying even in good times. As Robert Barton put it, "Firms like to cozy up to a winner to get in on the action."

So how to thwart their ability to "cozy up" to Monopoly?

Parker Brothers instinctively applied for and received a trademark for Monopoly, which provided exclusive right to use this name. (In prior years, no one had registered or properly commercialized this title.) But trademarks alone, such as for Ping Pong and Mah Jongg, had proved insufficient to deny competition.

Charles Darrow had already copyrighted his game board and had assigned it to Parker Brothers. This deterred competitors from copying his design—enlarged rectangular spaces with color bars along the top of each property, distinctive graphics for each corner space (some think Darrow also spoofed himself with the image of the man behind bars on the Jail space), the Chance question mark, the Waterworks faucet, the Electric Company lightbulb, and the iconic railroad locomotives.

George Parker now urged that a patent be applied for to protect its concept and deter competitors from introducing games that played like Monopoly. Robert Barton was not a patent expert, but Parker Brothers retained the services of an excellent intellectual property firm in Boston. Barton authorized filing an application with the United States Patent Office.

Fate intervened once more. A search of prior patents is essential to determine if there is prior art—older patents making the same or similar claims. Claims are questioned if prior art exists. The Patent Office search unearthed Lizzie's 1924 patent for the Landlord's Game, and George Parker realized he knew its inventor: Elizabeth Magie Phillips.

Parker remembered purchasing a card game from her a long time ago. And he recalled turning down her Landlord's Game twice. When Darrow was informed of the existence of the Landlord's Game, he admitted that he had redressed an existing idea of uncertain (to him) origin. Improvements in existing designs are common in industry and often make the difference between success and failure, especially in the toy and game business. But if it wanted to obtain a patent for these differences, Parker Brothers would first have to acquire the preceding patent. This became George Parker's mission.

On November 5, 1935, the game that arose in the creative mind of Lizzie Magie, that had cycled its way through colleges, wound through cities like Reading, Indianapolis, and Atlantic City, came full circle. Elizabeth Magie Phillips was about to reconnect to the offspring of her brainchild.

Parker journeyed to Washington, D.C., by train, preoccupied with the disappearance of his beloved dog, Nero. That morning, he received a telegram confirming Nero's safe return. Buoyed by the news, he was in good spirits when he met with Elizabeth and Albert Phillips at their home in Arlington, Virginia, near the Potomac River. It was a reunion of sorts. Elizabeth was about the same age as Parker (sixty-nine). Although he found her eccentric and a bit unsettling, they had much in common and her high regard for Parker was genuine (the "King of Games," she wrote of him.)

Lizzie admitted to being out of luck—and time—in her long effort to make America aware of the lessons imbued by her creation. Her 1932 edition had gone nowhere; few copies were sold. Parker was sympathetic but withheld criticism. (Of course the public did not want lessons.) He brought Lizzie around to considering a sale of her patent. What would it take?

Eventually this became clear. In return for assigning her patent to Parker Brothers, Lizzie accepted $500 cash and Parker eventually agreed to publish the Landlord's Game, as well as two of her more recent game inventions. Parker promised to place her name and/or picture on these games.

Satisfied, Lizzie and Albert joined George Parker at the Patent Office on November 6, 1935, and executed the assignment.

Armed with this, Parker's attorneys rushed through the Darrow patent (aided by the low level of patent work inside the office—a sign of the Depression's toll on innovation). The Monopoly patent was issued on the last day of the year, one of the last patents approved before the office closed its record books for 1935.

By the end of its first year, a quarter of a million Monopoly games had been made and sold by Parker Brothers. Based on this performance, it was sure to sell even more copies in 1936. To satisfy more demanding customers, Parker suggested three luxurious editions be added to the Monopoly line. Barton concurred.

But neither Parker nor Barton, nor anyone for that matter, anticipated just how well the many Monopoly editions would sell in 1936.

Shortly after New Year's Day, orders flooded into Parker Brothers, without letup, for Monopoly games from America's retailers and catalogs. Leading department stores capitalized on demand by setting up massive displays of the game. Trade journals, magazines, and newspapers excitedly reported its success, sparking even greater demand. Through a monumental effort, Barton and his staffers manufactured 1,810,000 copies of the game that year. It seemed that all who played the game with friends wanted their own copy immediately thereafter. To suppress demand until production could catch up, Barton raised the price of standard Monopoly to $2.50. As soon as supply caught up, a new $2.00 edition appeared. It contained smaller money bills and wooden playing pieces, but was otherwise much the same as its $2.50 cousin.

Many could not afford even $2.00 for a game, so Monopoly became a magnet drawing in friends and family to the homes of those who owned it. Some folks even made their own copy using play money, scraps of cardboard, bits of wood, and ersatz tokens. One of these, made in Ohio during 1936, remains extant (and is pictured).

Parker advertised Monopoly heavily in the leading publications of the day, including *Esquire, Time, Life, Liberty, Ladies Home Journal, Redbook,* and the *Christian Herald.* Radio commentators delighted in telling tales of its success. Monopoly was so "in" that Hollywood placed it in movies such as *Grand Jury, Meet Nero Wolfe,* and *Hot Money.*

The success of Monopoly benefited the entire game industry. As *Toys and Novelties* reported in May 1936, "The winter of 1935–36 will go down into history as the coldest on record, but toy buyers will long remember it as the season wherein game sales were at their hottest." The renewed popularity of games was both welcome and unexpected, the trade journal noted, and recognized the power of Monopoly to get consumers into stores and open their pocketbooks.

*Handmade Monopoly game from Ohio, made after
Parker Brothers published the game, c. 1936.*

Not all of the publicity was favorable. Letters to magazines like *Time* and *Fortune* disputed Monopoly's origin. And suddenly there was a similar game entitled Finance. Robert Barton wondered how a game so close in play to Monopoly could already be on the market. And who was Daniel Layman, the man who had written the letter to *Time* magazine claiming responsibility for Finance?

After a somewhat heated exchange of communications, Robert Barton returned to New York City and signed a deal to acquire all the rights to the Finance game from Electronic Laboratories on behalf of David Knapp of Knapp Electric and then to buy the game's complete rights from Knapp, in return for approximately $10,000. Ironically, Dan Layman got nothing from the windfall Barton paid Knapp Electric and Electronic Laboratories (as already noted, Layman had sold his rights to Finance for $200, three years earlier).

Looking to recover his sizable investment, Barton felt he had to keep Finance on the market and briefly marketed it through the Finance Game Company, with offices in the Parker Brothers showroom in the Flatiron Building.

After Barton learned of the Thuns in Reading, Pennsylvania, and their modest game production, he journeyed there and met Louis

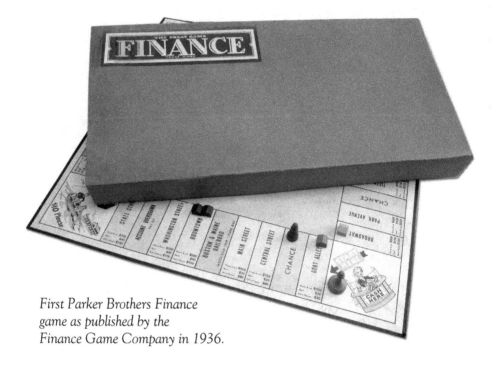

First Parker Brothers Finance
game as published by the
Finance Game Company in 1936.

Thun, who at the time had his hands full running the Textiles Machine Company (which included Berkshire Mills knitting factory). Barton purchased some of Thun's games from people in the Reading area. He also was directed by Thun to Paul Sherk, who sold a copy of his homemade version to Barton.

Of necessity, Barton reconvened with Charles Darrow to discuss the time, money, and legal effort Parker Brothers was expending to protect his game. But Barton approached these negotiations with care. Darrow's graphic additions and entrepreneurial efforts had made all the difference in Barton's mind. He acknowledged this the moment he compared the abstract design of Finance to the engaging appearance of Monopoly. Darrow had given the game "the perfect touch," as Barton termed it. Therefore, he proposed, and Darrow accepted, a smaller royalty in return for immunity from the legal expense Parkers Brothers might incur.

By so doing, Darrow effectively concluded his role in the game's development. Over the years, Charles Brace Darrow has been characterized as both a folk hero and a villain. It is easy to argue either characterization. You be the judge. But if measured by the yardstick of happiness imparted to others, his contribution to the game stretches beyond that of all others, especially the millions who suffered during the Depression's troubled times.

The Darrows soon moved away from 40 Westview Avenue. Charles purchased a farm in Bucks County, Pennsylvania, where he lived for the rest of his life and raised orchids when not traveling around the world.

In Salem, Parker Brothers began issuing joint credit for Monopoly to Charles Darrow and Elizabeth Magie Phillips. By emphasizing the patent George Parker had acquired from Lizzie, Parker Brothers strengthened its hand. To publicize this, Barton issued trade ads cautioning others from attempting to copy Monopoly, much as George Parker had used similar ads to publicize his firm's ownership of the Mah Jongg trademark. But Barton didn't think this would pay such a long-term dividend. As he later explained, "At the time, none of us, especially Mr. Parker, believed it would matter. We fully expected Monopoly to just be a pleasant memory after a few years, much like the Mah Jongg game that plagued Mr. Parker's memory."

Nevertheless, success is a magnet that attracts imitators. It came as little surprise to Barton that a game which played much like Monopoly, named Inflation, popped up in a trade ad. Barton demanded that it be withdrawn from the market but its maker resisted. Inflation was created by Rudy Copeland, who had learned the Landlord's Game while a student at Texas A&M. His game, its graphics, and text spoofed the Roosevelt administration by means of Monopoly-like rules. Copeland was familiar with the history of the Landlord's Game and told Barton he'd welcome a court trial against a Yankee. Barton met Copeland in Indianapolis and reminded him that he came from a long line of Virginians. Copeland was affronted by the idea of a southerner defecting to the North. Barton settled with Copeland, allowing Inflation to remain on the market with a license from Parker Brothers of the two Monopoly patents. (Inflation went nowhere and is today a rare collector's item.)

Parker Brothers succeeded in removing two other games from the market: New York, made by the start-up Amesbury Game Company, and Big Business by rival Transogram, which agreed to redesign its game so that it no longer looked or played exactly like Monopoly. Transogram eventually reintroduced Big Business in 1948; it sold modestly for many years. Parker's main rival, the Milton Bradley Company of Springfield, Massachusetts, also "cozied up" to Monopoly, according to Barton. In 1937 Bradley published a game named Carnival whose board layout and rules were entirely based on the expired 1904 Landlord's Game patent. It flopped. But the firm also published another game, similar to Layman's Finance, entitled Easy Money. Bradley executives were aware of Monopoly's past because of William Allphin's submission in 1931. Although Barton believed he could prevail against Bradley, he struck a deal to enable Easy Money to remain on the market. Friendship played a role. Barton had become close to George Fox, Bradley's representative to the industry's trade organization, of which Robert Barton was an active member. They agreed to license the Darrow and Phillips patents for Bradley's use on a modified version of Easy Money. While this move sanctioned a competitive game, it strengthened both patents. It is an axiom among patent attorneys that the more a patent is licensed, the stronger it is if challenged in court.

In fact, the Darrow patent was probably weak to begin with, and its filing date could have posed a problem, having occurred just beyond the grace period accorded a filer.

Nonetheless, Parker Brothers' rights to the game were firmly secured through its trademark and the copyrights on the game's visual design. This design was refined in late 1936 with the addition of a mascot—a friendly financier who sported a top hat, tuxedo, cane, and big white mustache. He was joined by his wife, three nephews, and several associates. The artist who created this character is unknown, but his inspirations were the calling cards he had previously designed for Parker sales whiz Albert Richardson and the clay figure, Little Esky, featured on the cover of each issue of *Esquire*—the top men's magazine of the era that ran several Parker advertisements.

Little Esky was modeled after the legendary J. P. Morgan, the greatest monopolist of all. Morgan had been gone for two decades, but the firm bearing his name (J.P. Morgan Company) continued to grow and prosper. It was destined to become a vital component of the Dow Jones Industrial Average and, aided by several mergers, achieved distinction as the world's largest bank.

And so, as fate would have it, the legendary monopolist and soon-to-be legendary Monopoly game were united. Ironically, J. P. Morgan joined the game whose predecessor intended to discredit him and his ilk. The public loved the twist and the resultant "marriage." The little Monopoly man, Morgan's alter ego, would forever grace the game's Chance and Community Chest cards and eventually its package cover, advertisements, and innumerable licensed products, plus a host of other Parker Brothers games. He would become as recognizable as any other cartoon figure on the planet.

John Pierpont Morgan
Financier, monopolist

The original Mr. Monopoly was modeled after J. P. Morgan.

Parker Brothers introduced more money games than Monopoly because there was a buzz in the air, as Barton put it. Consumers seemed receptive to making a paper fortune. In late 1935, his firm published a Monopoly-like game entitled Fortune. Its development was likely started before George Parker met with Elizabeth Magie Phillips as a precaution if she turned out to be stubborn or if she sold her patent to a competitor. David Knapp apparently was in the hunt. Even with

Lizzie's patent in hand, Robert Barton went ahead with Fortune because he liked its name and wanted to protect it as a Parker asset. About 10,000 copies of Fortune were sold; it played very much like Layman's Finance, which Parker Brothers also republished after improving its graphics and streamlining its play. Finance now became a "simpler Monopoly," according to Barton. In time, these two games were combined awkwardly as Finance and Fortune, or House and Lot. Eventually the long title was shortened to Finance. The final game retained a place in the Parker line for many decades.

The next order of business was Lizzie's Landlord's Game, which George Parker had obligated his firm to publish. This proved a challenge. Barton's salesmen were convinced they could not sell it without a major facelift, especially the removal of its political features. Leroy Howard and George Parker, distracted by the heady success of Monopoly, found this task unappealing and time-consuming.

However, Lizzie's Bargain Day and King's Men games were on display at the 1937 Toy Fair, both bearing the accolade "By Elizabeth Magie Phillips, famous originator of games." Her white-haired profile graced the cover of the latter. These endorsements meant little to the trade and even less to consumers because Lizzie—despite her thirty plus years of effort—was largely unknown and irrelevant to the American public. Further, most people couldn't care less who invented the games they played; it only mattered that they were fun. Even George Parker could not guarantee satisfaction by placing his picture on a game's box (which, by the way, he chose never to do). Bargain Day and King's Men sold modestly for a few years and then faded from view.

A similar endorsement ploy had been tried in 1936 to bolster the sales of a Parker stock market game entitled Bulls and Bears. In an effort to capitalize on the man who introduced Monopoly, it bore a photo of a rather dour-looking Charles Darrow with the caption: "Charles B. Darrow, Monopoly, etc." stating that Darrow had also invented Bulls and Bears (which he had not). The game included stock cards bearing the names of real companies, like General Motors, Dupont, and General Electric. Parker Brothers launched the game with much fanfare and in two different packages. When consumers didn't respond, it scrambled to reissue each version with a more flattering studio photo of Darrow. But this "improvement" also came to no avail. A large number of Bulls and Bears games were sold into the trade because game buyers were dazzled by Monopoly's success. But disappointing word of mouth led to the game's demise, which proved again that no matter how strong the hype, "the play's the thing."

Beyond endorsements and similar money games, there were licensed properties. The first was a clever tray designed by a Boston firm, Peel, Denton, Palmer & Hanscom, that a player could use to organize his money and deeds. Next came a Monopoly birthday card that use the imagery of the game to extend the sender's wishes (and perhaps a gift of real money). It wasn't long before a song entitled "Monopoly" emerged from Tin Pan Alley and gained airplay on the nation's radios; its sheet music was sold in many stores. Another accessory that hit the scene was a stock exchange add-on for use with any Monopoly (or Finance) game. This was the idea: place (or adhere) the Stock Exchange space on top of Monopoly's Free Parking space. Whenever you landed there, you were permitted to buy and sell cards representing shares in six companies. You could now make money in real estate and speculate on the side when playing Monopoly. Barton purchased it outright from the Capitol Novelty Company, which originally published it. But even Parker Brothers and a fifty-cent price tag could not make Stock Exchange hit the heights. It crashed to earth a year or two later.

Parker Brothers' experimentation with Monopoly-related games and its commitment to the real thing were akin to Darwin's theory of natural selection. Only the strongest survive. Monopoly prevailed and became the most significant money game in history. It also rewarded the firm with its strongest balance sheet in years. And thanks to an upturn in the general economy, Parker was not the only company to bounce back during 1936. A happy nation rewarded President Roosevelt with a landslide in the fall election. But business again slowed in 1937, and the warm glow of Roosevelt's fireside chats began to fade. Rexford Tugwell, feeling his job was done in Washington, accepted a position in the private sector before being persuaded by Mayor Fiorello LaGuardia in 1938 to head the New York City Planning Commission. Three years later, President Roosevelt appointed him governor of Puerto Rico.

During Roosevelt's second term, his New Deal faced increasing skepticism. While it had jump-started the nearly moribund economy, the nation's output had not roared back to 1929 levels. More misery set in as a vicious new recession gripped the nation in 1938. To stem the economy's renewed slide, Roosevelt asked Congress to approve another $5 billion for public relief and government-sponsored jobs. Many began to wonder if the United States could ever endure without government handouts (which were paid for by redistribution of income from rich to poor, and massive borrowing against the future). Meanwhile in Europe, two dictators were boasting of success with their fascist schemes: Adolf Hitler in Germany and Benito Mussolini in Italy. They seemed to have licked the Depression, much to the dismay of France and England, and communist Russia was boasting of "work for all." Capitalism was losing out on the Continent. Did that mean tough, dictatorial control was the wave of the future in North America?

Monopoly did not come through the 1938 recession unscathed. Its sales had waned by 60 percent in 1937, which Barton expected. Almost everyone who wanted a set had purchased one in 1936. But Barton was surprised when sales did not stabilize or bounce upward in 1938. Instead, Monopoly's sales declined further and slid again during 1939. When the books were tallied, it was found that only 151,000 units had been sold that year, 92 percent below peak sales in 1936. And sales of similar games seemed to stop altogether at retail. Out of context, sales of 150,000 units were very good by the standards of other game sales of this era, but for Monopoly it seemed to herald a day when the game would become only a "minor item," as Barton put it. To stem the tide, he lowered prices on some editions—a move George Parker opposed for good reason. Monopoly's prices had not risen since 1936, but material costs had (a byproduct of the economic bounce). Monopoly's price, adjusted for inflation, was now lower than in 1935. History would perpetuate this phenomenon. In terms of current dollars, Monopoly became increasingly cheaper for the consumer to purchase. Despite Parker Brothers' "monopoly" on the market for money games, Monopoly consistently disproved the price rise theory of monopolies (except for a brief period in 1936 when the price of the standard edition was raised by 25 percent to check demand).

No real change in the game occurred during this period except for the occasional use of nonstandard "pencil sketch" Chance and Community Chest cards (probably due to leftover inventory after the Monopoly man cards were adopted), and some rather crudely molded "composite material" tokens. Most of these tokens resembled their metal counterparts, although they were fatter and painted in primary colors. Among them was an occasional new design, such as an airplane.

The consumer benefited from not only Monopoly's improving value but also its otherwise rigid standardization. The long-term impact of Robert Barton's efforts to establish one superior design, coupled with George Parker's well-written rules, meant that consumers in every part of the country played Monopoly the same way (aside from the enthusiastic addition of certain house rules that didn't affect the core play of the game). This was true not only in the United States but overseas as well. Foreign editions in Europe and Asia maintained these ideals. Norman Watson of Waddington's wins credit for this (as you'll see). The Monopoly game was quickly becoming a common language, a shared reservoir of enjoyment and experience that players from the four corners of the earth could share with equanimity.

In 1939 the revised Landlord's Game finally appeared. It was packaged in an attractive pale green box with bright red letters and emblazoned with an attractive profile of Lizzie's smiling face. Its board had undergone a major facelift: its rectangular path of abstract spaces had been replaced by irregular spaces that wound through a scenic countryside. While this edition played much like Lizzie's 1924 version, the Prosperity version from her 1932 game was omitted before it was shipped. This angered Phillips because she had been sent a prototype with its rules enclosed. While this appeared to be a breach of promise, in reality it was an act of desperation by Parker Brothers to convince their trade to stock the game. With Monopoly on the wane, with the revised Finance puttering along, and with Bulls and Bears a failure, the trade did not want another property trading game, especially one espousing a tax theory. Parker Brothers resolutely printed 10,000 copies. But as the trade had warned, they remained "glued" to store shelves. Barton made the costly decision to take back all unsold copies in order to protect Monopoly's continuity at retail ("Take back Landlord's or we'll drop Monopoly," was a typical retailer's threat.) Virtually all of the 1939 Landlord's Games were then destroyed. The few that remain today are prized collector items.

The initial stage of Monopoly was playing out in the States, but thanks to Barton's foresight in building rapport with John Waddington Ltd., the game was in the thick of things in Europe, and elsewhere.

Well before the next war, this lone game was on its way to conquering much of the world. In just a few years, Monopoly would bolster the effort of those opposing the forces of tyranny that wanted it for themselves.

8

WATSON'S WAR

1936–1945

Monopoly began its spread around the world in December 1935, when Robert Barton sent a copy of the game to John Waddington Ltd. in Leeds, England. This was not an easy decision. For decades, George Parker had maintained a Parker Brothers export office in London. But Robert Barton did not think this facility had the means to distribute or license the Monopoly game throughout Europe, and he presumed Waddington did. This assumption proved to be another pivotal point.

John Waddington Ltd. had a history filled with ups and downs, including near-bankruptcy in 1913 (its founder, John Waddington, was taking money from the till). Waddington resigned and Victor Watson Sr. emerged and rescued the firm through sound management, devotion, and belief in the company's products. Early in the century, Waddington was known only as a printer of theatrical playbills. Watson aimed to expand this business and develop the printing trade by acquiring larger and better printing presses. In time he turned to the manufacture of playing cards. Thanks to superior lithography and reel-fed card stock, he broke up the British playing card monopoly owned

**Victor
Watson Sr.**

General mgr.
of
Waddingtons

**Norman
Watson**

General mgr.
of
Waddingtons

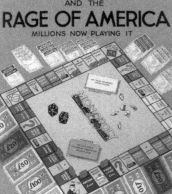

MONOPOLY
THE NEW GAME
AND THE
RAGE OF AMERICA
MILLIONS NOW PLAYING IT

U.K. Monopoly ad, 1936

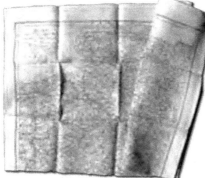

*Above: Waddingtons
Monopoly set,
used to
smuggle escape
tools to POWs.
Left: silk escape
map of Germany.*

1936–1945

by the De La Rue company. In addition, Waddington mastered the art of printing silk theater programs and cigarette cards. These developments would produce surprising consequences for both the Waddington company and Monopoly during the coming war.

Printed cardboard cartons soon joined the Waddington family of products. Waddington perfected the art of making cardboard jigsaw puzzles in the early 1930s, a difficult task because of the great pressure needed to die-cut the puzzles. Previously most puzzles—like Parker's Pastime Puzzles—were made from plywood and cut piece by piece with jigsaws. The new cardboard process dramatically lowered costs and provided cheap entertainment for idle millions during the Depression.

Because jigsaw puzzles were sold in game departments, it made sense for the Waddington company to try its hand at marketing games. By the early 1930s, Victor's son Norman was fully involved in the business, his role similar to Robert Barton's at Parker Brothers. Lexicon became his first choice. This word game was little more than a custom deck of cards, which was easy for Waddington to manufacture. It failed initially, apparently because it was too cheap to attract word game lovers. In a bold move, Norman upgraded the quality of the packaging (making it look like a little book) and doubled the price. Never before had a failure received such an investment. The new format sold spectacularly well and Waddington licensed Lexicon throughout Europe, and then to Parker Brothers following Robert Barton's inquiry.

By 1935 John Waddington Ltd. had the technology and the distribution to break the game market in England wide open. It just needed the right title.

Monopoly arrived in Victor Watson's office on a Friday in December that year; Robert Barton sent it in proposed reciprocity for Lexicon. Intrigued, Victor gave it to Norman to play with his family over the weekend. Norman and his seven-year-old-son, Victor Jr., were enthralled by its play. In fact Norman liked the game so much he continued to play it after his son went to bed, assuming the role of many hypothetical players. The following Monday morning, a transatlantic phone call was placed to Parker Brothers and a deal was clinched.

This marked the first time either firm had placed or received a transoceanic call. AT&T had inaugurated transatlantic service eight years earlier; a three-minute call still cost $75.

Barton licensed all rights to make and sell Monopoly throughout the United Kingdom to Waddington. Waddington registered Monopoly with the British Patent Office, secured its trademark, and dutifully made four versions using names of London streets, stations, and utilities. Its most expensive set featured alligator-skin paper on the package and back of the game board, and the rules were encased in a binder covered with the same luxurious material.

Within a year, buoyed by Waddington's initial success, Barton expanded its license to include Continental Europe, Australia, New Zealand, and South Africa. Although Barton assumed that Waddington possessed an established network of licensees on the Continent, it did not. Nevertheless, the Watsons, working through a few trusted partners, ensured that Monopoly found a home in every European country of note. Faithful to Barton's hope that Monopoly would look and play the same everywhere, Norman Watson provided his firm's graphics to each licensee and asked that its icons and layout be adapted to the greatest extent possible. His success in this effort was amazing, especially given a lack of face-to-face meetings or phone conversations (the post and telegraph being the norm).

The Miro company immediately licensed Monopoly in France; its game board would be graced with Parisian street names. Miro was founded by a Russian émigré named Mirovitch. (After the war an attorney named Michel Habourdin bought the firm and become a key contributor to Monopoly's later success in Europe.) Next came the Franz Schmidt company, Germany's most prestigious game maker. Schmidt chose Berlin names for its property spaces. Licensees in the Netherlands, Sweden, Denmark, Belgium, Spain, Switzerland, Italy, and Austria followed suit and chose names from their capital cities. But when Australia, New Zealand, and South Africa signed on, all three decided to retain London street names. Meanwhile, Parker Brothers licensed Monopoly to the Copp Clarke company in Canada and local game firms throughout South America. (It became known as Metropoli in some Latin American countries.)

Monopoly's invasion of Europe continued until a backlash developed in the fascist countries. Mussolini did not like the idea of foreign words becoming trademarks in Italy, nor did he approve of foreign companies owning Italian trademarks. Further, he frowned on capitalistic products being sold to his people. Emilio Ceretti of Editrice Giocchi circumvented these roadblocks by changing the spelling of Monopoly to Monopoli, registering the name himself, and including a few fictitious fascist street names on his game board (Via del Fascio, Largo Littorio, and Corso Impero), which otherwise featured streets from Milan, not Rome. Assuaged, Mussolini's bureaucrats dropped their opposition to its sale.

Franz Schmidt found the going more difficult in Germany. The most expensive space on his German board was unwittingly named for an island in Berlin where many leading Nazis owned homes. They didn't want their addresses to be associated with lavish capitalist-style wealth. Propaganda minister Josef Goebbels and Hermann Goering, Hitler's second in command, threatened to ban Schmidt's game. They encouraged the Hitler Youth to demonstrate against any shops that dared carry it. This threat effectively kept the inventory in Schmidt's warehouse. Few copies of the game were sold before World War II, and even fewer survived the war because the warehouse was destroyed during a Royal Air Force bombing raid. Only in Austria did the fascists ignore Monopoly, likely because its maker (DKT) wisely changed its name to Business and filled the center of the board with beautiful Viennese landmarks, such as its famous opera house.

Despite fascist opposition to Monopoly, citizens in these three countries continued to venerate game playing as a valuable tool in developing skills and knowledge. The versions in the fascist countries were made with finer components and materials than elsewhere on the Continent. To wit: Austrian Business game had money in the form of polished wood discs, not paper bills. Its playing pieces were large painted figures made of wood. One copy of the Austrian edition is known to have survived. It was the only luxury a little girl was permitted to hand-carry out of Vienna in 1937 when her family fled the Nazis after the German annexation.

In Shanghai another handsome—but unauthorized—version appeared, its box and board wrapped with paper resembling snakeskin. It was just starting to gain acceptance among the foreigners stationed there when the Japanese overran Shanghai and massacred its citizens. Few copies of this game survived because the Japanese regarded the game as tool of capitalist propaganda.

In 1939 World War II began after Germany invaded Poland, and France and Britain honored their alliance with the Poles. The following spring, the Nazis overran France, and England came under aerial bombardment. Monopoly sales plummeted on the Continent as the war emergency distracted people and diverted materials away from game production. In Nazi-occupied Europe, paper and cardboard were strictly rationed according to need and connections. Few game companies had the pull required to keep their presses running.

Across the English Channel, Great Britain fought for its survival. During these dark hours, Monopoly and John Waddington Ltd. were asked to join the war effort.

MI6 is the branch of the British Secret Service best known for espionage (Ian Fleming's character, James Bond, worked for MI6). Norman Watson worked with a real secret agent in a related branch of the British Secret Service known as MI9, whose mission was providing aid for escapes. From 1940 on, John Waddington Ltd. was involved in MI9's efforts to help British servicemen evade capture by the Germans or to break out and get back home after being captured. Waddington's ability to print on silk was responsible for its initial involvement in this clandestine effort. Later its license to manufacture Monopoly became equally important.

In mid-1940, a stranger arrived at Waddington's main factory at 40 Wakefield Road in Leeds (185 miles north of London). His name was

E. D. Alston, but his identity would not be made public for decades. He became known around Waddington as Mr. A. On his first visit he posed as a businessman and placed an order for calling cards. Waddington dutifully obliged, not realizing Alston was actually casing the firm to determine if it had the right "character."

A few weeks later, Alston returned and asked to speak in private with the principals of the firm. He then read them excerpts from England's Official Secrets Act. He asked the Watsons and the firm's management team if they would uphold the provisions of this act should they be called on to do service for their country. They did so without hesitation and agreed to never again call Alston by his real name. Mr. A now revealed his plan.

Soon Waddington began to print detailed maps of France and Germany on silk. Why silk? It was the material of choice because it did not tear easily, did not deteriorate in water, and weighed next to nothing. And unlike paper, it didn't rustle. A silk map can be silently unfolded with a shake in the air, alerting no one nearby. Waddington mastered the art of silk printing after finding the right grade of material, the right amount of "filling" to absorb ink, and the proper way to stretch it. Eventually the maps depicted much of western and central Europe. Only later did the Watsons learn that every British airman carried one of their maps on each mission he flew, sometimes sewn into his uniform, at other times in a flight boot. After D-day in 1944, countless foot soldiers carried them as well.

Mr. A forbade Waddington to record anything about this project in writing. Orders were transmitted verbally. Mr. A would bring the maps he wanted reproduced to Leeds, or Norman Watson would go to London and pick them up. Mr. A offered Waddington an armed guard at the factory, but both Watsons declined for fear it would arouse suspicion and worry among their mainly female workers.

With the silk map production humming, Mr. A asked the Watsons to make decks of standard playing cards to which were added maps and escape instructions. A tiny compass, which MI9 would provide, was hidden in their boxes. Waddington planned to discontinue making playing cards after Norway fell, since it was a prime source of the material Waddington needed to produce high-quality decks. But thanks to the encouragement of Prime Minister Winston Churchill, Waddington devised a linen-like replacement material and kept up its playing card production. Churchill and his wife played Bezique (a two-player card game) and believed card games were beneficial to British morale.

By virtue of this decision, Waddington was able to comply with Mr. A's latest request. But first a new obstacle had to be overcome: the paper material proved unacceptable for his specifications. MI9 preferred the cards to be highly flammable, so that a lighted cigarette could cause them to burst into flames. While this ran contrary to Waddington's commercial needs, the Watsons led an effort to make a volatile playing card. Pure gun cotton was the solution. Touching one of these cards to an ember (such as a lit cigarette) caused it to explode and vaporize instantly. MI9 was delighted, but the Watsons were worried about their workers inadvertently blowing up themselves and the factory as well. This they considered more likely than the threat of a German bomb finding its mark. Consequently men with foam fire extinguishers were always present during the production of these flammable novelties. (Fortunately they were never needed.)

However valuable a map, escape instructions, and a compass were to a flyer downed behind enemy lines, they were of little use if the airman was captured and imprisoned in a POW camp. In this situation, cutting tools and bribe money had to be smuggled into the camp.

MI9 concluded that Monopoly would be an ideal means to transport these items. Mr. A requested Waddington to construct special editions of Monopoly games with low-profile escape tools, maps, and compasses hidden inside their game boards, and real currency tucked under the game's colorful bills. The Red Cross would deliver these games to Allied airmen housed inside Nazi stalags—prisoner of war camps. Norman asked how these games could pass inspection by the prison guards. Mr. A explained that the Nazis considered games and puzzles "pacifiers" that kept prisoners occupied with something other than escape schemes. Further, the Germans had stopped inspecting packages that the Red Cross delivered because they depended on the Red Cross to supplement the rations in these camps to achieve the minimum level specified by the Geneva Convention for prisoners. Being found in violation could harm Germany's ability to get needed goods in exchange for prisoners. MI9 was therefore confident that these Monopoly games would arrive without incident.

This reassurance was important to the Watsons. While there was no obvious way for the Germans to link escape maps and playing cards to their factory, Monopoly was another matter. There was no doubt which firm made Monopoly in England. A revenge raid by the Germans would destroy their plant and kill the workers.

To hide the tools, skilled mechanics cut precise openings for them in the cardboard liner of the game boards. Money pads were assembled with a few Monopoly bills on top and currency supplied by MI9 underneath. The currency was French francs, German marks, or Italian lira, depending on the destination of the game.

Once a prison camp took delivery, POW leaders could designate a group of prisoners to make use of the games' escape aids. The files would cut through barbed wire, and the map would guide the escapees to the coded locations of partisans. The compass would fix direction, and the money would buy train tickets and food, as well as bribe those who might endanger their progress.

One of six area maps was hidden inside each game. To innocuously tag each game board and signal which map was inside, a period was added after the title on one of its spaces. For example, a period after Mayfair might signal a map of Scandinavia and upper Germany.

Here is a typical production order to Waddington as orally provided by Mr. A:

12 Monopoly ITALY
Reference "Marylebone Station" full-stop [period]

12 Monopoly NORWAY, SWEDEN and GERMANY
Reference "Mayfair" full-stop

12 Monopoly NORTHERN FRANCE, GERMANY and
FRONTIERS
Reference "Free Parking" full-stop

12 Monopoly straight
Reference "Patent Applied For" full-stop
[These "straight" games were used as decoys.]

Ironically, the intense secrecy of the British war effort prevented MI9 from knowing that Waddington was also making shells, flares, and cartridges at the behest of the army. Neither service learned of the other's procurement thanks to Waddington's internal security precautions.

Not until forty years after the war was the British public informed of the secret use of card games and Monopoly to aid escapees during the conflict. Sadly, no visual or written record of these games was made. The memories of those involved, a few reproductions, and a handful of leftover silk maps were all that remained. By the time the war ended, 35,000 Allied airmen had successfully escaped captivity. Given the intense secrecy of the Monopoly project, there is no record of the number who owed their freedom to the game.

Although the war in Europe inflamed American isolationists, President Roosevelt and his cabinet believed neutrality would prove fatal for Great Britain and ultimately for the United States as well. If England fell, the Nazis could take Iceland and Greenland, and then march into Canada at will.

During the sharp recession of 1938, President Roosevelt had initiated a plan to bolster the nation's armed forces, which were smaller than Portugal's. Military spending finally injected a dose of real growth into the economy. By 1939 millions had gone back to work or joined the military. A national joke at the time went like this: If you're not working to build the military, you are the military. Roosevelt won an unprecedented third term the following year.

Roosevelt's top priority in 1940 was Britain's survival, and his Lend-Lease Act was approved in the nick of time. England's monetary reserve had just run dry, and the act enabled Roosevelt to send massive aid to Britain in return for leases on military bases. As a result, companies like John Waddington Ltd. continued to receive funding from His Majesty's government, and the war against Germany continued to be prosecuted from British soil, not American.

Even this emergency aid to a friendly nation met stiff opposition. Cries of war profiteering soon rang anew. Scott Nearing issued a proclamation that "the world role of the United States since 1918 has been a logical outcome of the evolution of monopolistic capitalism . . . Necessarily, it has been shameful. The United States is the world's number one war profiteer. We are forever shamed."

Nearing was aware of Monopoly's immense success and didn't care for it. Most aspects of modern society disturbed him. In 1932 he and wife Helen had moved to rural Vermont to live a self-sufficient life on a secluded farm. To earn cash for the few transactions they needed to make, Nearing wrote and published many books and papers that made people think about their values. But the Japanese surprise attack on Pearl Harbor on the morning of December 7, 1941 drowned his outcry of war profiteering and silenced his fellow isolationists.

Roosevelt asked for and got a congressional declaration of war against Japan. Among those immediately affected was George Parker. While Parker had been as vocal a pacifist as Nearing, he was far more sanguine in his outlook and more practical by necessity. Even as he wrote to many congressmen urging neutrality, he was stocking up on raw materials because he remembered how tough it was to get them during the Great War. Even so, once the war began, shortages of certain materials forced Parker Brothers to revise Monopoly. The game's metal tokens were replaced with wooden pawns. A diecut cardboard insert bearing a printed apology replaced the cellophane that had sealed the box bottom and prevented its components from spilling. But Parker's foresight enabled cardboard and paper to be in ample supply to satisfy the surprisingly strong demand for the game during the war years. Monopoly was always kept in stock.

Across the Atlantic, Waddington managed to keep Monopoly in production by employing similar measures. It replaced the metal tokens with a composite of cardboard and wood and substituted a cardboard spinner for the dice. On the Continent, Monopoly remained in production in the Netherlands, albeit in a smaller version featuring tiny playing equipment. Its licensee, Smeets Drukkerijen, was a printer in the town of Weert. The firm managed to secure a K permit from the Nazis (number K2507) to maintain a supply of paper and was able to manufacture 4 million games of all types during the war, including "Junior" Monopoly.

While Parker Brothers had paper and board, George Parker wisely focused production on a handful of his best-sellers. "Evergreen" card games like Pit, Flinch, and Rook were kept in stock, and so were a few board games, such as Sorry!. Monopoly received top priority.

The military purchased large quantities of these select games for its PXs and rest camps. But the servicemen's top choice was Monopoly. A typical letter mailed from a serviceman was posted in a 1943 trade ad. "Your game of Monopoly has given us much enjoyment . . . this set is in great demand . . . and has come through the campaign, though not unscathed." General George Patton even telegraphed George Parker to thank him for Monopoly's morale-building effect on his troops.

Happily for Parker Brothers, more and more people at home bought these select few titles. Since they were fun to play, people spoke highly of them and unit sales began to strain Parker's ability to produce. George Parker, at age seventy-five, devised a "we must focus on our strengths" plan. He found himself once more in complete command of his company. (Robert Barton, despite being overage, had joined the navy, as did the younger members of the Parker family.)

One new game George Parker fostered during the war was Dig, a frantic word race that featured the Monopoly mascot (still nameless) on its cards. Dig became the first of many "flanker products" that benefited from Monopoly graphics.

By the time the war ended in 1945, Monopoly's sales had rebounded to 800,000 copies a year. Material constraints prevented a similar rebound in the United Kingdom. John Waddington Ltd. may have survived the war without damage to its factories, but it lacked materials to rebuild sales. Significant rationing in the United States ended in 1946, but restrictions continued in England until 1952. Its economy—like those of all European nations—was exhausted and bankrupt. It would take time for Waddington to regain its prewar energy and its licensees to ramp up production of Monopoly.

By contrast, American commerce was purring when the war ended. Nevertheless, a significant price had been paid to correct the chronic economic dilemma of the 1930s. Under Roosevelt, the national debt soared over 1,000 percent (from Hoover's $22 billion to $259 billion). More than a million American men and women gave their lives or were wounded. True, the unemployment rate had fallen from nearly 15 percent in 1940 to less than 2 percent by 1944, but 16 million citizens were pulled into the military and they represented *22 percent* of the total workforce. And they risked their lives for very low wages.

But wars must be fought to preserve a way of life. The price tag is a moot point if defeat is the outcome. Roosevelt had led the Allied effort to victory. Liberty and capitalism were preserved. Industry responded to the military's demands for better weapons and materials and, in the process, created computers, better medicines, and lighter metals. After the war, plastics technology became so advanced that it revolutionized nearly every household item, including toys and games (even Monopoly).

After celebrating the Allies' victory, people everywhere wanted to forget the past and rebuild their lives. Most had endured a decade of economic misery followed by four years of bloody conflict. All yearned for shortages to end and for store shelves to fill once more with goods. Money was not an issue; most pockets were filled.

Among those with money to burn were the returning GIs. They quickly readjusted to civilian life and spent like there was no tomorrow.

And Monopoly would be a prime beneficiary of their spending.

9

GI GAMERS
1945–1958

President Harry Truman concluded the war and brought home the troops. The economy, with war production terminated, braced itself to absorb the impact of countless GIs reentering the workforce. Millions of women who had kept factories humming while the men were away gladly returned to their homes. But others wanted to keep their jobs. A recession ensued as the transition to peacetime goods jolted industry. Despite this, shortages pushed up prices for two years while controls and rationing were phased out. Capitalism suffered through yet another jolt.

The soldiers, sailors, and airmen who returned home didn't seem to mind. They were ready for a better life, at any price Their dreams included leisure time, a car, a family, and a home. However, many couples had to delay marriage for a while because they could not find a place to live. Prefab housing, such as Quonset huts (metal military buildings) and Lustron homes (made from aluminum blocks), was introduced to relieve the shortage. The situation improved in 1947 when builders like William J. Levitt erected entire communities of low-priced homes, providing affordable housing for first-time homeowners. Veterans could purchase Levitt's houses for next to nothing down and $56 a month.

PARKER GAMES
The MOST FAMOUS and LARGEST SELLING Games in the World

MONOPOLY

On All Fronts . . . At Home and Overseas
Relaxation with Unequaled Entertainment

1944 trade ad

Early mainframe IBM computer

FAMOUS PARKER GAMES

DIG

Hilarious New Action Game

The Pick Does the Trick! Just dig letters from a pile with the Magic Pick, and be first to form a winning word. Any number can join the hilarious scramble! The more players, the faster the fun and excitement! **Buy DIG Today — De Luxe Edition** $2 (Players) $2, Standard Edition (4 Players), $1. Add more Picks for extra players — 8 Picks, 50c.

The plastic revolution altered Monopoly in the late 1950s when wood houses (left) were replaced by plastic ones (right).

These modest homes could be expanded when the owner's financial condition improved. Never before had so many prospective homeowners been able to buy so many houses so early in their adult lives. After a few years, half of the residents of these towns were children—the first of the baby boomers. They would forever change the nature of the toy and game industry.

Truman narrowly won reelection in 1948, defeating Republican Thomas Dewey and Progressive Henry Wallace, who had been Roosevelt's vice president prior to Truman and had served as Truman's secretary of commerce. Bad blood developed between the two after Wallace criticized Truman's economic policy. To Wallace's credit, he was a staunch advocate of civil rights. He was endorsed by the U.S. Communist Party, but this did not help his voter appeal. Elizabeth Magie Phillips would likely have voted for him, but she passed away a few months before the 1948 election. The patent she had assigned to Parker Brothers had quietly expired seven years earlier, and so did memory of Lizzie's achievements.

During Truman's elected term, the economy began a strong, long-lasting boom generated by returning GIs. As they reentered the workforce, their spending multiplied and created more and more jobs, exactly as economists had predicted. Industry grew rapidly to satisfy the demand they created. The Federal Reserve bolstered the nation's money supply; more money in circulation also meant more spending on entertainment. The pursuit of happiness shifted into high gear: vacations, boats, and home additions for some; movies, books, and games for many.

The games GIs played during the war became must-have purchases for their families, with Monopoly being the most coveted of all. The game that distracted people during the Depression came to symbolize good times. An infectious spirit of getting rich arose as the 1950s dawned. In 1952 a million copies of Monopoly were sold and sales climbed in each year of the new decade.

In Europe, Monopoly limped back to health wherever commerce was reestablished. But this recovery was spotty. Entire cities, such as Warsaw and Berlin, had been heavily damaged or destroyed. The fire bombing of Dresden caused worse damage than the A bomb did in Hiroshima. Transportation networks lay in ruin. Ships, vital to resupply, lay on the ocean floor. The Truman administration realized it had to help out the devastated economies of Europe, or poverty, disease, and dissent would foment widespread support for the communists. The Soviet Union had also suffered greatly in the war. It kept troops in the eastern European countries it occupied, and its influence hung like a giant shadow over the battered democracies of western Europe, threatening to plunge them into totalitarian darkness. This concern led the United States to extend massive aid, beginning in 1947, to Turkey and Greece (both faced serious communist threats) and then thirteen additional countries. This great humanitarian effort was named the Marshall Plan, after Truman's secretary of state, George Marshall, who had been army chief of staff during the war. Marshall's organizational skills shone brightly during the implementation of his namesake.

The Soviet Union and its satellites were also offered economic aid. But Stalin would not allow them to accept it, requiring the nations it occupied (e.g., Poland, Hungary, and Czechoslovakia) to look to Moscow for aid (although little was forthcoming). The Soviet secret police and military occupation ensured that Stalin's will was obeyed. Consequently the countries of eastern Europe recovered slowly and fell behind their western neighbors.

By all measures, the Marshall Plan was a marvelous success. The years between 1948 and 1952 saw the fastest business growth and greatest improvement in living standards in European history. Poverty and starvation disappeared. The appeal of communism diminished. Capitalism reemerged. Free trade between the nations of the plan led to today's system of international finance and promoted European unity. Concomitantly game makers regained the means to make and sell games and the marketplace resumed selling them.

Waddington rebuilt its relationships with its many licensees. The Miro company not only relaunched Monopoly in France but also provided production for Franz Schmidt until it could rebuild its factory in Germany. In a controversial move, Schmidt decided not to reintroduce its ill-fated Berlin edition. In its place, it designed a game whose streets bore no connection to any specific German city. This was a misstep. Without the identity of its capital city, sales were lackluster. Henceforth Monopoly would be less significant in Germany than in other European countries.

Monopoly now appeared for the first time in countries such as Spain, Greece, Finland, and Israel. The countries of eastern Europe were forbidden by Moscow to license the game because of its capitalist—and therefore anticommunist—nature. Nevertheless, enterprising souls in various countries such as Poland and Hungary made a few underground copies.

Worry over real monopolies survived the war. As late as 1949, roundtable discussions among economists considered the likelihood of new players amassing economic combines, not unlike those created by J. P. Morgan. NBC Radio broadcast one such event, held at the University of Chicago in January 1949, where a consensus emerged that it could happen. This possibility further enhanced the relevance and sales of the Monopoly game.

Low ratings convinced President Truman to bow out of contention in the 1952 presidential elections, and the nation elected popular war hero Dwight D. Eisenhower. "Ike" had held together a diverse group of opinionated, egotistical leaders while commander of Allied forces in Europe. He was an organized man, a born negotiator and diplomat. He was also a consummate Monopoly player and found the game to be a perfect stress reliever. He now applied his negotiating skills and love of capitalism to running his country.

Eisenhower balanced the budget for three of his years in office (a rare achievement for any modern president) and oversaw an expanding economy in six of his eight years. He built interstate highways, and he witnessed the first jet airliners, the first business computers, the development of plastics, and the spread of television into most homes in the country. And he became America's first true TV president through his televised press conferences.

Monopoly benefited from the economic good times of the Eisenhower era. Television advertising enhanced the game's popularity, and the plastics industry affected the way it was made. These new "miracle" resins made household goods cheaper, easier to care for, and more durable than the glass, rubber, and metal materials of their predecessors. And their time-saving advantages freed up more time to have fun.

The toy industry was reborn, thanks to plastics. The use of high-impact, nonshattering materials in dolls, play sets, musical instruments, and cowboy guns replaced metal components and made these playthings more popular than ever. Games also benefited. Monopoly's wooden houses and hotels gave way to shiny injection-molded plastic buildings. Parker Brothers whimsically became the nation's largest prefab house and hotel builder. If all the little houses and hotels Parker produced in one year were lined up end to end, they'd reach from Salem, Massachusetts, to Chicago, Illinois. The nation's love affair with plastics even inspired the firm to introduce a special edition in 1965, packed inside a plastic briefcase.

Consumers flocked to stores to stock up on the "good life." Modern retailers had to adapt to the growing volume of goods passing in and out of their stores. The time-honored tradition of a knowledgeable sales clerk assigned to each department's counter was no longer tenable. These trained specialists gave way to cashiers and stock clerks. Consequently informative packaging was required to sustain sales. For Monopoly, this meant phasing out the utensil box format. Only a full-size box containing the game board and its components could be merchandised. (Its lid could still be removed and the board lifted to inspect the components, which were again sealed under cellophane.) Shrink-wrapping was a decade away.

Parker Brothers chose not to add selling copy to its package. By now, an entire generation of game players had accepted Monopoly as a standard, and they were buying it for not only their own amusement but the next generation's as well. Parents and grandparents were teaching the baby boomers how to play according to George Parker's rules.

In September 1952 George S. Parker passed away at age eighty-six. Son-in-law Robert Barton assumed full control of the firm, aided by descendants of the other two Parker brothers (notably Eddie Parker, who had joined the firm in 1935 and served with distinction in the U.S. Navy during the war).

With Lizzie and her patent gone, the current leadership of Parker Brothers decided to stop mentioning her, and Darrow reemerged as Monopoly's "inventor." In time, naive publicity people accepted this as gospel, and undoing this mistake would later prove troublesome.

The Darrow patent expired in 1952. Parker Brothers braced for new competition for Monopoly. Rival game makers could now market games with similar play. As it turned out, none launched a worthy rival (Milton Bradley's Easy Money, regarded by many as an easier Monopoly, continued to sell). Monopoly was secure at Parker Brothers because the Monopoly copyrights and trademark were carefully protected. A tagline was introduced on the package to further its validity: "Parkers Brothers Real Estate Trading Game" (later changed to "Property Trading Game from Parker Brothers").

Patent and trademark issues aside, Monopoly had gained a monopoly among financial games. One reason was the charm of its mascot character. A few years earlier, Parker Brothers finally gave him a name. In 1946 he appeared on the cover of Rich Uncle, a new stock market game (which was destined to be marketed for the next twenty years). Inside, purchasers learned that his given name was Rich Uncle Pennybags, which endured for the next half century.

American capitalism was humming, the threat from bad trusts a thing of the past. However, some notable firms powered ahead and dominated their industries in near monopolistic fashion. They reached the top by aggressively applying the rules of capitalism and investing heavily to exploit its strengths. It was as if each had acquired a valuable color group and put hotels on it, overwhelming their opponents.

One of these new emerging companies was International Business Machines, which in the space of eight short years became the world's most powerful maker of computers. IBM began life in 1911 as the Computing Tabulating Recording Corporation. The name International Business Machines was adopted in 1924, when its main products were timekeeping systems, weighing scales, and punch card equipment. In these precomputer days, punch cards were the primary means of tabulating data. Businesses like Parker Brothers would eventually purchase IBM tab machines to compile orders, track inventory, and print invoices.

IBM did not invent computers. The first acknowledged American computer was built after the war. The ENIAC (electronic numerical integrator and calculator) was built at Nearing's alma mater, the University of Pennsylvania. IBM won a contract to develop and build fifty-six computers for the air force (at $30 million each). By so doing, it gained access to computing research at MIT. Benefiting from its technical expertise and chairman Thomas Watson Jr.'s realization that the outside world would need more thirty computers (as some experts concluded), IBM won over big business to its machines. By 1960 it had become so large that its seven closest competitors were known as the "seven dwarves."

IBM's dominance sparked antitrust inquiries by the government, but the man on the street had little interest in such concerns. Computers were more the stuff of imagination and science fiction. (Would a computer ever think like a human or rule the world?)

But just as the Landlord's Game fascinated college students in the early 1900s, so computers sparked students in the 1960s to think how a computer might be programmed to play games, especially Monopoly. The realization of this dream would not be far off.

General Motors was another American corporation that dominated the nation's economy in midcentury. General Motors and the game of Monopoly were fated to share a stage in the summer of 1959.

10

THE GENERAL'S GAMBLE
1959–1972

In 1959 the battle for hearts and minds waged by the world's rival economic systems reached a crescendo. Scott Nearing and Rexford Tugwell were but two of many well-educated Americans who perceived merit in the notion of a government-run economy. Communist governments ran much of Asia and nearly half of Europe, their economies centrally planned. The movement retained momentum.

But while communists crowed about five-year goals achieved, they resorted to smoke and mirrors to deflect attention from the totalitarian control they wielded over their citizens. Communist leaders everywhere had *seized* power rather than receiving it from the people. Further, the main prop holding up their economies was a disproportionate amount of military spending, despite the peace. What about consumer goods for their people? Oh well.

Soviet papers made it seem that everyone in modern America was as destitute as the dirty West Virginia children photographed on the broken steps of a ramshackle house amid ugly coal mines. *Pravda* neglected to mention that this photo was taken by Roy Stryker's team during the Depression, or that the mines were working again, or that

The General's Gamble

Khrushchev and Nixon at Moscow Trade Fair

MONOPOLY...*Greatest Game Ever!*

The version that went to Moscow in 1959.

The Beatles played Monopoly during their 1964 U.S. tour (George Harrison pictured).

1959–1972

kids today were clean and attending school. The American National Exhibition in Moscow was an attempt to break through the veil of Soviet misinformation.

The exhibition showcased American images, products, ideas, and cultural icons. It was made possible by a cultural agreement signed by both nations the prior year. The exhibition site, Moscow's spacious Sokolniki Park, was often used for Soviet trade fairs. In the past, the tsars had employed falcons to hunt foxes on these very grounds.

The featured attraction at the fair was a model American home. Wide passageways separated its rooms so visitors could flow through it and absorb its furnishings and appliances. A Monopoly game lay open on a game table in the living area.

The Monopoly game ruffled the feathers of many Soviet officials who considered it an insidious tool of capitalism. They were aware that Monopoly was played underground in eastern Europe. Monopoly's "own it all" goal clashed with the "for each according to his means, from each according to his ability" mantra of communist doctrine. Never mind that Soviet leaders seemed to follow a credo based more on George Orwell's observation that "some are more equal than others" or that their own taste ran the gamut from Levis to Hollywood movies to Marlboro cigarettes.

The open land on which the American exhibition rose was considered U.S. property during the six weeks of the fair. Consequently Soviet officials could do little to prevent Monopoly's appearance, except to effect retribution elsewhere.

The verbal clash between Vice President Richard Nixon and Soviet Premier Nikita Khrushchev at the fair has become the stuff of legend. Khrushchev felt compelled to defend the prospects for communism in the face of the tangible success of capitalism, represented by a wealth of products and pictures. The debate peaked when the two leaders reached the kitchen in the model U.S. home.

Khrushchev: We always knew that Americans were smart people. Stupid people could not have risen to the economic level that they've reached. But as you know, "we don't beat flies with our nostrils!" In forty-two years we've made progress.

Nixon: You must not be afraid of ideas.

Khrushchev: We're saying it is you who must not be afraid of ideas. We're not afraid of anything. . . .

Nixon: Well, then, let's have more exchange of them. We all agree on that, right?

Khrushchev [tries to lighten the mood]: You look very angry, as if you want to fight me. Are you still angry?

Nixon [smiles, relaxes]: That's right!

Each day 75,000 Russians visited the fair, exceeding their leaders' fears by 50 percent. Polling after the fair jolted the Soviet leadership. Not only did the average Russian realize his American counterpart had a better life and more options ("Why can't we have Monopoly?" many asked), but the communist leadership felt obligated to promise more consumer goods to meet Western consumption levels. This promise proved empty, as the Soviet leadership continued to pour diminishing funds into military spending.

Lack of fun times was a fact of life behind the Iron Curtain. It is not difficult to understand why all the copies of Monopoly brought to Sokolniki Park were stolen before the fair was half over!

Like a player bankrupted in Monopoly, Khrushchev was forced out of the game after expending his political capital. He paid the price for miscalculating the will of the West to protect capitalism and its way of life against the spread of communism. He was deposed in 1964 and spent the remaining seven years of his life under house arrest. His successors would perpetuate communist rule for two more decades before their system finally went bankrupt.

Capitalism was destined to prevail. And so was the Monopoly game. Monopoly was officially published in Russian in 1987, sixteen years after Khrushchev died. The entire Soviet system was dismantled three years after the ban on Monopoly was lifted.

Presidents Eisenhower, Kennedy, and Johnson oversaw substantial growth in the U.S. economy. However, deficit spending on Lyndon Johnson's Great Society and the Vietnam War set the stage for high inflation and slow growth by the time Richard Nixon was elected president in November 1968.

Charles Darrow did not live to see Monopoly published in the Soviet Union. He died on August 28, 1967, at age seventy-eight, at his country estate in Ottsville, Pennsylvania. His obituary appeared nationally and erroneously credited him as the inventor of Monopoly, rather than its stylist and original publisher.

By 1968 the Parker and Barton families were stretched financially. The cause was not a business slump but the opposite: relentless growth. Since the firm's early days, Parker Brothers had religiously adhered to conservative financial management. The Parker family satisfied the cash needs of the business by using its own savings, eschewing bank loans. This worked fine when growth was moderate. However, by the 1960s, demand for toys and games was growing at 20 percent or more per year. The children of the GI generation were the reason. And they were plentiful.

Growth of this magnitude has an enormous appetite for cash. Inventory must be purchased months before stores pay for it; the workforce needs to be augmented and payrolls increased. Factories require expansion to house all the new activity; expensive new production equipment becomes necessary. For example, by 1968, the price tag of a modern five-color offset press approached $1 million, compared to the $5,000 Robert Barton paid for a one-color press in 1934.

By now, Barton had help in running the business—his son Randolph, great-nephew Eddie Parker, and great-nephew Channing Bacall. The four wanted to declare an annual cash dividend, but the demands of growth made this frustratingly difficult.

Monopoly sales tracked the exploding number of baby boomers. From 1 million units in 1953, 2 million units a year were being sold by 1965 (surpassing the record level set in 1936). The standard self-contained edition became the bellwether in the Monopoly lineup, accompanied by a deluxe edition or two. In 1935 Monopoly had retailed for $3.00. If its price had increased along with inflation, it would have been selling for $7.50 in 1967. Parker Brothers suggested retail price, however, was $6.00. With the emergence of new discount chains (like Kmart), it often retailed for $4.99. Fierce competition was largely responsible.

The year 1967 also marked the last time the firm could post suggested retail prices in its trade catalog. Most states were outlawing fair trade laws. This meant that manufacturers could no longer encourage or compel a retailer to sell a product for a minimum required price. Back in the 1930s, states like California adopted fair trade laws to prevent large variety chains from using their economy of scale to underprice small stores. The continued existence of small retail stores was essential to protect the jobs of the many men and women who ran them. The worry then was that prices in general were too low (Tugwell's lament).

By 1967, with the economy performing soundly, consumers were able to demand lower prices. In 1975 the remaining state fair trade laws were found in violation of the Sherman Antitrust Act. Discounting was here to stay, and blue laws forbidding stores to open on Sunday also vanished.

Low prices posed a subtle but real problem for Parker Brothers. When Monopoly was offered at a substantial discount, it created an unfavorable comparison with the prices of brand-new games, which stores typically sold at full markup. Further, stores were reluctant to carry new games unless they were advertised on television. Consequently Parker was forced to invest in such advertising, and this further drained cash.

After taking these business dynamics into account, the leaders of Parker Brothers decided it was time to sell their firm to a bigger company with "deep pockets," as Robert Barton put it. He and his staff ruled out a public stock offering because of the red tape involved. The sale must be private, outright, and preferably to one buyer.

At this moment, the General arrived.

In 1928, the Washburn-Crosby Company merged with twenty other flour mills, and the new enterprise was christened General Mills, Inc.

The new firm purchased a radio station and developed a knack for advertising brands like Gold Medal flour and Bisquick baking mix. General Mills quickly became a dominant maker of flour and cereals, though it never achieved monopoly status. However, its consumer marketing expertise made it aspire to become a monopoly of a different sort. By the mid-1960s, General Mills wanted to become a conglomerate.

Spawned by tough antitrust laws, low interest rates, and a repeating bear/bull market cycle, conglomerates were amalgams of seemingly unrelated businesses acquired in leveraged buyouts (hopefully at deflated values during bear markets). The leaders of General Mills watched with great interest the steady growth of the leading "conglomerators" of the 1960s—Ling-Temco-Vought, Litton Industries, GE, Teledyne, ITT, plus Gulf and Western.

For these firms, the best way to grow was through synergy, a novel idea at the time. A popular college text of the era (*Corporate Strategy* by Professor Igor Ansoft) defined synergy as $2 + 2 = 5$. It worked something like this: A major firm with a high price–earnings ratio buys a smaller, lower-valued firm. It pays partly with debt, partly with newly issued shares. The new shares and debt temporarily dilute the interest of shareholders, but the profits of the acquired firm more than make up for this. Let's say the buying firm is earning $1.00 a share and trading at twenty-five times earnings. This means its fair value is $25.00 per share. Let's also assume that the interest on its loans drops existing profits to $0.90 per share. But after the profits of the newly acquired firm are added in, earning increases—despite the larger number of shares outstanding—perhaps to $1.10 per share. Thus the stock will *rise* in price to $27.50: $2 + 2 = 5$. The higher stock price makes it easier to buy yet another firm, add it into the conglomerate, and jolt the share price upward once again. Economic heaven!

The financial model of conglomerates was based on this alluring premise. And the idea of synergy could also be applied to less obvious gains by virtue of such mergers. In the case of General Mills, its advertising and marketing savvy could immediately help increase sales and pump up profits for Parker Brothers. Its large bank account could fund modernization of the Parker factory. General Mills was in the process of buying other toy companies; bringing them together under a common management team would bring about further economies and spark even more growth.

Investment bankers of this era noted the staying power of board game companies, since their core products sold well year after year. (Toys, by contrast, tend to have short lives since many are based on licenses with fleeting appeal.) Bankers also noted that families, not shareholders, owned most toy and game companies. This made purchasing them less intricate. Parker Brothers was singled out for praise because of its family ownership and its many staple games, especially Monopoly.

Armed with this knowledge, General Mills ultimately agreed to pay $47.5 million in cash for Parker Brothers. Insiders later admitted that if all they had gotten was the Monopoly game, the price would have been fair.

Robert Barton now retired and Eddie Parker assumed leadership of Parker Brothers. Barton's son Randolph (who preferred to be called Ranny) became executive vice president. Both men worked in harmony with their new superiors at General Mills. In the ensuing five years, Parker Brothers flourished as never before, thanks to General Mills' systems, procedures, and dollars. With fresh advertising and bigger promotions, sales of Monopoly regularly exceeded 3 million units per year. In 1975 sales bumped up again thanks to a special Fortieth Anniversary edition of the game.

In 1971 inflation so threatened the entire economy that President Richard Nixon ordered wage and price controls. They didn't work, and the nation's economic future turned cloudy. Uncertain times always seem to foster a rise of interest in game playing. Games remind people of happier times. Perhaps foremost among the beneficiaries of the economic uncertainty of the 1970s was Monopoly.

And soon a brainstorm by Waddington's new leader would remind the world of the enduring appeal of its favorite game.

11

VICTOR'S VISION
1972–1985

I n 1972 Boris Spassky of the Soviet Union faced off against Bobby Fischer of the United States at the World Chess Federation Championship in Reykjavik, Iceland. Fischer, whose initial recalcitrance almost led to forfeiture, won the match through novel moves that exhilarated chess fans in the West. Capitalism and democracy hailed their new hero.

The popularity of this event, as well as the resultant uptick in sales of chess games, did not go unnoticed by Victor Watson II. Victor, engaging and erudite, was the son of Norman Watson and had recently become managing director of John Waddington, Ltd.

As a young boy, Victor had helped his father play the first Monopoly game to arrive in the British Isles. Thirty-seven years later, Victor realized that Monopoly had achieved a level of universal acceptance sufficient to warrant championship competition. Given the locale of Bobby's Fischer's triumph, Watson believed a Monopoly world championship would also garner press attention if held in Reykjavik. The event needed to be cobbled together as soon as possible, while the buzz about Bobby was strong. Victor had an idea of how to do this, having organized a Tycoons championship event at Waddington two years earlier.

Victor's Vision

Victor H. Watson II

General mgr. of Waddingtons

Randolph Parker Barton

President of Parker Brothers 1974–1985

First organized World Monopoly Championship, 1973.
From left: Don Lifton, George Tatz, Lee Weisenthal (judge), Brian Nuttall, Lee Bayrd.

Them that has, gets, in game

By Bill Fripp
Globe Staff

LIBERTY, N.Y. — Getting Out of Jail and Not Passing Go took on global significance over the weekend as our favorite childhood game was elevated to the cerebral realm.

About 40 grown men — and one child — gathered at Grossingers Hotel-Country Club for the first World Monopoly Championship, an event that established Los Angeles TV writer Lee Baryd as the greediest entrepreneur in the universe. Bayrd, 33, bested three other finalists in a tense three-hour game, winning when his opponent landed twice on his outrageously expensive hotel on Park Place.

The affair was part high camp, part masters' chess as hotel guests, the press (10 newspapers and magazines were represented and television gathered in Nightwatch Parlor for the Sunday final, necks craning for a clear view of the board.

The tourney was cosponsored by

the US Monopoly Assn. and Parker Bros. of Salem, Mass. the Monopoly producer. And there was considerable disagreement as to what constituted criteria for participation.

Association officials said players were chosen from regional championships. But Bayrd said the Beverly Hills regional championship was "open to anyone who happened to notice the sign announcing it," which was posted in a restaurant window.

George Tate, 35, Long Island College food-service head, said he only played Monopoly a "couple of times a year" and "I'm not sure what the hell I'm doing here."

Adam Himber, 11, of Short Hills — the only child in the child's game and a loser in the semifinals — was apparently here on his ability to beat his father.

However suspect their credentials, there sat the four finalists at their roped-in table, awaiting the first role.

Lee Bayrd (the champ) and daughter Jodi

Boston Globe, November 20, 1973

1972–1985

At Parker, Robert Barton's affable son, Ranny, endorsed the idea. Like Victor, Ranny had learned the inner workings of business by observing his father and grandfather. And like Victor, he had also grown up with Monopoly in his blood. (Within two years, Ranny would become president of Parker Brothers when Eddie Parker died of lung cancer.) Watson and Barton agreed to expedite plans for the contest.

The problems confounding this first tournament were many. Not the least was the question Is there anyone who plays the game scientifically? Followed by Do such players employ winning principles of tactics and strategy, or is the game beyond analysis, aside from the need for negotiating skills?

Purists argue that reliance on chance should disqualify a game from serious competition. The smarter player should always win a game of precision. They point to chess, whose rules bring about a game of uncompromising strategy. Yet contract bridge and backgammon, both highly respected games, have components of chance. In bridge the randomness of the deal determines the type of strategy to be employed during bidding and play. (This luck is eliminated in tournament play by use of the duplicate system of hands.) In backgammon, the roll of the dice compels a player to make the best move based on probability and statistics with each throw.

It turns out that winning a game of Monopoly does require considerable skill. And Monopoly has one attraction the others lack: the need for social interaction. And there were players everywhere who took the game seriously, even if their methods—like the rules of the game during its formative years—were still largely unrecorded. After finding players of merit, Watson and Barton forged ahead.

What began as a publicity stunt achieved a life of its own. A groundswell developed after the 1972 tournament to do it again, sparked by keen media interest. Men and women from TV and radio stations as well as magazines and newspapers felt far more connected to Monopoly than they did to chess, contract bridge, or backgammon. They were eager to cover another event. In their reports, they referred to Monopoly as the "game of the masses" and rallied behind the idea of a common man, or woman, becoming its champion.

Media acceptance provided the third pivot of Monopoly's enduring success. Tournaments would showcase the game's best players, and media coverage would elevate Monopoly's stature to rival the world's elite games.

In November 1973, the first officially organized World Monopoly Championship was held at Grossinger's Hotel and Country Club in New York. Press coverage was overwhelming. Among the journalists present was Charles Osgood of CBS *Evening News*. Osgood began his commentary with a quote from President Richard Nixon: "I've been exposed to insurance salesmen and stock salesmen, but believe me, you've never been exposed to a salesman 'til a realtor gets at you." Osgood then introduced the four "shrewdest real estate traders in all the world," gathered to play Monopoly for keeps.

Despite its name, the tournament was not quite a global event. Three regional U.S. champs were to compete against the British national champion. When the dust settled, Lee Bayrd—a game nut from Los Angeles—benefited from good fortune and smart play and won the crown. More tournaments soon followed. Typically students comprised the majority of players at these events. Among the most notable were two from Cornell University—Jeff Lehman and Jay Walker. In 1975 they collaborated to author a paperback titled *1,000 Ways to Win Monopoly Games*. Lehman went on to serve as his alma mater's president from 2003 to 2005; Jay Walker founded priceline.com in 1998.

As the title of the Lehman–Walker book suggests, players wanted to know how to improve the odds of winning at Monopoly. Key questions became topics of serious analysis. Were certain property groups better buys? Did some properties offer a better "return on investment"? How many houses should a player erect on a group? When should a player stay in jail rather than pay to reenter play?

Examination of Monopoly's principles may have been in its infancy, but success in the economy had been defined and analyzed for decades.

As the 1970s began, indicators once again pointed to a downturn. The United States was about to experience its worst economic spell since the Depression. Terms like *inflation, devaluation, productivity,* and *stagflation* became household words. Each contributed to eroding the value of the dollars in consumer wallets.

Prices of goods and services rose relentlessly. Only in a sheltered domain, like the realm of Monopoly, did prices remain firm. Second prize in a beauty contest still paid $10 (unless you had a very old set, in which case $11 was the prize). For $50, release from jail was guaranteed. Rent on Pennsylvania Avenue, improved with three houses, was securely fixed at $1,000.

But outside Monopoly's idealistic domain, inflation had been eating away at the dollar since the Depression. Everything from automobiles to gasoline to bread and milk seemed to triple in cost. Wages increased too, but taxes took an ever bigger bite due to progressive tax rates. This prompted demand for more wage increases, which in turn led to higher prices. This vicious cycle was new to America, but frighteningly similar to the onset of runaway inflation in other societies, like ancient Rome or post–World War I Germany and China.

Normally prices in free enterprise economies respond to an imbalance between supply and demand. In good times, people have more money so they demand more goods and services. This makes prices rise. In bad times, less money cools demand, so prices fall. But in the 1970s, prices just kept rising.

Inflation begins when too many dollars are injected into the economy. Lyndon Johnson started the vicious inflation–wage increase cycle when he tried to bankroll the Vietnam War and the Great Society by turning on the government's printing presses. Eventually this led to massive government deficits. (The debt during Johnson's administration reached $358 billion.) Although Johnson did not run for reelection, his successors were unable to stop the runaway inflation express he had set in motion. Two other causes exacerbated the problem. In 1973–1974, oil prices spiked after the Organization of Petroleum Exporting Countries (OPEC) launched an embargo against the West in response to the Yom Kippur War between Israel and the Arab countries. At the same time, America became serious about conservation and pollution (a development that pleased Scott and Helen Nearing, now living on a new homestead near the Maine seacoast). Tough new laws were enacted requiring industry to stop dumping chemicals into rivers and releasing pollution into the air. Exploration and deforestation came under scrutiny. Consequently even mundane materials like paper and cardboard doubled in price and so did plastic resin, a by-product of petroleum.

Board games are largely made of paper, cardboard, and plastic. Rising prices meant that Parker Brothers had to raise the price of Monopoly. Stores resisted, exercising their growing influence over manufacturers desiring to avoid consumer sticker shock.

Parker's management, however, considered the quality of the game's components as essential to its appeal. Their reasoning went something like this: consumers play games to escape from problems and uncertainties posed by the real world. Downgrades in the Monopoly game would be noticeable, and every time consumers played the game they would be reminded of problems they were trying to forget. Parker Brothers did make one concession. To save labor, an automated folding style of box was introduced that was not as sturdy as the traditional setup box style. As more assembly automation was introduced, the labor needed to make each game was reduced. These measures held down cost increases for decades. Nonetheless, the cost of Monopoly crept upward along with other toys and games. But Monopoly's core appeal showed through the gloom, and sales remained near peak levels.

Desperate to stop inflation, Richard Nixon devalued the dollar by refusing to exchange dollars held by foreign governments in return for gold bullion. Arthur Burns, the chairman of the Federal Reserve, opposed the move out of his belief that the Russians would trumpet the action as a signal of the imminent collapse of capitalism.

Gerald Ford succeeded Richard Nixon and quickly abolished the gold standard. Americans could once again own gold for investment purposes and the price skyrocketed. The decoupling of the nation's coins and bills from silver and gold meant that their intrinsic value would henceforth be based solely on confidence and supply. Throughout the 1970s, these forces fell out of balance.

Both experts and crackpots warned of a coming monetary crisis (massive devaluation). The experts predicted runaway inflation and advocated that the nation's citizens benefit from the new law by hoarding gold coins, bars, and pre-1965 silver coins. They believed that the U.S. government would have no recourse but to establish a new fixed exchange rate for gold. What could it be: $1,000 an ounce? $10,000 an ounce?

Inflation continued despite declining economic output and increasing unemployment. This phenomenon became known as stagflation. Spiraling prices and wages led many to question the sense of never changing the prices, rewards, and penalties in Monopoly. Why didn't they increase to keep pace with their real-life counterparts? After all, the $1,500 each player received at the start of the game had been the equivalent of an average income in 1935. Shouldn't it be $12,000 now, or more? Shouldn't passing Go be worth $1,600 and property prices and rents commensurately higher, as well? Parker Brothers decided that the real world should retain exclusive control over uncertainty. Worry about devaluation, productivity, and stagflation did not exist in Monopoly. A Monopoly dollar was always worth a Monopoly dollar and would be for the next thirty years.

President Ford tried to rescue the economy by promoting his WIN program (Whip Inflation Now). He urged citizens to wear WIN buttons (much as Roosevelt encouraged NRA signs and buttons during the Depression). However, most people regarded this as a gimmick, not a solution to the problem. Ford's presidency was short-lived, and in January 1977, Democrat James E. "Jimmy" Carter entered the most demanding office in the country. He arrived in time to preside over the worst economy in forty years. Inflation and interest rates touched new highs. He adopted a gauge of economic health known as the Misery Index. It was intended to benchmark steps he took to fix the economy, but the index, which Carter expected to fall, actually rose 50 percent during his four years in office.

In 1974 mighty AT&T—the last of the big regulated monopolies—felt the misery of a federal suit filed under the Sherman Antitrust Act. Conviction was growing that allowing one firm to monopolize the nation's communications was detrimental to progress. The long battle to break up AT&T moved into the courts.

The Monopoly game fell victim to a misery index of a different sort. On November 15, 1976, Monopoly entered the United States District Court of Northern California. Anti-Monopoly Inc. had filed suit against the parent company of Parker Brothers—the General Mills Fun Group. At stake was the continued existence of Anti-Monopoly's game by the same name and the validity of the Monopoly trademark owned by Parker Brothers.

In late 1973 Ralph Anspach, an economics professor at the University of California, began to market a game of his creation. Originally he intended to call it Bust the Trust but finally decided on Anti-Monopoly. His game was intended to express his concerns about the lessons taught by the Monopoly game, which he regarded as bad. Unwittingly, Anspach had embraced the same concern that led Elizabeth Magie Phillips to create the Landlord's Game seventy years earlier. Anspach would try to educate consumers about the wrongs of real-life monopolies. Consequently the first page of his rules folder was mostly devoted to explaining monopolistic practices; the final page defined a list of economic terms, such as *indictment, net social credit, oligopoly,* and *supervisory payment*. While the nature of his game should have posed his biggest obstacle to its commercial success, the legal right to market his game took that honor.

In February 1974, following good publicity and strong retail sales of its game, Anti-Monopoly Inc. received a letter from Oliver Howes, Parker Brothers' trademark attorney, requesting that the game Anti-Monopoly be withdrawn and the value of orders refunded.

Parker Brothers became aware of Anti-Monopoly from Anspach's publicity and communications with the trade. Many stores were selling Anti-Monopoly side by side with Monopoly. The Parker Brothers sales force believed the game was unfairly capitalizing on the fame of Monopoly by stimulating sales among the curious.

Parker Brothers' executives and attorneys agreed to take action, and Howes issued the ultimatum. Anspach and company resisted because compliance would force bankruptcy. Parker Brothers then requested a temporary injunction to stop shipment of Anti-Monopoly, which was denied.

While coping with this challenge, Anspach became superficially aware of Monopoly's history prior to its publication by Parker Brothers. His understanding began with a call from a listener to a radio program in Portland, Oregon, while Anspach was in the studio. Soon Anspach would cross the country to visit many of the now quite elderly people who had played and influenced the game in the 1920s and early 1930s. He wrote Scott Nearing, pursuing a hunch that Nearing might have invented the game. Nearing wrote back that while he remembered playing an antilandlord game during his Arden days, he did not invent it. Anspach soon learned of Elizabeth Magie Phillips. Armed with his knowledge and bolstered by the sale of 419,000 of his games, Anspach concluded that the way to counter the threat from Parker Brothers was to attack the Monopoly trademark. Monopoly's day in court was at hand.

At the outset of the trial, Anspach's lawyers produced many of the people the professor had interviewed. The witness list was a veritable who's who of the game's early days. Dan Layman described his role in playing the game at Williams College, before devising and selling the rights for the game of Finance. He mentioned his affiliation with the Thun brothers and their game. Catherine Allphin, the wife of William Allphin (the MIT player), appeared next, followed by her husband. William described his notion of publishing a version of the game and his 1931 attempt to interest Milton Bradley in licensing his idea. Introduced into evidence was an article he had written about his knowledge of the game's history, which appeared in the March 1975 issue of a British magazine, *Games and Puzzles*.

Dorothea Raiford then took the stand. She spoke of her role in helping her husband, Jesse, and Ruth Hoskins make the Atlantic City prototype. Next came Charles Todd, who had been stewing for many years over Darrow's lack of appreciation for introducing him to the game and providing copies of its rules. He described in detail how the Atlantic City game had come into his possession and how he played it with his old schoolmate Esther Jones and her husband, Charles Darrow. (Esther, widowed for nine years, declined to appear.)

Finally Robert Barton took the stand. Called out of retirement to defend the game he had acquired, he described the legal steps taken by Parker Brothers to protect its name, design, and play. Robert also noted the Barton family's long tradition of lawyering, qualifying this by stating that his father's firm practiced general law, including the filing of copyrights and trademarks, but not the application of patents, which required specialization. He noted that George Parker had handled the Darrow filing and the acquisition of Elizabeth Magie Phillip's patent. Undeterred, Anspach's attorney accused him of fraudulently acquiring a patent for Monopoly in Darrow's name. Barton was affronted. Judge Williams did not find favor with this charge, and it was withdrawn. And having expired in 1952, the Darrow patent was now irrelevant. Anyone could market a game that played in similar fashion to Monopoly—for example, Anspach's game. It was the name that was in question.

Barton was a savvy witness, and while his memory may have been convenient, the prosecution could not ruffle him. He resolutely believed in and affirmed the crucial role Darrow had played in the establishment of Monopoly and his unique contributions to its appeal.

The case now turned to its core: the Monopoly trademark. Anspach and his attorneys argued that the name Monopoly had frequently been used to identify the game among its cadre of players while it was evolving from the Landlord's Game. Barton testified that no individual or firm had ever reduced the name to meaningful commercial application and that it had not been subject to prior trademark activity before Parker Brothers registered it. Therefore Parker Brothers was perfectly within its rights to apply for and be granted the use of this name. Further, his firm had invested substantial money to protect the name through publicity and had practiced good trademark protocol for forty-one years. His testimony concluded, Barton was excused from the stand.

Several members of the retail trade rounded out the case, responding to the assertion that Anti-Monopoly caused confusion in stores for Parker Brothers and its Monopoly game.

The goal of the Anspach team was a declaratory judgment canceling the Monopoly trademark. This would remove any restraint from selling and promoting Anti-Monopoly. The goal of the General Mills Fun Group was verification of the trademark, along with an injunction barring Anti-Monopoly Inc. from selling any more copies of its game, plus the destruction of all existing inventory. The impact of the outcome would be punitive, no matter who won. Anspach stood to suffer a major financial setback if the judge ruled against his petition. He was a small businessman who had persuaded other small investors to back his venture, and he had applied significant personal money to fight this battle. As the trial neared its conclusion, he began to worry that Judge Williams would rule in favor of the General Mills Fun Group. Anspach's attorneys offered to settle; Parker's lawyers declined.

Several months later, Judge Williams rendered his verdict. He set aside the testimony of the old-timers because the issue at hand was the Monopoly trademark and infringement upon it.

Judge Williams upheld the validity of the Monopoly trademark, stating it was not a common or generic name when registered by Parker Brothers. He disputed the claim that Monopoly had become generic—like the terms band-aid, thermos, or aspirin—because it was the title of a *particular* real estate trading game, not every real estate game. He also found a likelihood of confusion caused by the use of the name Anti-Monopoly. He noted that Anspach chose Anti-Monopoly as his game's name and not Bust the Trust in hopes that its sales would increase due to inclusion of a popular name.

In summary, Judge Williams granted Parker Brothers the injunction it sought and restrained Anspach and company from using the name

Anti-Monopoly or leveraging the equity in the name Monopoly. He ordered the inventory and related selling materials to be destroyed in the presence of a Parker Brothers representative, the site of which was a snow-covered Minnesota landfill. Anspach then appealed.

The media followed this trial faithfully and reported its outcome nationwide. As an unintended consequence of this trial, the Monopoly game had become a courtroom celebrity, almost as if a Hollywood star was defending his or her honor.

The appeal offered an opportunity for Anspach's team to refute Judge Williams's conclusion. Before the Ninth Circuit Court of Appeals, they presented a consumer survey (a "purchaser motivation" test) they had sponsored, which revealed that most people did not associate the Monopoly game with its maker, Parker Brothers. They argued that if consumers could not identify a maker with the name of its product, the name had become generic. The Ninth Circuit was swayed by this argument and ruled in favor of Anspach and sent the case back to Judge Williams.

This decision temporarily cleared the way for the Anti-Monopoly game to return to market. The following year, it was off again after Williams defied the court of appeals and reinforced his earlier ruling. The case was appealed once more. Again, the court of appeals ruled in favor of Anspach. The media had another field day.

The General Mills Fun Group now attempted to persuade the Supreme Court to hear the case because more than the validity of a board game's name was at stake. The method used to dispute its legitimacy threatened any brand name if consumers didn't know the identity of the company that made it. Try answering these questions: Do you know who makes Pepsodent toothpaste? Or ChapStick? Or Norelco shavers? The answers are Church and Dwight, A. H. Robins, and Philips Electronics, respectively. If the makers of these brands, and thousands of others, suddenly had to worry their trademarks would be declared generic via similar purchaser motivation tests, competitors would unfairly benefit from the substantial investments these firms had made to popularize and strengthen their marks. And they would be copied with impunity.

When the Supreme Court refused to hear the case, General Mills, together with a legion of other companies, convinced the U.S. Senate of the severity of the issue. Congress was swayed and amended the trademark law, disallowing this type of research and reasoning. Monopoly might have brought about this larger good, but it did not benefit from the congressional ruling. The final date was approaching when enforcement of the Ninth Circuit's decision would be declared official in Judge Williams's chamber.

Finally, for practical reasons, Anspach elected to reach a settlement with General Mills. He had expended his financial resources and lacked the means to get his business moving again. Consequently on August 15, 1985, in Judge Williams's courtroom, the final judgment— privately agreed to by both parties—became official and was entered into the record.

Monopoly remained a valid trademark, and Anspach agreed to help protect it. He assigned the Anti-Monopoly mark to Parker Brothers, which licensed it back to him, agreeing to protect it as well. A financial settlement was reached, and both Anspach and General Mills agreed to retain the terms of the agreement in confidence for a limited period of time. As a result of this settlement, no one else but Professor Anspach had unfettered access to the Monopoly trademark, which was likely the best outcome he could have hoped for.

Thus ended the saga of the Monopoly game's ordeal in court.

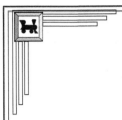

The
MONOPOLY®
Gallery

A Century of Monopoly and Related Games

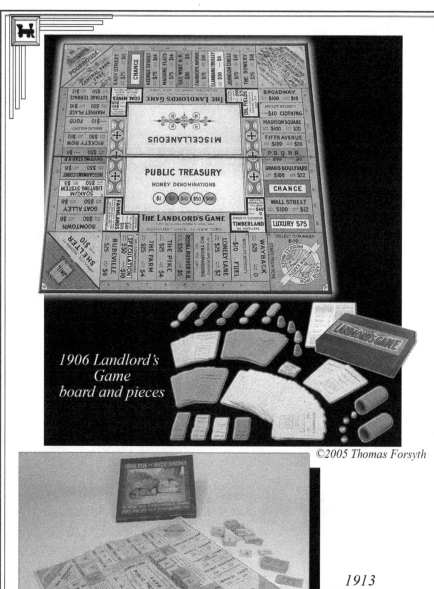

1906 Landlord's
Game
board and pieces

©2005 Thomas Forsyth

1913
Brer Fox
game
from
Scotland

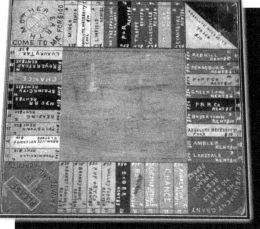

Print of the Buckwalter wooden board, circa 1910. The original is in the Forbes Gallery.

Title deeds from the Thuns' game

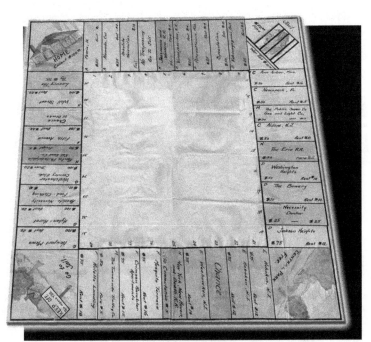

Alice and Roy Stryker's Landlord game oilcloth board, circa 1925

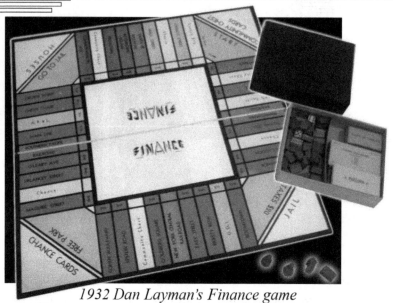

1932 Dan Layman's Finance game

Three early Finance and Fortune editions

1936 Fortune game by Parker Brothers

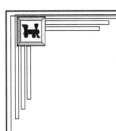

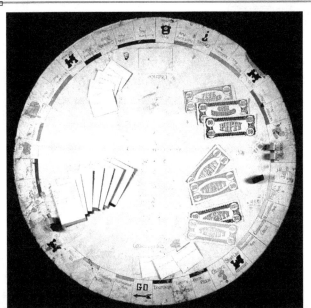

1933 Darrow original round oilcloth game

Todd game graphics above, Darrow graphics below

1933–1934 Darrow tie box set

Dowst Favor Cake Mix with metal tokens

*1935, first number nine deluxe edition by Parker Brothers
(Darrow graphics)*

*These 1935–1936 number six standard Parker editions each bear
a different legal line, according to date of manufacture.*

From left (earliest to most recent):
Trademark, Patent Pending, single patent, double patent, patents plus copyright.
Their rarity is commeasurable with age.

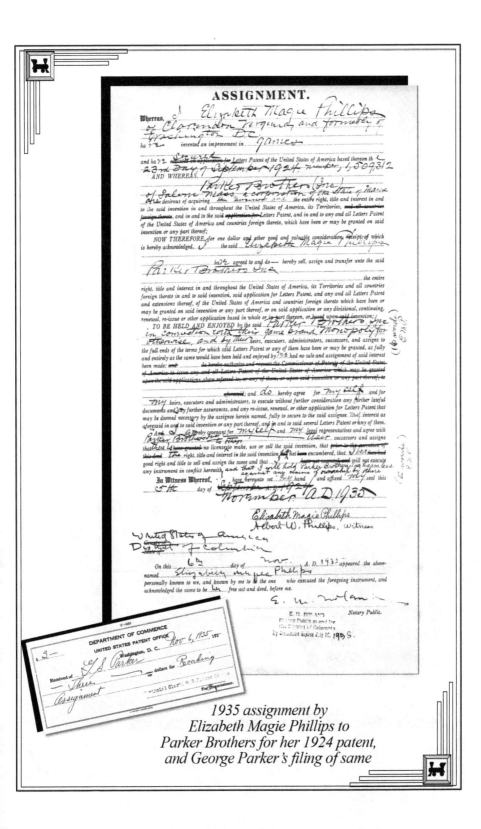

1935 assignment by
Elizabeth Magie Phillips to
Parker Brothers for her 1924 patent,
and George Parker's filing of same

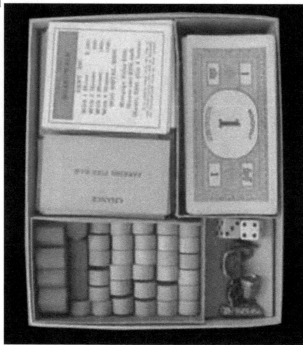

Octagonal hotels from another 1936 improvised set

1936 round houses set, issued when regular wood houses were in short supply during height of demand

December 1935 Jordan Marsh Department Store display

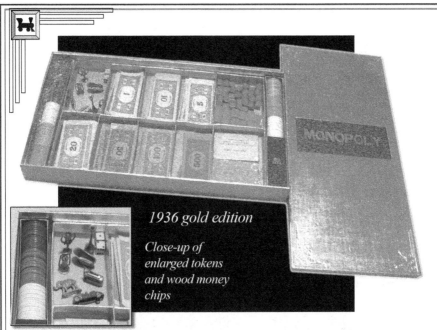

1936 gold edition

Close-up of
enlarged tokens
and wood money
chips

*1936 deluxe number twenty-five
wood edition*

Simpler case from 1939 version

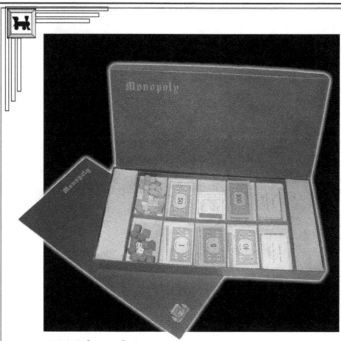

1936 fine edition

*1930s Cracker Jack charm
featuring little Esky*

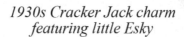

*1937 library edition
and 1936 Stock Exchange accessory*

1936 Darrow-endorsed Bulls and Bears games
(Plain Darrow photo on larger box; airbrushed on smaller box)

1937 King's Men and
Bargain Day by Elizabeth Magie Phillips
(Note her photo on King's Men)

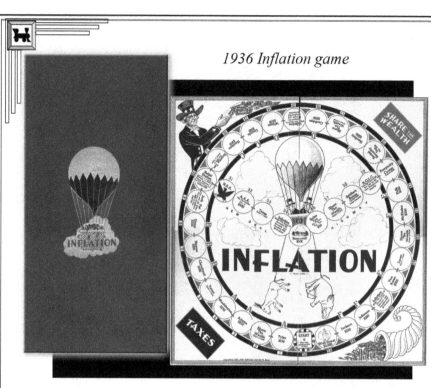

1936 Inflation game

*1937
Milton Bradley
Carnival game,
based on
the 1904
patent of
E. M. Phillips*

KNAPP

Announces

1935 Knapp Electric ad for Finance

*1936
ad for
Inflation
game*

1936 Waddington's first U.K. Monopoly edition

*Fall 1936, Waddington's U.K. gold edition
(The ill-fated 1936 German edition
was similar in appearance)*

1937 revised Big Business game by Transogram

*1939 Parker Brothers Landlord's Game
as played by the firm's officers*

1936 Easy Money
with Monopoly patent numbers; small and large packages

1946 Rich Uncle and 1941 Dig
brand extensions
(1961 Rich Uncle package shown)

1936 Austrian edition

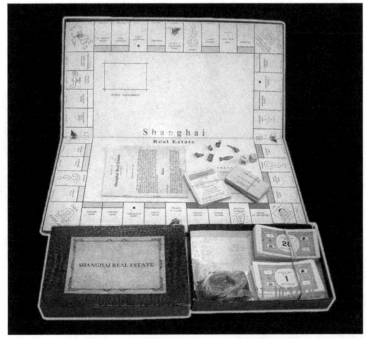

1936 unauthorized Shanghai edition

1936 Zurich Monopoly, first bilingual (French–German edition
1936 Australian Monopoly, first Asian edition (on right)

Clockwise from bottom left: 1936 Uruguay edition,
1937 French edition (first to include "quad-fold" game board),
1938 Swedish Monopol, 1961 revised German edition

Monopoly, late 1930s and early 1940s editions

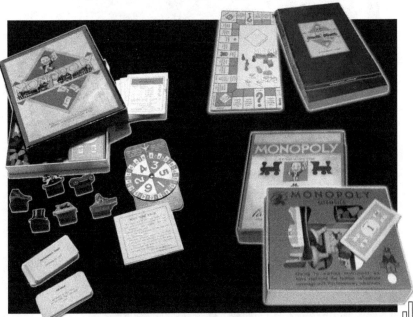

Wartime editions: U.K., Dutch Jr., and U.S. Each used substitute materials and smaller printed components. The Dutch game also miniaturized the game board.

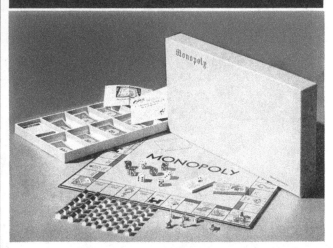

FAMOUS
Parker Games
THE MOST FAMOUS AND LARGEST SELLING GAMES IN THE WORLD

Most popular real estate trading game in the world!

MONOPOLY   PARKER BROTHERS' TRADE-MARK NAME FOR ITS REAL ESTATE TRADING GAME

You are assured of the constant popularity of

Monopoly! Year in, year out, the many novel and

original features of this exciting REAL ESTATE

GAME continue to appeal to players of every age.

New De Luxe Edition. A most attractive and unusual set! Distinctive playing pieces include beautifully designed *Inwood* Grand Hotels and Houses imported from France. Sturdy, removable Bank Tray, Board bound in rich, wine-red batherette. Complete Rule Book. 3 to 10 players.
Price **$10.00**

White Box Edition. Removable Bank Tray, Grand Hotels stamped in gold. Double supply of "Money." New Short Game rules included. 3 to 10 players.
Price **$4.00**

Popular Edition. Complete equipment in separate box. 3 to 8 players.
Price, **$3.00**

Parker Brothers, Inc. SALEM, MASSACHUSETTS
200 FIFTH AVE., NEW YORK 10 • MERCHANDISE MARTS, CHICAGO AND SAN FRANCISCO

1953 trade ad, featuring new deluxe edition

*1954,
last small
box edition
with
cellophane
wrap
over
utensils*

1957 train cover, short-lived but picturesque

*1961
library
edition*

"FLAMELESS ELECTRIC HOME HEATING HELPS KEEP OUR HOUSE CLEANER THAN WE EVER DREAMED"

1962 industry ad featuring Monopoly game

Experimental tokens from the 1940s;
U.S. postal stamp, 1998

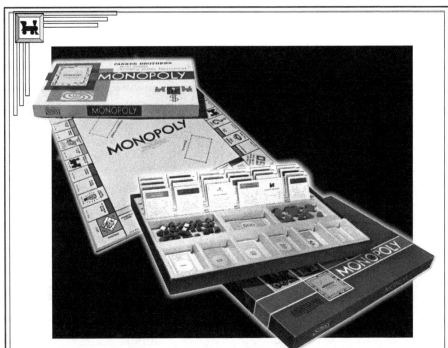

Standard edition from 1961, "better" edition from 1964

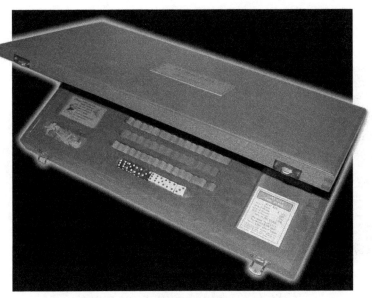

1971 deluxe edition with wood case

*1966 U.K. ultra deluxe Thirtieth Anniversary edition,
featuring stippled foil wrapping paper and bejeweled tokens*

*1993 U.K. standard edition;
1986 U.K. deluxe edition (on right)*

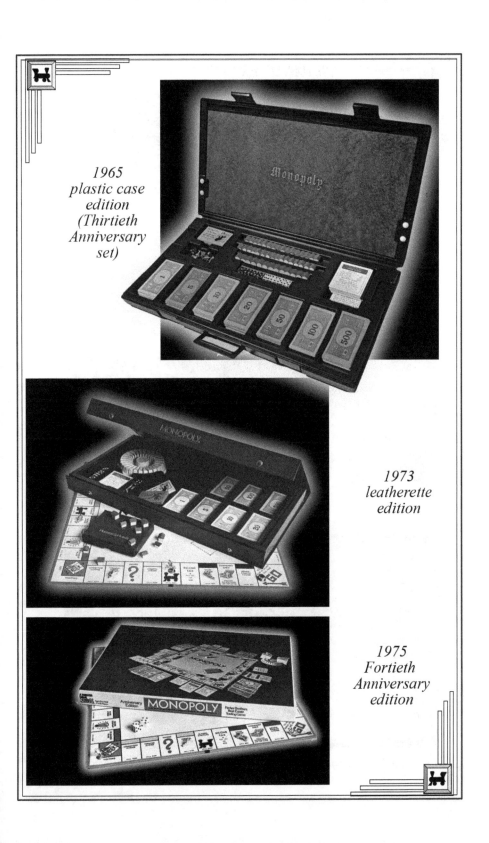

*1965
plastic case
edition
(Thirtieth
Anniversary
set)*

*1973
leatherette
edition*

*1975
Fortieth
Anniversary
edition*

1982 Monopoly Playmaster electronic accessory

1986 Advance to Boardwalk and 1988 Free Parking card game

1990 Monopoly Junior; 1991 Don't Go to Jail

*1990s Franklin Mint luxurious collector's edition,
with portfolio for title deeds*

*Last number nine edition made in Parker's Salem factory, 1992.
650 copies were made and given to employees.*

1992 and 1996 deluxe editions

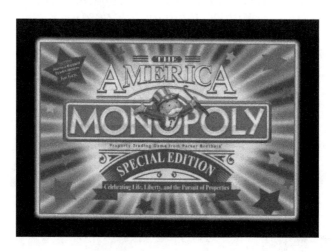

America edition, 2002

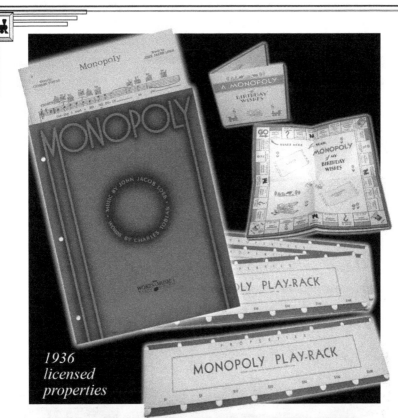

*1936
licensed
properties*

Examples of modern era licenses

$100
1999 heirloom
edition,
packed in a
wood chest.
It also included
a family
game log
to record
games for
posterity.

*2000 car tin
edition included
a revolving rack
for the title
deeds and a
six-fold game board.
2003 Train tin, below*

*2001 nostalgia edition
in wood case*

*2003 Target—Michael Graves
designer edition*

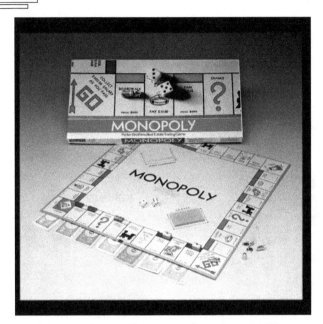

Monopoly number nine from late 1970s

Compact number nine editions;
2005 above, 1999 below with new moneybag token

*Four Anniversary editions, plus
Seventieth Anniversary board and booklet*

*2006 Monopoly: The Mega Edition
Biggest and fastest playing version of the game*

12

THE REAGAN ROLLS

1979–1991

My bond to Monopoly was strengthened when I accepted an offer to join Parker Brothers in March 1979 to manage the firm's new product research and design group. The job was right up my alley, and I anticipated staying in it for years. But Parker was experiencing another round of breathtaking growth with electronic games like Merlin and Stop Thief! American consumers were in love with early handheld computer games, including Milton Bradley's Simon and Mattel's Electronic Football. Meanwhile, the first wave of video games was about to take the nation by storm. With business booming, Parker's organization was bursting at the seams. After a year, I was promoted to vice president of product development. While the business side of my job grew and grew, my first love remained a sideline I stumbled into shortly after joining the company.

I was surprised to learn that Parker Brothers had no in-house Monopoly expert. Parker's head of marketing, Ron Jackson, soon asked if I knew much about the game. When I replied affirmatively, he proposed that I assume the role. After I agreed, he asked me to shape up the rules and procedures for the forthcoming series of tournaments

The Reagan Rolls

President Ronald Reagan

Bankrupted his chief opponent

Communist Save game (as in "being frugal") from Hungary. Published during Russian occupation beginning in the early 1960s. Aimed at deterring interest in Monopoly.

First official Russian language version, 1988.

Version of Anti-Monopoly, which came to the attention of Parker Brothers and led to a famous lawsuit, settled in 1985.

1979–1991

and serve as its chief judge. Awed by the prospect, I studied the game every night, trying to prepare for the day when a crafty player's stratagem would test my mettle.

My prep wasn't overdone. In my first tournament (the eastern regionals), a player slyly hid a $500 bill in his shirt pocket after the game began. During play, he leveraged his apparent poverty to win sympathy when making deals. At the opportune moment, the $500 bill reappeared and the fortunes of the game swung immediately in his favor. The two most disadvantaged players promptly converted the contest into a "best out of three falls." I jumped in to stop the fisticuffs and had to disqualify the manipulator.

When all four rounds of play concluded, ten-year-old Angelo Ropolo of Staten Island was declared the winner (he had withstood every attempt at intimidation by his adult opponents, including a smoker who blew pipe smoke in his face).

Going home that night, I realized that player protocols were needed to shape up the next tournament. I also needed to clarify the intricate play situations I had observed. I could now appreciate Jackson's description of prior tournaments as "loose affairs."

Nine out of the twelve tournament points I would compile came about because of incidents from the first event. No longer would bills appear magically from pockets or would one player abuse another. No one would use lucky tokens other than those included with the game, or sell a Chance and Community Chest card to an opponent before drawing it, or trade nongame assets like options and free passes.

These are perfectly fine as private house rules. But they do not belong in serious tournament play. Jackson liked the controversy-free tenor that marked subsequent tournaments, and I was asked to stay on as judge indefinitely.

After the four regional U.S. champions were determined in 1979, they would play against the reigning champion (Dana Terman) at the U.S. finals. The new U.S. champ would go on to compete for the world title against thirty or more foreign champions. No longer were world tournaments stacked in favor of the United States, as in the days when all four regional champs were invited to the finals against a lone foreign champion.

Alan Aldridge, a student from Dayton, Ohio, was the last U.S. player to win the world championship (1974, Washington, D.C.). The following year, again in D.C., a tipsy merchant banker from Ireland named John Mair took the prize home to Europe (Mair once errantly tossed the dice into his cocktail). In 1977 in Monte Carlo, a sales executive from Singapore named Cheng Sheng Kwa became the first Asian to win the world championship. Monopoly had inspired players around the world to master it. In the fall of 1980, I met the newest group of global masters at the world championship in Bermuda.

At the U.S. finals in November 1979, Angelo Ropolo bankrupted three of the adults competing against him at the Palace Restaurant in New York. He then found himself alone against Dana Terman, the reigning U.S. champion. As the game approached its climax, Ropolo, with hotels on the light purple properties, went to Jail—a safe haven late in the game. The crowd applauded; the ten-year-old was clearly their favorite. Terman was a crafty player and knew Monopoly inside out, but he was out of cash, barely clinging to the dark blues with a hotel on Boardwalk. Although the odds were against him, he still had a slim chance, provided he did not land on Angelo's properties. If he suffered this misfortune, he'd have to break down his hotel and sell houses to pay the rent. This would assure the boy from Staten Island the prize. But defeat was snatched from the jaws of victory when Ropolo rolled a double six, forcing him to leave Jail and placing him on Chance. Even before Angelo drew the top card, Terman grinned, having memorized the fifteen previous Chance cards. The sixteenth read "Advance to Boardwalk." Angelo was wiped out. Terman repeated as U.S. champ.

At the world tournament in Bermuda, Dana Terman held the lead through much of the contest, but an Italian exchange worker named Cesare Bernabei charmed his opponents, avoided bankruptcy, and ultimately knocked out Terman. There was a brief moment of suspense at the conclusion when the table was jostled and Terman's token vibrated forward one space. Terman had not moved his token after rolling an eleven because the roll landed him on the knockout rent; his bankruptcy was obvious. Bystanders unaware of the jolt thought Terman was still in the game. I agreed to review the action on videotape (an innovation at the time). The instant reply verified my ruling.

After the 1980 competition, I took time to reflect on what I had observed. I calculated the odds of Ropolo rolling double six and drawing the one card that could destroy him (1 chance out of 576). A long shot. I again pondered the enduring question, Is luck too prevalent in Monopoly? The games I observed suggested it isn't. For example, players who acquired the orange group seemed to fare better than those who acquired the greens. Better players did not buy hotels until late in the game. They typically built three or four houses per property and stopped, despite being cash rich. Why was this?

I decided, before the 1982–1983 championship season began, to study the math behind decisionmaking used in the game. Several people, including Jeff Lehman and Jay Walker, had been tinkering with computer analysis of Monopoly for years. A twenty-seven-year-old Ph.D named Irvin Hentzel was one of the first to publish results of a computer simulation of the game ("How to Win at Monopoly," which appeared in March 1973 in the *Saturday Review of the Sciences*). *The Monopoly Book* by Maxine Brady also included elementary statistics and odds when it appeared in bookstores in 1974.

But I wanted to go beyond statistics to report my observations of how human nature played a role in winning. And I wanted to describe how best to apply the odds of winning tactics and strategies. I needed a computer to play the role of hypothetical players and engage in hundreds of mock games. The results could then be studied and conclusions drawn.

They opened my eyes. Boardwalk and Park Place are not the best properties to own, in part because there are only two of them and they aren't landed on as much as groups with three properties. Furthermore, players do not spend as much time on that side of the board because of the Go to Jail space on its first corner. Many cheaper properties have a better return on invested dollars than the expensive greens and dark blues. Also, a property with three houses enjoys a huge rent increase over two houses. While four houses or a hotel pay higher rents, the jumps in rent aren't as dramatic. Another reason why smart players often do not buy hotels is that the rules prevent hotels from being purchased if insufficient houses are available to qualify for them. By retaining twelve houses on a three-property group, a "housing shortage" would be more likely to occur, which would deny wealthy opponents high rents.

In addition to establishing itself on the tournament scene during the 1970s, Monopoly became a fixture in the world of entertainment. Two years into the decade, John McPhee wrote a brilliant essay for the *New Yorker* entitled "In Search of Marvin Gardens." His lead character (his alter ego) plays countless games of Monopoly against a loyal opponent. In surreal fashion, McPhee mixes action on the game board with a journey through contemporary Atlantic City. The city envisioned by Osborne and Pitney in 1852 has fallen from grace and is as unpleasant as the smell coming off its marshes at low tide. McPhee describes ghetto street scenes resembling Cologne after World War II. The avenues he visits seem to slide from grand to ghastly as he moves inland (west) from the Boardwalk and from the southern end of town to its northern tip.

When Jesse Raiford laid out the spaces on the Atlantic City Monopoly board, he arranged them to reflect this pattern of riches to rags. But by 1972, the difference between the extremes was as sharp as a black-and-white television with its contrast control turned up to the max.

McPhee's hero is determined to find Marvin Gardens. But it eludes him until he finally learns that it is the name of a suburb south of the city and that its name on the board is misspelled.

That same year, 1972, the movie *King of Marvin Gardens* appeared in theaters, starring Jack Nicholson and Bruce Dern. Just as McPhee's essay had elevated Monopoly to a topic worthy of literature, the movie used the game's imagery to enhance its allegorical story. Dern's character

(Jason) is playing a high-stakes game of chance not unlike Monopoly. He says to Nicholson (David), who is in jail, "You notice how it's Monopoly out there? Boardwalk, Park Place, Marvin Gardens."

"Go directly to jail?" David replies, and Jason plays along.

"That's me—don't pass Go, don't collect $200." Jason sees life in AC as a game, complete with play money and punishments as sharp as Angelo Ropolo's bad luck roll.

In 1980, when Atlantic City was struggling to recast itself, it became the setting of another movie, this one starring Susan Sarandon and Burt Lancaster and simply called *Atlantic City*. The action shifts between Monopoly properties like Boardwalk, Kentucky Avenue, and Pacific Avenue. Monopoly references abound as Sarandon works at a casino and struggles at home.

Hollywood recognized Monopoly as an American icon. This isn't difficult to understand. Monopoly features evocative names on its spaces. Its play is like a three-act drama. The first act is buoyed by the actors' excitement and hope of victory. The middle act dashes these dreams as competition and uncertainty mount. Suddenly the final act arrives—the endgame where every move threatens bankruptcy. The audience moves to the edge of its seat. Now comes the final blow; elation courses through the veins of one player while the others lie lifeless on the stage. The crowd is stunned; the curtain falls. But everyone looks forward to the next performance because the play is guaranteed to have a different ending next time.

Monopoly is both visceral and allegorical. It has flair; it speaks without uttering a sound. If the dice don't roll our way, Monopoly appears as an unreliable friend. But when they do, Monopoly is our buddy, our trusted pal.

The nation's new president, Ronald Reagan, took charge and rolled the dice, determined to leap over the obstacles that had blunted the nation's progress. He entered the White House with the promise of bolstering America's shaky reputation overseas and revitalizing its inflation-ridden economy. High interest rates broke the back of inflation, and Reagan's belief in supply-side economics ignited growth (albeit at the cost of higher deficits).

As jobs were lost and the core industries that dominated America at the turn of the century disappeared, the nation's future came to depend on the service, computing, and information industries. A small software firm named Microsoft developed an operating system for IBM to use in its new home computers—an innovation made possible after hi-tech firms like Texas Instruments perfected the first microprocessors in the mid-1970s. These little brains changed how America worked and played. Microsoft became a giant and then became the target of antitrust investigations. It made concessions to remain intact.

Armed with economic strength, Reagan now rolled an even bigger set of dice. He took on the Soviet Union (the Evil Empire, he called it) intent on bankrupting communism, once and for all. His effort was destined to succeed. He won congressional support to accelerate the military buildup begun by President Carter, convinced the Soviet Union would exhaust itself trying to keep up.

Scott Nearing was appalled by this new wave of militarism, but not for long. Having attained the ripe old age of one hundred on August 6, 1983, Nearing decided it was time to go. He stopped eating and gradually refused nourishing liquids. Eighteen days after his centennial birthday, he died. His lifelong protest against perceived injustice came to an end. His wife, who lived a few more years, willed their home in Maine for a study center of their advocacies (The Good Life Center). Scott Nearing outlived his protégé, Rexford Tugwell, who had died in 1979 shortly after his eighty-eighth birthday. Roy Stryker had departed even earlier, in 1975, at age eighty-two.

Monopoly was jolted by consumers' fascination with electronic games. Sales declined for the first time in decades. Many speculated that Monopoly was finally losing popularity.

In response, Parker Brothers took several steps to bring Monopoly into the electronic age. First, we created an electronic accessory named the Monopoly Playmaster. My goal was to make the game play faster, accompanied by the bells and whistles electronic fans expected. The Playmaster unit was positioned in the center of a Monopoly gameboard, making it easy for all players to roll its electronic dice and react to its commands.

Next we licensed the rights to make a video game version of Monopoly to Sega Enterprises, a leading provider of video game hardware and software. (Eventually this license would transfer through many hands.)

Third, we designed a special edition commemorating Parker's fiftieth anniversary of Monopoly. Since 1975, no changes had occurred in the Monopoly line, which consisted of a standard edition (the descendant of Darrow's White Box edition), an earlier anniversary edition, and an expensive wood case set with minimal sales. The new Fiftieth Anniversary edition would be packaged in a large, embossed cookie tin and feature graphics from the original 1935 Parker edition.

Sales expectations were modest, given downturns in the board game market. But consumers reacted strongly to the look and feel of the new version; over 350,000 were sold at $40 to $50 retail (five times the price of the standard edition). This unexpected success provided a wake-up call. Maybe Monopoly's lull wasn't entirely due to electronic games. Maybe it was also due to inactivity.

More action followed. The Franklin Mint—a leading producer of collectibles—took notice of the Fiftieth Anniversary edition and came forward with a proposal to license Monopoly for an even grander set that would sell for over $600. Franklin's game would be a large, hand-crafted wooden platform, with the game's track printed on its open top surface. A central, felt-lined depression would serve as a casino-like area to roll the dice. The components were made of fine materials, the tokens 24-carat gold plated, the houses silver plated, the money luxurious paper. The components were stored in drawers, tipped by brass knobs, under the platform. A $300 stand for the game was also available, as well as special Monopoly chairs for $100 apiece.

After this concept cleared the Franklin Mint's extensive research and testing process, the game was offered to its mail-order clientele.

To everyone's amazement, over 100,000 were sold! Franklin Mint continued to market the game for many years.

Parker now began to market Monopoly flanker products—a practice that had been discontinued when the Rich Uncle game left the line in 1968. Many at Parker thought flankers to Monopoly would harm sales. However, General Mills believed that Monopoly, Clue, Sorry!, and Boggle were begging for line extensions because consumers loved them and would have confidence in new games based on their appeal. Finally the right game appeared on our doorstep—Advance to Boardwalk (submitted by an inventor named Charles Phillips). It became Parker's best-selling board game of the 1980s and was followed by two more: Free Parking and Don't Go to Jail.

At this time, McDonald's restaurant chain approached Parker Brothers and suggested using Monopoly imagery for a retail promotion. McDonald's proposed giving away little property tags customers could match up to win prizes (including substantial cash awards). The promotion became the most successful in McDonald's history and has endured ever since. The most recent grand prize was $1 million. Parker Brothers now knew conclusively that Monopoly's appeal had not faded and extended far beyond the game board.

But there were limits. Monopoly did not succeed as a TV game show coproduced by Merv Griffin and King World Productions (of *Wheel of Fortune* and *Jeopardy* fame). And Parker was not happy with Hollywood scripts that turned the game into a movie (to their credit, these rejected scripts were more upbeat than *The King of Marvin Gardens* and *Atlantic City*).

Monopoly itself underwent a facelift of sorts. At the time I joined the firm, the Anti-Monopoly trial was in the appeals stage. While I had brought with me some knowledge of the game's history, most members of the firm, myself included, were not privy to the legal aspects of the case. But many of us were soon made aware of a new graphic strategy to reinforce the Monopoly brand, regardless of the outcome in the courtroom. Monopoly's logo would be enhanced by an image of our mascot, still known as Rich Uncle Pennybags. Monopoly

Parker Brothers expanded the Monopoly name and logo for use in other products, such as this Massachusetts lottery ticket.

games would henceforth feature J. P. Morgan's successor popping out of the central O in its name. Simultaneously the unique graphics on the game board, especially the corners and pictures on many spaces, became registered trademarks. These steps would ensure that Parker Brothers' Monopoly would be seen as "the real thing" because no other company could legally utilize these famous images.

Following the settlement with Ralph Anspach, Parker's legal team acted against competitors who had banked on the name becoming generic, for example, Medical Monopoly, Main Street Monopoly, and Gay Monopoly. And to further strengthen its trademark, it began out-licensing its imagery—a development that would flourish as a major business in itself.

Parker Brothers preserved Charles Darrow's unique graphics on the Monopoly game board, which became protected as registered trademarks.

In the United Kingdom, Victor Watson and John Waddington Ltd. issued new versions of the Monopoly game similar to Parker's, and out-licensed such wares as stationery, carpets, chocolates, and even socks.

My role on behalf of Monopoly tournaments expanded. In addition to judging the U.S., World, and occasionally Canadian Championships, I was asked by the Loews hotel chain to help with an imaginative plan to use Monopoly as a fun means of raising money for charity. Loews planned to conduct lighthearted tournaments at several of their hotels. Local celebrities and leaders were invited to donate to a local charitable cause and, in return, gain a seat during the competition. My agreement to preside over these events led to travel from coast to coast. Unlike those at official Monopoly tournaments, the players in these worthy efforts did not always know the rules. I remember comedian Jackie Mason participating in the very first event at Loews' Regency in New York City. He had never played Monopoly, and I quickly taught him the basics; he came in second and lamented missing out on "this wonderful game" during his childhood. Ed Koch, former mayor of New York, played well in Nashville during a book-signing tour. Unlike Mason, he knew the game well and said it had helped him hone his negotiating skills in politics. In Santa Monica, California, the stars of Hollywood came out to support the effort (more money was raised there than in any other venue).

In between these events, I judged the 1984 U.S. championships in Palm Beach, Florida, and the 1985 world event in Atlantic City (a memorable occasion for me because my parents attended). After this tournament, I was approached by an agent and asked to author a book about Monopoly, including everything I knew about its play, tournaments, and the winning strategies employed by its champions. At first I balked; I did not want to write an educational treatise. Monopoly was a source of enjoyment for most of us. But after thinking it over, I came up with a fun idea. I'd write The Monopoly Companion as if Rich Uncle Pennybags had imparted his knowledge to me during interviews at a mythical home in Marven Gardens. The concept was accepted and Parker's president at the time, John Moore (a Canadian with no links to the game's past), supported my efforts.

I included my knowledge of the game's history as I understood it at the time. While I did not have access to transcripts or depositions from the Anti-Monopoly trial, I was able to glean information from Oliver Howes (Parker's trademark attorney) and eighty-four-year-old Robert Barton—who revealed a sharp memory, once coaxed, during several days of interviews.

The world of Monopoly collectors opened up to me at an auction of antique games held in Bolton, Massachusetts. While attending on behalf of Parker Brothers, I met Andy Egandorf, who purchased a fine Darrow White Box set. I managed to buy several games Parker needed for its archives and a collection of old Parker sets for myself. Andy and I became friends. Andy was a hi-tech entrepreneur who decided he'd like to own an old Darrow game. After he purchased it, he decided to dig into its Philadelphia origins. He let me know what he discovered, and that's when I learned about MacDonald and the role of the John Wanamaker Department Store in Monopoly's history. This interested me and I wanted to know more.

Over the next few years, I connected with many people who regarded the history of America's Game to be as important as that of American art, literature, or music. I remain grateful for their friendship.

Institutions now began to value Monopoly and its history. During a two-year period beginning in 1991, the Forbes Gallery in New York City acquired at auction a prestigious collection of one-of-a-kind Monopoly games. For the princely total of $123,000, Forbes purchased the original round Darrow oilcloth game, the blue oilcloth board on which Charles Todd taught Darrow how to play, a square Darrow oilcloth board, and the Buckwalter wooden game board. A Forbes representative explained the reason for these purchases: "We thought the games were appropriate for the collection of a magazine about money." All are now displayed in the Monopoly Room of the Forbes Gallery. Admission is free during the several days each week the gallery is open to the public.

While the history of Monopoly interests some people, many more want to know how to win it. This was the main goal of *The Monopoly Companion*. I shared with its readers a mathematical analysis of the game, especially in the form of picture charts. At about the same time, Kaz Darzinskis published *Winning Monopoly*. While I had run hundreds of mock games, Kaz had gone deeper by conducting thousands of computer-played games. Our results were nearly identical. *The Monopoly Companion* was used as a player's reference in the 1988 championships held in London and won by Ikuo Hyakuta of Japan—an amazing accomplishment because Monopoly only appeared in Japan after World War II and had not yet developed a significant a following.

That same year, an exclusive $2 million Monopoly set was created by the jeweler Sidney Mobell of San Francisco. Sidney inlaid 23-carat gold and rubies into its finely crafted wooden board and inserted sap-phires into the tops of the chimneys of its solid gold houses and hotels. Oh, and the forty-two pips on the dice were full-cut diamonds.

Monopoly was again set to incite a bidding war over its ownership. The quest to own America's Game began as General Mills shed its con-glomerate skin. Its misguided efforts to micromanage its nonfood groups led to losses and riled the firm's many shareholders. In response, General Mills spun off Parker Brothers, Kenner Toys, and their inter-national affiliates in 1986. All were combined into a new company, Kenner Parker Toys, whose shares began trading on the New York Stock Exchange in November of that year. Parker was now part of a moderate-size public company. Any investor could purchase its shares on the exchange. Or offer to take them all. Within two years, Tonka, another toy company, gobbled up Kenner Parker after winning an auc-tion against New World Productions, a Hollywood movie producer. New World had offered to buy all shares of Kenner Parker at $44, a big premium over the $23 price on the day it made its offer. With few op-tions, Kenner Parker sought out a more compatible acquirer. Tonka rose to the opportunity and bid $52 a share.

Tonka was financially weakened by the massive acquisition. It could not pay its debt burden and went into bankruptcy. (Many in the press commented on the irony of Monopoly going bankrupt.) In early 1991, the nation's second largest toy company—Hasbro Corporation—acquired Tonka, and thereby Kenner Parker.

How all this happened is described in detail in *The Game Makers: The Story of Parker Brothers*, which I wrote in 2003. The events were very much influenced by the nation's economy, and trends on Wall Street. And because General Mills tried to manage its toy companies as if they were cereal firms.

After nearly two decades of experience, I had learned that deep knowledge of this industry and its marketplace was crucial for endur-ing success. My peers and I had seen many entrepreneurs wander into the game industry, enjoy initial success, conclude it was easy to make a killing, and then blunder. Afterward, they would blame unfair competition or some external cause for their demise. In truth, the road to success, however pretty, is heavily mined. The core reason for the industry's existence is to provide fun and entertainment. What constitutes fun changes quickly in the entertainment field. Kids in particular often change their interests from week to week. Survival and growth in the industry depend on nimble feet and fast thinking. Bigness alone provides little assurance of rising above the fray. For one thing, retailers don't care where hit products originate. They just want them in stock so shoppers can take them to the registers.

Beyond Kenner Parker, the Reagan economy was climbing higher in 1987. Household income and housing prices had risen 30 percent in the prior three years. Inflation and unemployment were tame. Following the Reagan tax cuts, more and more money found its way into the consumer economy. Stock prices soared following years of stagnation. The Dow Jones average rose 170 percent in sixty months. Before this expansion, most big companies had downsized (which is why unemployment took a while to subside). Their new efficiencies made them very profitable during the boom. To put their newfound money to work, corporations began to buy each other. This time, the attraction was not only the high stock price of the acquiring company, but the treasury of each firm that was gobbled up. Many companies could be purchased in part with their own money due to sizable bank accounts, overfunded pensions, and a high rate of profitability. Kenner Parker Toys was one of them.

Parker's top management—including myself—departed during the Tonka years, before the Hasbro deal closed in January 1991. But turmoil in management and ownership did not dim the luster of our star product. Monopoly was again in the hands of a strong parent and poised to fly even higher; some said to cloud nine.

13

NUMBER NINE, NUMBER NINE

1992–2002

The number nine is hallowed among those whose hands have made and sold Monopoly games since 1935.

Mention number nine to Dave Wilson, and he will likely reply with reverence. He may tell you that one of his goals in life was to leave number nine in strong hands and possessed of even brighter prospects when he turned over the reins of command.

Dave Wilson had been associated with Monopoly for much of four decades when he retired from Hasbro Games in December 2005. He had been vice president of sales at Parker Brothers before joining Milton Bradley as its general manger in 1981. Ten years later, he was reunited with his former employer when Hasbro acquired Parker Brothers. (Hasbro acquired Milton Bradley in 1983 and the games division of John Waddington Ltd. in 1994).

Wilson presided as president of Hasbro's North American game operations. Under his leadership, Hasbro's Milton Bradley and Parker Brothers brands retained their position as the world's largest makers of nonvideo games, producing up to a million games and puzzles per week in the factory in East Longmeadow, Massachusetts. The massive factory

Number Nine, Number Nine

E.David Wilson

Legendary leader of Hasbro Games

MONOPOLY

WORLD CHAMPIONSHIP

BERLIN 1992

October 3rd Thru 6th

Number nine, number nine

1992–2002

often operated around the clock, employing over 1,500 workers. Its assembly lines produced such favorites as Trivial Pursuit, Operation, the Game of Life, Risk, Boggle, Scrabble, and the one that meant the most to Dave—Monopoly number nine, its most enduring edition. (Originally, it designated Parker's first deluxe edition—the one featuring Darrow's White Box graphics.)

If Dave had taken you on a tour of his 150,000-square-foot facility, the highlight for him would have been the assembly line cranking out number nine. Gears turn, levers pivot, mechanical arms push components into trays, a machine swallows games in its open mouth and spits them out the other end, enclosed in shrink-wrap, ready to be packed into shipping cartons. Dave's presence would not have distracted the workers on this line. He had shown them off to guests since 1992, when this line was transferred from Parker's factory in Salem, Massachusetts. (Hasbro would suspend all game manufacturing at the venerable Parker plant later that year and eventually demolish it.)

To this day, a mighty effort goes into preparing Monopoly for the line. Large injection molding machines spit out millions of plastic houses and hotels every day. Precision scales weigh out the correct number of each before they are enclosed in plastic bags. Huge rolls of colored paper are fed through presses that print sheets of Monopoly money. A guillotine blade neatly cuts them into pads. Title deeds, yellow and orange cards, instructions, platform, box, and game board labels are also produced in the print shop, one of the largest in the United States. Custom machines cut and collate the cards into decks before they go to the line. In the game board department, a special machine glues the board's label to a die-cut piece of cardboard after encasing it in a sheet of the light blue wrap on its rear side. The newly made boards are then whisked over to the line. A beefy machine wraps box labels around "tortured" cardboard to form each box top and bottom (making the boxes as they are needed avoids storage and handling).

Assembly can now begin. A box bottom makes its way down a conveyor belt, and a platform and plastic tray are loaded into it. Next the game components are dropped into the trays, with board and rules placed on top. The box top seals the deal once an inspector checks for accuracy. The completed game is shrink-wrapped and packed into a shipping carton with eleven others. Another conveyor lofts these cartons overhead and into the next room—the huge distribution center. A truck will soon pick them up and take them across America to a store near you.

This automated process is a reflection of the times. For all of Monopoly's unique success, it is affected by the "no price increase" trend for toys and games that has influenced the industry since Wilson and his team began making Monopoly under this roof. Retailers often use popular toys and games as loss leaders: value-priced items that lure consumers into their stores. Monopoly is the loss leader of choice for many store chains because demand is so predictable. Since the late 1980s, number nine has gone on a forced diet of sorts. Its board became a bit thinner, its box smaller, the tray more compact (and less convenient to use as a bank), the paper used for its money no longer slippery. Consequently in real dollars number nine often sells for less today than at any time in its illustrious history: $8.99 or lower. Its 1935 retail price, adjusted for inflation, would be $40 today. So rejoice. This prized game has become a great bargain.

If you had asked Dave, he would have told you this is a good thing. It encourages people to buy a fresh Monopoly game to replace that old dog-eared one. But number nine can no longer carry the Monopoly brand by itself. It needs help from higher-priced editions and innovations to keep the brand vibrant.

In 1968 John Lennon of the Beatles had number nine on his mind when he recorded "Revolution 9." The number is spoken many times during the song's eight-minute length. The captivating, bizarre collection of looped sound effects and voices has baffled and enthralled listeners ever since. The title of this avant-garde work had nothing to do with the nine muses in Greek mythology, or the expressions "dressed to the nines" or "the whole nine yards," or with nine being the ultimate masculine number in Chinese mythology, or in tribute to the alignment game Nine Man's Morris, or to the mathematical magic that occurs whenever nine multiplies another number (the resulting digits always total nine), or even cloud nine (a meteorological term).

No, Lennon's chaotic epic was named when a sound engineer said "revolution number nine" to begin the ninth take of Lennon's prior hit song about revolution. Lennon loved the sound of this phrase. He looped the engineer's words to form the basis of a new song. It was a fortuitous accident.

Monopoly number nine also gained its single-digit product number through a lucky accident. By 1935 Parker Brothers had used up all 999 of its product numbers. In this preautomation era, larger numbers couldn't be keyed in on its manual tabulating machines. Rather, the company started over by reassigning the lowest numbers of products that had dropped out of its line. It happened that a discontinued shooting toy called Firing Line had been number nine, which was reassigned as the product number for the White Box edition of Monopoly.

Perhaps Lennon's affection for the number nine began years before when the Beatles played Monopoly number nine between shows on a U.S. tour. They enjoyed the game so much they gave Parker Brothers publicity photos of them playing it.

Lennon's "Revolution 9" did not advocate revolution; it criticized violence. As Lennon explained, its jarring content was actually a commentary on the communist student movement that had instigated bloody riots in 1968, beginning in Paris. If Lennon had lived until Hasbro purchased Parker Brothers and the Monopoly game, he would have seen vindication for his message when communism came undone.

Capitalism's greatest threat finally collapsed under its own hollow weight. How this happened is easy to see in hindsight.

Momentous change unfolded in 1985 when the younger, less militaristic Mikhail Gorbachev took command of the Soviet Union. He faced up to the looming economic disaster confronting his country and its satellite nations by improving relations with the capitalist nations of the West. Reykjavik, Iceland, again became the scene of a match with global implications when Gorbachev and President Reagan arrived there in 1986. The two initiated a sweeping reduction in nuclear arsenals. Gorbachev's willingness to end the Cold War was a reflection of his nation's inability to match Reagan's military spending. But it was also a reflection of the failure of the communist system. Gorbachev soon permitted private ownership of business in Russia and allowed his eastern bloc allies to manage their own internal affairs. Both of these moves were designed to get more goods (especially food) onto store shelves in the Soviet Union. Instead, they resulted in a largely peaceful revolution that brought down the Iron Curtain and saw the Soviet Union collapse.

Monopoly was there to celebrate the victory of capitalism over communism. In 1988 Parker Brothers published the first Russian-language edition of the game, one of its tokens being a Russian bear. (The communists had published a couple of sanitized, unauthorized versions in the early 1980s, one of which was named Manage.) In 1992 the World Monopoly Championship was triumphantly staged in the formerly divided city of Berlin, Germany.

After a four-decade ban, Monopoly number nine was officially welcome east of the Brandenburg Gate—a stately monument that has symbolized Berlin since 1795 (except for eight years when Napoleon Bonaparte removed it to Paris). The wall separating East from West Berlin had been torn down, and the Brandenburg Gate was located just inside its former eastern side. When the Monopoly champions arrived in October 1992, the gate was weathered with age and maintenance lapses. Its condition was symbolic of the drab, nearly moribund economy East Berliners had suffered through since 1945. During the 1992 Monopoly event, Turks on Pariser Platz were plying Russian military trinkets in front of this monument. Russian soldiers had sold them before returning home to an uncertain future (no housing, few jobs).

Hope and expectation filled the hearts and minds of Berliners. Construction cranes filled the skyline. Museums, government buildings, office buildings, and infrastructure were rapidly being restored in the former communist section of the city. Within this atmosphere,

Monopoly and its champions celebrated a victory for freedom, democracy, and capitalism.

Thirty-two nations were represented at the championships, including three from eastern Europe (Hungary, the Czech Republic, and Slovakia). A confident investment banker named Garry Peters represented the United States. Peters had won the 1991 New York finals. Also present was reigning world champion Ikuo Hiyakuta. A cheerful and devoted student of the game, Hiyakuta-san had replied, "Most pleased," when a reporter once asked this business manager how it felt to be the world's number one Monopoly player.

True to tradition, neither Peters nor Hiyakuta reached the 1992 finals. The new champion was Joost von Oren of the Netherlands, a smart and focused competitor who played the game with aplomb.

Von Oren's victory was heralded throughout Europe; it enhanced the official licensing of the game in many other nations, including Poland, Latvia, Lithuania, and several former Soviet republics.

Hiyakuta had been champion number eight; von Oren became number nine.

Back in America, Monopoly's retail presence was expanded through broad application of its brand imagery. The outlicensing begun by Kenner Parker Toys accelerated under Hasbro's leadership. The Monopoly brand began to adorn a multitude of products, including tote bags, earrings, Christmas ornaments, soft goods (blankets, sheets), rugs, shirts, hats, purses, and even underwear.

Affinity editions of Monopoly became a market mainstay, the first being launched in 1992 with the publication of Monopoly: New York City Edition. Within a dozen years, over two hundred versions of Monopoly appeared with property spaces associated with cities, states, colleges, sports teams, special events (e.g., the Alaskan Iditarod), TV shows (e.g., I Love Lucy and The Simpsons), and even other products (e.g., Harley Davidson, Chevy Corvette, and Coca Cola). A California-based company that adopted the name USAopoly published these U.S.

official editions. (In Europe, Winning Moves International has published dozens of comparable versions in several languages.)

But a legal slip during the brief Tonka years resulted in the word
Opoly becoming available for public use. Soon it seemed that for every
official version marketed by USAopoly, an unofficial Opoly version
appeared lacking Monopoly's distinctive graphics.

*Affinity editions of Monopoly
were introduced to the
market by a California-based
company called USAopoly.*

Dave Wilson lamented the spread of the unofficial games, but Monopoly's appeal and sales appeared resilient to all the clutter. George
Parker would have been worried too. "The public does not like confusion," he explained when Mah Jongg suffered under the weight of so
many variations. There is, of course, a simple explanation for the demise of Mah Jongg versus the endurance of Monopoly. George could
not establish an official set of rules for the former. With Monopoly, he
did. The game has since weathered all storms.

In 1995, to commemorate the game's sixtieth anniversary at Parker
Brothers, a beautiful gold foil edition was introduced, complete with
an aged graphic for its game board and reproductions of the large tokens used in expensive 1936 sets.

Hasbro Games also marketed selected affinity versions of Monopoly, such as NFL Monopoly and Monopoly: All-American Edition.
The most successful by far were the various Monopoly: Star Wars editions, which transported the Monopoly board to a galaxy, far, far away

and provided its players with detailed pewter tokens of the movie's famous characters.

Monopoly sailed smoothly through the George H. W. Bush and Bill Clinton years as electronic and computer versions were launched. They were small, compact, and highly intelligent. Programmers in the 1960s who simulated the game on the hot, massive, and expensive mainframes of the day would have drooled at the attainment of such goals.

Three newsworthy events occurred in Monopoly's world before the millennium turned. First, with the aid of Internet voting, a new token was added to number nine: a die-cast moneybag. Over the years, dozens of token designs had been included in the game, especially in its upscale editions, but never a moneybag. Some of them were made of wood and some of composite plastic. But most were of shiny silver-colored die-cast metal. Originally made in Chicago, the tokens were now molded in the Far East and shipped in giant containers to the States for assembly into newly printed games.

Second, Parker Brothers was consolidated under the roof of Hasbro Games in East Longmeadow, thus ending over a century of tradition on Boston's North Shore. This was a jolting experience for the remaining 150 Parker employees. While all were offered relocation packages, only a few accepted. Eight years earlier, following Hasbro's acquisition of Parker Brothers, the venerable factory in Salem, Massachusetts, was closed and Monopoly's production equipment moved to the former Milton Bradley game plant in East Longmeadow. Now its brand management was moved there as well.

Third, Rich Uncle Pennybags became Mr. Monopoly. The change occurred after extensive research revealed that his new name was easier to remember and that many people already referred to him by this nickname. His full name had been Milburn Pennybags and his wife was Madge. His three nephews were Randy, Andy, and Sandy. Presumably their first names weren't affected, but from now on they all would bear the Monopoly surname. Separate research revealed that Mr. Monopoly's likeness remained one of the most recognizable in the world. (One wonders if J. P. Morgan could have imagined the recognition he inspired.)

Monopoly celebrated the new millennium with not one but two special 2000 editions and a graphic refresh for number nine. This change resulted in the ninth version to be marketed since 1935.

Number nine for number nine.

14

MCNALLY'S METHOD

2003–2004

As the new millennium started, hundreds of millions of people around the world had played Monopoly. The best players compete periodically by nation to determine a champion. These champions gather every few years for a rousing global tournament. Most significantly, Monopoly championships can be won by anyone, even *you*.

If you can imagine yourself as a champion of this great game, fasten your seatbelt. This chapter will take you on a ride behind the scenes of the recent U.S., Canadian, and World Championships. Our first stop is Chicago. The date was Thursday, October 16, 2003.

Matt McNally, a graduate student from Wisconsin working on his master of fine arts degree at the University of California–Irvine, was pacing nervously inside the great hall of Chicago's Union Station, along with forty-seven other hopefuls.

On the opposite side of the broad marble floor a colonnaded staircase rose. At any moment, it seemed, Treasury Agent Elliot Ness would appear, intent on rescuing a baby whose mother loses control of its

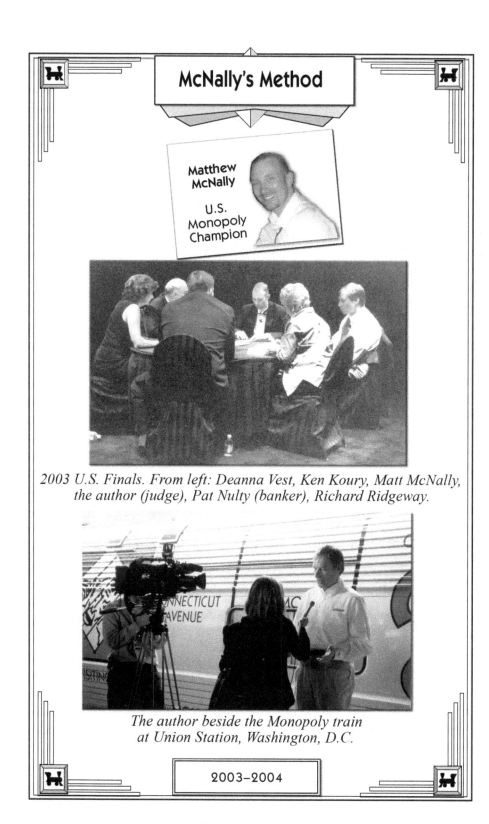

McNally's Method

Matthew McNally

U.S. Monopoly Champion

2003 U.S. Finals. From left: Deanna Vest, Ken Koury, Matt McNally, the author (judge), Pat Nulty (banker), Richard Ridgeway.

The author beside the Monopoly train at Union Station, Washington, D.C.

2003–2004

carriage at the top of these stairs. This scene from *The Untouchables* played out in the imagination of many of those standing in line, myself included. But none of Chicago's legendary mobsters—headliners during Monopoly's early days—arrived to give the carriage a shove. Instead, we heard marching music. A high school band emerged from an unseen hallway, led by a strutting Mr. Monopoly. He was dressed in top hat and tails, waving a cane in time to the Roosevelt-era refrain "We're in the Money."

The 2003 United States Monopoly Championship had kicked off with a bang. As Mr. Monopoly and the band passed by, the other contestants fell in line. I followed. Matt was somewhere ahead of me; I hadn't met him yet. I prefer not to socialize with the players in advance. Impartiality is essential in my role as chief judge. I waited to size them up when they were on the clock, hunched over a game board. They came to Chicago from the four corners of the continental United States and points in between. They ranged in age from eleven to fifty-nine. Thirty-six of them were male and twelve female, a typical ratio at a Monopoly championship. What was not typical was their origin. None were state champions, as in past tournaments. Rather, these were the game's most proficient players, regardless of state, as determined by an Internet Monopoly challenge. Modern times, indeed.

We marched to platform 1, where the Reading Railroad was waiting—a train unlike any other. While its rear car was a vintage 1920s private car, the others were sleek aluminum-sided Amtrak cars decorated with large, eye-catching graphics of Monopoly spaces. Properties, Jail, Go, Chance—they were all onboard. Each graphic was bright and perfectly applied. They made the train look like pure fun, a life-size child's plaything. The intent was to startle and amuse during the long journey from Chicago to Pittsburgh, Washington, D.C., and finally into Philadelphia's 30th Street Station. Judging from the expressions on the faces of early morning commuters disembarking on nearby platforms, it was working.

Alongside the silent diesel locomotive was a speaker's platform. There to provide opening remarks was Frank Bifulco, newly hired president of Hasbro Games, Dave Wilson's successor in training. Frank held the distinction of being the ninth leader of Parker Brothers and therefore of the Monopoly brand. Leader number nine for number nine.

I saw Matt McNally up ahead, standing next to two contestants I came to know—John Meyer of Indiana and Shelly Testa of Georgia. As Matt later told me, he became aware of Monopoly tournaments while completing his undergraduate degree and made up his mind to enter the next one. He took only two hours to complete the Monopoly qualifying test when it was posted online in July. He passed the test easily and was invited to compete.

Mr. Monopoly (portrayed brilliantly by actor Merwin Goldsmith) welcomed everyone and introduced Frank Bifulco. Frank described the upcoming tournament schedule, introduced my fellow supporting judges and me, then stood aside when Mr. Monopoly christened the train and asked all those departing to go aboard. We departed the station's darkness into the light of a new dawn.

Tables in two of the dining cars were organized for game play, two tables per car. Four players huddled around each board, racing the clock for ninety minutes to roll, deal, and build their way to a strong finish. Qualifying points are awarded according to assets held when time expires, plus a bonus for each opponent bankrupted during play. If all were vanquished, a perfect score of twenty-eight points would be earned by the table winner. Every player's goal is to sweep the field three times, in order to earn the ultimate score of eighty-four points. Rumor had it this class of players was sharp, and I suspected there would be few sweeps.

The top four players were announced on the afternoon of the second day following the third round of games. They vied for the championship the following morning in a casino ballroom in Atlantic City.

Among those who aroused early attention was Matthew Gissel of St. Albans, Vermont. Gissel was the reigning U.S. Monopoly champ, having prevailed in Las Vegas in 1999, where he defeated the 1995 champ, Roger Craig of Illinois. Gissel, I soon learned, had set his sights on the game's four railroads. He liked to capitalize on the bountiful cash they generate and used it to secure and develop a powerful group of properties. Like Matt McNally, Gissel was attending grad school. Unlike McNally, he did not fare well in this tournament. Gissel's reign ended on Saturday.

Matt McNally, lean and tall, had a friendly face and affable disposition. Matt had done his homework, playing countless warm-up games and researching local events around the nation. He wanted to have more to talk about with his fellow competitors than the weather. Demeanor and preparation are aids when playing Monopoly. Unlike other classic games played around the world, Monopoly depends on negotiations. For many, the art of negotiation does not come naturally. They view driving a hard bargain or selling something—anything—as painful, like a dental procedure. The sum total of negotiating skills employed by many people is learned from playing Monopoly. But the pain of negotiating is easier if you expect to be treated fairly, with respect. An opponent who possesses a pleasant style stimulates a certain comfort level. As it goes in real life, so goes it in Monopoly.

Matt's negotiating skills, however acute, played only a small role in his first game because luck shone on him. He landed on all three yellow properties and gained a natural Monopoly (one acquired without trading). Armed with this strong base, Matt took command: his feel for the game, his touch, his "method." For Matt, the method took years to develop. But it seemed worth it.

What is McNally's method? As Matt puts it, "At its core are strategies and statistics that make luck work for me, not against me. While I always show respect for my opponents, I also look for nonverbal cues to reveal their thinking. With luck in my favor and an understanding of the other players, I apply rote tactics in developing my first color group." How so? "By building intelligently, not greedily. I don't want to motivate the others to trade and build, until at least one goes bankrupt to me. Thereafter, I should be in a commanding position and I must exploit this to the fullest to drive the others out of the game."

Matt applied his method flawlessly in the finals. He did not develop the yellow group, even though he had cash to buy houses. Why? If he did so, he would sound an alarm bell in the minds of his opponents, stimulating a frenzy of trades among them. If a better color group was monopolized by one of them, Matt could have ended up paying a huge rent—and down his houses would come to pay. A better color group than yours is one that gets landed on more often and can be developed for less money. The yellows are good, but the reds are better and the oranges even better. Even the light purples are good to own early in the game. These groups share something in common: all lie after the Jail space and in front of the Go to Jail space. Since players frequently go to jail, these groups get landed on more than the other four groups on the board.

So Matt bided his time and his opponents sat tight (including one who coveted the race car token because race car is a palindrome—spelled the same forward or backward). Then slowly Matt began to develop. First one house per property, then two. He paused. Small rents came in: $110 or $330. He checked the clock. Plenty of time left. This fact provided false hope to Matt's opponents, who believed a color group could be theirs without the need to trade.

Matt now struck. He built a third house on each yellow (this level offers the best return for money invested, regardless of group). One opponent landed there, went bankrupt, and then pushed his cash and properties Matt's way. In that instant, Matt took full control of the game because he owned at least one title deed from each of the other groups. Before the hour expired, Matt swept the board. He owned it all and was awarded the maximum twenty-eight points.

After all players had finished their first game, the scores were posted in the lounge car. Because nicknames were posted on the board, each player knew only where he or she stood, while the identity of the others remained a mystery. This prevented collusion (a problem at earlier tournaments). I noticed that Cash Conductor was at the top along with Iron Horse and Big Spender.

Game two proved to be a nail-biter. The dice took vengeance on Matt as he landed on few properties and struggled to get a color group.

The other three players seemed on the verge of multiple one-for-one trades that would deny Matt any chance of winning. But Matt recognized this and persuaded one player to accept every property he owned except Park Place in return for Boardwalk. He achieved this by pointing out the possible trades she could then make to improve her position. Matt also convinced her that if the trade was made, either she or he would win and not the other two players, whom she happened to dislike. Matt immediately built houses on the dark blues. His unfortunate trading partner landed on Boardwalk and Matt took possession of her lucky yellows. His opponents, sensing doom, slowed their play and tried to milk the clock, hoping to hang on until the bell and garner a few points. But just before the clock expired, Matt bankrupted his final opponent and came away with twenty-eight more points. At another table, a player nicknamed Big Spender did likewise. These two became the favorites after the first day's competition.

The Reading Railroad Express rolled into Pittsburgh hours late, due to a freight train that blocked the tracks. As Matt's head hit the pillows, he realized that he had achieved his goal of playing in a tournament and had a good shot at making the finals. While other players closed their eyes and caught some needed sleep, Matt lay awake, figuring out his strategy for the third and final preliminary game. A simple plan developed: Do what it takes to survive the game. Just earn a few points and make the finals.

The next day, Matt played a leisurely game. He had decided not to advocate trades of any sort unless threatened with bankruptcy. He hoped to block trades by acquiring a rainbow Monopoly—one deed from each group. Matt has a name for this novel tournament tactic— the McNally maneuver—having encountered few players who employ it. In this contest, however, the dice did not bestow a rainbow Monopoly on Matt. But no player acquired a natural Monopoly and eventually Matt controlled enough key properties to deter trading. (A key property opens the door to a successful trade. A key player is one who must be included in a trade to bring it off.) Matt owned several keys but choose to sit on them.

With time winding down, a sense of urgency gripped his table. Matt had to act. He offered a trade to a sharp opponent named Deanna Vest. Matt had carefully figured out the merits of this trade. If accepted, it would assure him of a second-place finish in the match and guarantee Deanna third place. But Deanna declined. Only later would Matt learn that Deanna was Big Spender. She was employing a strategy similar to his: just survive. Deanna liked the railroads. In this game, she owned several and counted on the cash they produced to keep her in the game. Her plan worked. The match ended with all four players still standing. Matt finished last, earning only three points for a three-game total of fifty-nine—just enough to qualify him.

After two long days on the rails, the Reading Express pulled into Philadelphia's 30th Street Station. We climbed aboard buses for box lunches and a ride to the World's Playground.

Atlantic City appeared on the horizon an hour later, its flashy casinos lighting up the sky beyond the broad salt marshes that edge the New Jersey mainland across from Absecon Island. The rail line built by Richard Osborne a century and a half earlier cut across this very marsh. The streets named by Jonathan Pitney awaited us. I held my breath. I had my reasons.

We traversed a bridge, entered the city, and headed north on Mediterranean Avenue. For most of my fellow travelers, this was their first sight of the Las Vegas of the East. I worried that they would be disappointed, perhaps even horrified, when they glimpsed the back side of Atlantic City. While I didn't think it would appear as desolate as the bombed-out Cologne of John McPhee's essay, I fretted that it might look as grim as it did in the movie bearing the city's name. I had last been here a year or two after that film was released in 1980. I hoped, perhaps unrealistically, that the wealth along the Boardwalk had finally extended to the dogs—Baltic and Mediterranean.

And it had, sort of. The neighborhood looked surprisingly clean: no grime, no broken glass, and no transients. But as we passed a row of adult bookshops and video stores, the driver jokingly advised, "Eyes straight ahead, kids."

The bus turned east, and ahead loomed Harrah's Showboat and Casino Hotel spanning the entire block between Pacific Avenue and the Boardwalk (Pacific being the first major avenue inland of the Boardwalk). Because Absecon Island has an irregular shape, the distance is greatest here. We clambered out of the bus, entered the glittering casino, and lined up to register. Ten minutes later I was lying on a comfortable bed.

Meanwhile, the finalists were being fitted for the tuxedos or formal dresses they would wear during the contest the next day. Then they were free to explore. The city awaited us. The casinos were waiting expectantly for our money, and the city beckoned with many other venues capable of exciting sleepless eyes. I passed.

Matt McNally ventured onto the Boardwalk but only to touch it for good luck. He then returned to his room and fell asleep. The next morning he rose early and began reviewing his knowledge of the game. His ordered room service but barely touched the hot meal after it arrived. The knots in his stomach were tightening.

In the morning I looked out my window, which faced north. The adjoining blocks had been leveled and all that remained were the streets, as if the owners of the former buildings had been forced to sell them off to raise a rent. Many of these barren streets had been made famous by Monopoly: Connecticut, Vermont, Oriental, St. Charles Place, St. James Place. Inevitably, new casinos would be built on them. The smaller streets will likely disappear forever under these massive structures. Sadly the Monopoly character of Atlantic City had already been altered. Illinois Avenue was renamed Martin Luther King Boulevard, while Park Place was reduced to a stub road, with Bally's Park Place Hotel consuming the park made famous by the game.

The next morning, Christy Newton seemed to be everywhere at once. She was the marketing whiz at Hasbro Games charged with pulling together the entire tournament, a complex juggling act. Several other talented folks from Hasbro Games and their PR agency, Fleishman-Hilliard, were present to assist Christy. But if anything went wrong, she would shoulder the blame. It was always like this at Monopoly tournaments. When the tournament ran smoothly, the people who made it happen went unnoticed. When a glitch occurred, they were caught in the searchlight like escaping prisoners.

Among those Christy gave last-minute instructions to was Merwin Goldsmith: Mr. Monopoly. His mission was to kick off the championship game with a grand welcome for everyone, especially the press and sizable audience. Merwin had a twinkle in his blue eyes and a voice both rousing and confident. He had begun his career with Monopoly by mouthing an animated Mr. Monopoly for TV commercials in the 1980s. In 1995, on a whim, he was asked to don a costume and bring the character to life for an interview. An accomplished actor who had performed on stages from New York to Liverpool, Merwin was admittedly scared when he showed up near Wall Street for the session. But passersby smiled and called him by name. That's when Merwin Goldsmith *knew* he was meant to play the role. He and Mr. Monopoly became one and the same.

At the stroke of nine on this Saturday morning, Merwin led the players into Harrah's ballroom, accompanied by a local marching band. "We're in the Money" reprised the buoyant mood from Chicago. The finalists and I, much like contestants in the recent Miss America pageant, wore identification sashes. Mr. Monopoly and representatives of Hasbro Games introduced each of the forty-four nonqualifying players and paid them proper respect. The four finalists were then announced and joined head banker Pat Nulty of Citibank and myself on the dais.

Matt felt ready. He had memorized the odds of landing on any property, of going to Jail, of drawing a good versus a bad card. He'd mastered techniques of persuasion, argumentation, and nonverbal communication. And he'd sharpened these skills "in combat" by playing hundreds of games against a talented training team back home. But was it enough? Matt knew that the other finalists—Deanna Vest, Ken Koury, and Richard Ridgeway—had been sharpening their saws for months as well.

America's Game beckoned. By 9:45 the winner-take-all contest was under way. By 11:10, it was over. During the intervening eighty-five minutes, the best championship game I have ever witnessed took place.

Matt was upbeat and energetic, even after he failed to secure his favorite token (the race car). This little setback proved to be his only distraction in the game. It was Ken Koury who raced out of the starting blocks, and he soon owned a natural Monopoly on the cheap dark purples and built hotels. Next he drew a card that invited him to "take a walk on the Boardwalk," and the dice obligingly carried him to Park Place. He now possessed the coveted dark blues and wanted to build on them, but he lacked cash. To raise some, he offered to sell four properties to Richard Ridgeway. Richard made the deal in hopes of landing on properties currently in the bank, which would complete one or more color groups for him. But Richard's luck ran out. He owed the bank $75 for luxury tax, which he couldn't pay. In a pivotal moment, he eschewed offers from Deanna and Ken and elected to go bankrupt to the bank. Why? Likely because Richard had become acquainted with Matt during the preliminaries and the two had developed a mutual respect. Richard, vanquished, apparently did not want to harm Matt's chances.

The rules require the banker to immediately auction properties it reacquires through a bankruptcy. Matt was already thinking hard. While Richard transferred his assets to Pat Nulty, our banker, Matt counted his cash discreetly: $402. He quickly evaluated what could happen, property by property, if his opponents purchased them. None posed an immediate danger, except the orange deed. If this one got into the hands of either opponent, Matt would not be able to block an orange monopoly, the best on the board. The printed value of Tennessee is $180, but Matt bid an astounding $400 when it came up for auction. Deanna Vest and Ken looked at Matt as if he had blown a fuse. Neither challenged his bid. A few turns later, Matt landed on the final red property and bought it. From that moment on, he controlled the game.

I could visualize the outcome of the game. Matt couldn't lose because the only groups that threatened him were the railroads, utilities, and low-price dark purples (which Ken had owned since early on). None of these could knock him out of the game. Ken was a sharp player and recognized his need to deal to improve his chances. Deanna, who loved the railroads, owned three of them. She knew they would produce a steady supply of cash for her. So she was in no rush to deal with Ken. Matt, of course, had no desire to make a deal with either of his opponents. The calm lasted for only a few rolls of the dice. Now even Deanna grew concerned. Without a color group, she couldn't hope to win. The trading buzz resumed. Matt remained quiet for the duration, except when he occasionally distracted Ken and Deanna with halfhearted offers.

No deals were made and Ken soon went bankrupt to Matt. Ken's bankruptcy destroyed Deanna's last chance to own a color group. Amazingly, she prolonged the game through an exceptional run of the dice. Whatever roll she needed, she threw, avoiding Matt's rents. The audience got into the game, cheering each time she escaped the hangman's noose. But as sure as Sunday, the board, which Matt designed with his trades and auction victories, prevailed. Deanna's luck ran out when she landed on a light purple topped by a hotel.

Matt McNally became the new U.S. Monopoly champion. He won not only a Monopoly game filled with real money ($15,140) but an all-expenses-paid trip to the upcoming World Championships as well. In the course of the next few days he appeared on several TV programs and over sixty radio shows. During the next year, he made many personal appearances on behalf of the game he loves. All the while, he prepared for the World.

In June 2004, I reprised my role as judge at the Canadian Nationals, held inside a beautifully restored locomotive roundhouse near the waterfront in downtown Toronto. Toronto was also the site of the last World Championships in 2000. On an October day that year, economist Yutaka Okada of Japan had overpowered his opponents and won the crown.

In this Canadian Championship, thirty-three-year-old Leon Vandendooren prevailed. Leon was a quick thinker and every bit as proficient as Matt NcNally. He also knew the game's odds and mechanics inside out. In addition, he possessed the rare ability to get inside the heads of his opponents and alter his game face in order to rattle their psyches. In one preliminary game, he won by being gentle. In another, he drove a multiplayer trade that broke the game his way. In the finals, he took a surprisingly tough stance. At one point, I needed to restore order by reminding the other players and him of their need for mutual respect. Leon responded immediately and graciously. But the twinkle in his eye told me that his rough tactics were intentional. Leon was pitted against Jason Kirsh—a formidable opponent—and he was trying to distract Jason into a miscue. The game rapidly distilled down to the two of them, and the ebb and flow became fantastic. Each built up a powerful color group, only to land on the other's and suffer a massive rent, inevitably paid for by tearing down houses. This happened time and again. The two players pounded each other like prizefighters in a ring, trading heavy punches but unable to deliver a fatal blow. But when the knockout finally came, it was Leon who delivered it. The crowd collectively exhaled, exhausted from this lengthy exhibition of powerhouse Monopoly.

As October rolled around, Matt, Leon, and I—along with hundreds of other people from around the world—descended on Tokyo for the 2004 World Monopoly Championship.

A Japanese billionaire named Mori built a sparkling city within a city in Tokyo's fashionable nightlife section of Roppongi Hills. The tournament would take place high up in cylindrical Mori Tower. Everyone was sheltered at the nearby Grand Hyatt. If the weather didn't cooperate, participants could walk from one to the other through an underground walkway. We were informed that a typhoon was approaching Japan, but before we could even worry about that, an earthquake vibrated our beds at one o'clock in the morning on Friday. For those of us unaccustomed to the experience, it made for animated discussion over breakfast. But no damage was done and the tournament was not delayed. The Mori

モノポリー世界選手権

東京

The logo of the 2004 Monopoly Championship in Tokyo featured Mr. Monopoly in samurai dress.

Tower was built to take far worse than this early morning jolt.

Many talented champions were present, including several from behind the former Iron Curtain. Monopoly, like many icons of Western culture, had become a fixture in these countries. They wasted little time catching up. Bartlomiej Korczak of Poland reached the finals, along with Bjorn Andenaes of Norway, Antonio Fernandez of Spain, and Anthony Redmond of Ireland, for an all-European match.

Japan's reigning champ, Yutaka Okada, did not repeat. Matt McNally and Leon Vandendooren—two of the best players I ever watched—also missed qualifying for the championship round. It was not because opponents ganged up on them or their play was less than flawless. It was because certain opponents made glaring errors in judgment, trades didn't break their way, or lady luck found other partners to dance with.

Those of us who had hoped to see the best of North America go head-to-head in the finals were disappointed. However, it is a testament of the broad appeal of this game that in any given match, any player (including you) can win. This boast cannot be made on behalf of chess, backgammon, or bridge.

The finals were held in the ballroom. Giant projection screens overhead were ready to display the action for the audience. Flags of all competing countries flanked the playing area, a Kabuki band and actors performed during the pregame ceremony, and geishas wearing lovely kimonos escorted the players to the elevated table, where banker Yumiko Suzaki and I awaited. Mr. Monopoly energized the large crowd and the game began.

Within thirty minutes Fernandez had clinched a win. The Spanish champion landed on all three orange properties and gained a natural monopoly. The other players struggled to cope, but the other color groups were blocked, broken, or partially owned by the bank. Redmond of Ireland had played countless endgame possibilities in his head in preparation for this contest, but he never got a chance to use even one. He cursed his bad luck well before his final bankruptcy-inducing throw and fourth-place finish. Korczak of Poland played the best possible game under the circumstances. He came in third. Bjorn held on a while longer but inevitably landed on Fernandez's oranges. The Spanish champion's hands flew into the air in triumph. "I'm extremely happy, and proud," the new champ proclaimed.

The game may have ended crisply, but for many, there was an incomplete sensation in our stomachs. The feeling was akin to seeing Muhammad Ali knock out Joe Frazier in the second round. The outcome was thrilling, but you had hoped for more of a battle.

I congratulated Antonio and stepped aside. My job was done.

Outside, the typhoon had blasted its way across southern Japan and was now having its way with the capital city. I returned to the hotel safely through the underground passage. When I emerged in the lobby, I saw an awe-inspiring sight. The sky at 5:30 p.m. was pitch black. Young saplings were bent to the ground by winds hurling sheets of rain sideways. The blast of the storm was worse than any hurricane I ever endured as a kid growing up near the Jersey shore. But Roppongi Hills didn't flinch. The rain pounded fruitlessly, like the Big Bad Wolf attempting to blow down a house made of unyielding bricks. In an hour the worst had passed.

Only then did this event reach an unexpected high. Matt McNally, his training friends Jason Chan and Cory Casoni, and Adrian Prince—flamboyant U.K. champion—invited me to join them in a final Monopoly game. I had no reason not to accept, and I felt honored.

The game was an eye-opener; Matt employed a strategy I had never seen before. He tore down his expensive houses on the greens and sold the group just to get the light blues, where he quickly built hotels. Suddenly they loomed ahead of me, and I hit them twice on one turn (thanks to doubles followed by a roll of 3). My newly built houses on Park Place and Boardwalk came down to pay for the damages. Matt claimed victory, and I was awed by his brilliant play. He departed Tokyo a winner once more.

As we flew home, the game continued to spin in my brain, along with the realization that Monopoly now seemed as important in Asia as it was in the Americas, Australia, and Europe. I continued to think about our American-bred game, and I looked forward to sharing my impressions of the tournament with my other Monopoly friends—those who research and collect its past.

15

WILLIAMSON'S WORLD
2005 AND BEYOND

There is more to Monopoly than making, selling, or playing it. Studying this activity also fascinates many. Growing numbers of Monopoly historians and collectors are found everywhere in the world, and the Internet is their forum. Like any good pastime, this one does not require the investment of a lot of money or time. But like any passion, it is capable of monopolizing all of your free time (and cash) in its pursuit.

On a typical Sunday morning in Chillicothe, Illinois, Chris Williamson rose early to get a head start on a busy day. He woke up the little one, Abi, age four, and shook fifteen-year-old Erik into coherence. Already awake were wife Julie and thirteen-year-old son Nathan, who both help him in his profession. After he assembled his family and checked everyone's preparation, Chris's mind turned to Monopoly—his favorite hobby.

Then he opened his Bible and studied the verses he planned to preach from that day. He wrote down notes and checked if any words in the Scripture should be explained according to their Greek or Hebrew

Chris Williamson, preacher

Monopoly historian

portfolio 2/98 zomer 1998
(F. van Lanschot Bankiers)

*Albert Veldhuis on right.
Below, excerpt from a typical entry
on Albert's site (Monopli, Italy).*

Edition: Standard Editions of the "fascist period"
Publisher: Ed.Giochi S.a.S. - 1936 till 1946
The game: The picture was submitted by Paolo
Coletti and Spartaco Albertarelli, former director of
Editrici Giochi's R&D department, who tells about this
original edition:

"When in 1935 Arnoldo Mondadori, owner of the most important Italian book publisher,
received from Waddingtons a copy of Monopoly, he showed it to his best translator:
Mr. Emilio Ceretti. Mr. Mondadori decided that he was not interested in publishing a
game but he gave this opportunity to Mr. Ceretti, who wanted to start his own business.
It's important to note that in 1935, Italy was ruled by the "fascist laws" that did not allow
the use of foreign names and titles. Nor did they like the distribution of foreign products,
particularly those coming from the English or American markets...."

*Part of a devoted
collector's
display of
Monopoly
games.
This one belongs
to Dan Fernandez.*

2005 and Beyond

meanings. Chris understood both languages and especially appreciated the humor that colors the Hebrew Scriptures. There are few subjects Chris has not studied, explaining why only the brave or the foolish challenged him to a game of Trivial Pursuit.

At their small church, Julie led worship and strummed guitar while Nathan played an orchestra's worth of instruments—from guitars and piano to percussion—and Erik ran the overhead projector to display the song lyrics. When Chris stood up, Bible in hand, he preached without the aid of his notes. The discipline of writing them merely guided his sermon, which he attempted to keep as short as possible. He knew attention waned otherwise.

After completing the Lord's work, Chris returned to the history of Monopoly. Back at home, he immediately went to his computer and checked the current eBay listings of his favorite game. An e-mail backlog awaited his replies. Many people in the world of Monopoly have found Chris. He has become a clearinghouse of knowledge. His airtight, Trivial Pursuit–advantaged mind has absorbed and retained every imaginable fact about Monopoly's history. These details began to accumulate only three years ago, when Chris—a fan of Monopoly during childhood—learned that Elizabeth Magie Phillips hailed from nearby Canton, Illinois. (Chris tracked down her childhood home and photographed it.) He began to contact other Monopoly aficionados and follow eBay listings in order to learn all he could about the many versions offered for sale. Chris did web searches on all the people whose names peppered these listings—Henry George, EMP, the Thuns, the Dowst company, Darrow, Barton, Parker. So quickly did Chris become an expert that senior Monopoly historians began coming to him to sharpen their facts. When Ralph Anspach decided to sell the files he compiled during his lawsuit against General Mills, Chris helped document them for listing on eBay.

Chris views collecting as a sideline to demonstrate the history and changes that have occurred in the game. Actually, Chris would love to collect as well, but having chosen to serve God rather than money, his means are limited. His many skills, three degrees, and varied business experience benefit him in other ways than making a monetary fortune. Nevertheless, Chris has amassed an impressive collection of prints, scans, books, and articles about Monopoly and games of special value to him. And he has connected with the individuals who own the rare Monopoly games described in this book.

Once he answered his e-mail, Chris made some calls, including one to Thomas Forsyth in Oregon. Thomas is best known for his award-winning photography and animation work, but for those of us in the Monopoly world, Thomas is the owner of the holy grail.

The grail entered his life during the 1998 holidays while he was home for a visit in Sequim, Washington. His father suggested the family have a game night. In the garage Thomas found a stack of games, including a very old game his father characterized as "much like Monopoly." Moments later, Thomas was gazing on an original Landlord's Game (the one pictured in this book). It looked like Monopoly but was patented in 1904, three decades before Monopoly appeared. This discovery led him to uncover the game's history, its rarity, and its place in American history. Subsequently he launched a website devoted to it and many of the early games described in this book.

The preservation of the Forsyth family game began with Thomas's grandmother. She kept everything while raising her family in the Park Ridge suburb of Chicago, including a game her husband's mother had purchased in 1910, most likely in Chicago. Thomas's grandfather was a high school student at the time. Elizabeth Magie Phillips was living in Chicago with her new husband, Albert, and chances are she persuaded local stores to stock her game.

Ninety-two years and three generations later, the Landlord's Game entered the life of Thomas Forsyth. Initially he attempted to sell the game on behalf of his parents, thinking it might be worth some money. But no reference existed to this game and its value could not be established. Thomas wasn't even sure other copies existed. (Three more are now known—and perhaps a fourth—according to Chris Williamson.)

Urged on by dealers, Thomas researched the game and eventually made contact with Ralph Anspach. Forsyth probed deeper and, with the help of fellow historians, tracked down many Landlord-Finance-Monopoly games made between 1904 and 1933.

Today they are pictured and described on his website (his and related sites are listed in the appendix). "I've relied on the generosity of others, yourself included," Thomas related to me. "It's a group effort. My website grows with donations of rules, photos, and historical information. I find myself in the middle of a hub and am blessed with new friends whose homes span twenty time zones."

All this because of a family game night on a winter's eve.

Back in Chicago, fellow historian Dave Sadowski checked Thomas's site to see if anything new had been posted. Then he logged on to eBay. A relative newcomer to the club of Monopoly historians, Dave has rapidly come up to speed thanks to the exploding popularity of this online auction site. EBay is a time machine of sorts, offering a peek into the past at the click of a mouse and a search word or two, such as "Monopoly vintage." Today Dave searched carefully. He was not interested in big-ticket items but less obvious listings of Monopoly components and editions overlooked by collectors with deep pockets. Recently he had discovered gems such as cylindrical green houses and octagonal hotels from the 1930s (Parker Brothers apparently ran short of the familiarly shaped A-frame houses and hotel pieces). Slowly but surely, he and Chris Williamson had traced the source of the game's metal tokens to the Dowst Manufacturing Company. (Author's note: I had been told a vendor in the Midwest made the tokens, but the Parker old-timers I interviewed couldn't recall its name.) Consequently Dave and Chris established a link between Tootsie Toys (a Dowst company), Crackerjack prizes, and Monopoly. A significant accomplishment, shared by a man who belatedly caught the Monopoly bug.

"How did this happen?" I once asked him.

Dave explained by referencing his past. He was born in Chicago in 1954 and spent his entire life in the area. His dad was an amateur historian, and Dave discovered that he too liked reliving history. "We are truly standing on the shoulders of giants," he offered. A confirmed bookworm, once Dave developed an interest in Monopoly, he read everything he could find about the game. When he found no reference with the level of detail he sought, he decided to self-publish *Passing Go*, under the pen name Clarence B. Darwin. (While he sometimes offers it on eBay, it is best to go direct via davidsadowski@yahoo.com.) Dave also made reproductions of printed components from old versions. Dave has been an entrepreneur and a manager, working in the photo industry and advertising. He stays active in his church and considers his role as the single parent of a teenage son to be his top responsibility in life. He values his good relationship with his son, and he values the friends he's made in the world of Monopoly—especially Chris Williamson, whom he regards as a mentor.

As on most days, with each free moment Dave once more logged onto eBay. Something new might have emerged from the shadows of history while life distracted him. He is not the only one afflicted by this compulsive habit.

Another is Scott Bernhart. During his college years, he and friends would often visit Chicago. On one occasion, he came across a store selling foreign editions of Monopoly. They fascinated him, so Scott began saving money to buy one or two with each trip.

Scott had been hooked on the game since he first watched his parents play with friends. Eventually he bought an early home computer and learned how to program a side game for amusement. Today Scott is an attorney and owns over four hundred licensed Monopoly games and early Parker Brothers editions. (Unfortunately rats nibbled at some items in his collection while it was stored during a move a few years ago.) He also owns a Monopoly pinball game, which he plays with his eight-year-old son, Parker. Scott is teaching Parker the board version as well. As a former tournament player, Scott's advice to his son is succinct: "Buy everything."

In California, Ken Koury has struck pay dirt. Ken is a practicing attorney by day and a Monopoly buff by night. You'll remember Ken as a finalist in the 2003 U.S. Championships. Two summers later, he found a gem on eBay. A seller offered a set of handmade deeds, cards, and houses. Ken grabbed it for a song and contacted me. I noticed that these cards bore a striking resemblance to the typed, hand-painted components fashioned by Charles Darrow in 1933 and early 1934. While their origin was uncertain, there were several clues. They seemed to be the work of someone in a hurry. There are misspellings ("Illonois") and the paint on the title deeds was sloppily applied—exactly what you would expect from someone impatient with performing this task day in and day out. The typeface resembled that on the hand-typed Darrow cards on display in the Forbes Gallery. While these clues were not conclusive, Ken Koury may well have found a rare set of components handmade by Charles Darrow.

Dave Sadowski and Chris Williamson were skeptical because the instructions on some of the Chance and Community Chest cards were post-Darrow, meaning they were not found in Darrow's published editions or even in the first editions of Parker Brothers. However, it is

Monopoly collector and champion Ken Koury discovered a rare handmade version of the game, complete with misspelled "Illonois" title deed card, on eBay.

known that Darrow wrote as many as sixty different Chance and Community Chest cards and used different combinations of them in his handmade games. And Parker Brothers continued to tweak the copy on these cards in 1936 and 1937. It is possible the firm consulted Darrow's old variations before locking in the cards we know so well today.

Bargains like Ken's are tougher to come by as more people become aware of the value of unique Monopoly items. But the thrill of a good buy is eternal and it drives those devoted to this cause. For example, college student Jordan Gonzales purchased a rare Darrow–Parker Brothers hybrid edition for $25 at a local auction. It is likely worth hundreds of times this amount. Karen Powers came across a pristine Darrow White Box edition, bought it for $9, and resold it for $8,400 on eBay. "Candlecrazygirl" has picked up many a bargain on this electronic forum. EBay spans the globe and unites collectors everywhere. But it provides a ready selection of common Monopoly collectibles, and this availability drives down established prices. On the flip side, when a truly rare item surfaces, it stimulates a bidding frenzy among the devoted.

The world of Monopoly collecting has its share of pros—fans bent on owning the best and most sought-after Monopoly items in their area of interest, be it Parker editions, affinity editions, or Monopoly paraphernalia.

Dan Fernandez (no relation to the current world champion) typifies this growing field. In 1990 he and wife, Anita, left the Empire State Building and Dan's New York City roots. They moved to Colorado and purchased the Sundown Farm and Ranch. There they found their good life, much as Scott and Helen Nearing found theirs in New England. Unlike the Nearings, they did not eschew wealth. They brought their things with them—collections of furniture, coins, World War II memorabilia, gasoline pumps, and Old West artifacts.

Dan is a brilliant guy who holds three degrees and has worked for several university systems. He once served his country in the Peace Corps. History has special meaning for Dan and Anita, which partly explains their varied collecting interests. Their interest in Monopoly began after their move, when they noticed a small collection of Monopoly games at an estate sale and decided to buy it, only to discover components were missing from some of the sets. In this pre-eBay era, it took them years to find all the missing components. By then they were hooked. EBay has made it possible for Anita and Dan to expand their collection as quickly as they want.

They decided to limit their purchases to games published between 1934 and 1954 and then set out to complete their quest. They have since collected over seventy historic games and variations, all of which can be seen on their website.

Back on the East Coast, Rich Scozzari is proud to have spent the four decades of his life in New Jersey. (He beats me on this count; I moved away for college.) He's been a fan of Monopoly since his parents and grandparents introduced him to the game when he was eight. He fondly recalls trips to Philadelphia and the same John Wanamaker Department Store that gave Darrow his big break. His family bought their Monopoly sets there as well. Visions of money always seem to float through Rich's head; he's now a corporate controller. The money theme of Monopoly inspired his choice of vocation and defined his avocation.

Rich and his friends once designed an elaborate money game. Knowing of this interest, family and friends began giving him money-related games as gifts. Today Rich owns over seventy editions of Monopoly, including a 1934 Darrow set on the early end and the most recent Parker editions on the other. He plans to polish his playing skills and compete in a Monopoly tournament too. (Matt McNally, take note!)

Jerry and Libby Teal have a Monopoly collection room in their home, complete with a wall-mounted map of the United States marked with 115 pins. Each pinpoints a town or city where they purchased a game for their impressive collection. Jerry's interest in Monopoly began when he was eleven and he lost out on winning a Monopoly game in a bingo competition at school. Determined, he made a deal with the winner and came away with the game anyway. His curiosity was piqued in 1985 when he bought the Fiftieth Anniversary set and, like many other purchasers, was struck by the brief history included in its illustrated booklet. From that moment on, Jerry and Libby decided to collect in earnest. Their favorite is a Darrow Black Box game, like the ones pictured in the booklet. As a business graduate from the University of South Carolina, Jerry sees the parallel between Monopoly, economics, materials technology, and world conflict. He appreciates not only the differences these factors wrought by way of the editions he owns, but knowledge that other families played with these same sets many times before he acquired then. Libby and their three kids may be supportive of his passion, but they cut Jerry no slack when the dice roll for real in their household.

Richard Biddle's life seems to run parallel with the Landlord's Game. Richard has the distinction of having been a student in Colonel Gene Raiford's chemistry class at Westtown School. Richard currently serves as the director of the Henry George Museum in Philadelphia. He is a tenth-generation Quaker and is familiar with Quaker connections to both Georgeism and the history of Monopoly. He once hosted a Georgist conference where Thomas Forsyth's game was displayed. His personal collection includes a partial 1910 Landlord's Game and one of the few extant 1939 Parker Brothers Landlord's Games.

Bruce Whitehill discovered a rare 1950s Spanish version of Monopoly, but he is better known for founding the organization that became the American Game and Puzzle Collectors (AGPC) association and for helping many a game collector get his bearings in the field. The AGPC has become the single most significant organization to serve the needs of serious game and puzzle collectors, including Monopoly aficionados.

One of the organization's departed alumni was my friend Sid Sackson, who passed away in 2002. Sid's collection included over 18,000 games of every imaginable theme. It filled every spare foot of his home, plus the former rental apartment above it and his basement.

(When I visited, stacks of games had come to within six feet of his oil burner.) With the aid of Bruce Whitehill and others, Sid's widow and children auctioned off this massive anthology a few years ago. Sid's avid fans purchased most of it.

The AGPC holds an annual convention, which in 2005—thanks to the addition of several British and European members—convened in London and honored Victor Watson for his efforts on behalf of John Waddington Ltd. and Monopoly. (Previously the AGPC inducted both George Parker and Elizabeth Magie Phillips into their Game Inventors Hall of Fame.)

A year earlier, the AGPC met in Philadelphia. Among those attending was game author/inventor Tim Walsh. The first thing I noticed about Tim is his height—six feet seven inches. Tim was an athlete at Colgate University, where in 1987 he pitched a no-hitter and caught the longest touchdown pass in the school's history. He went on to play professional baseball in Mexico. Three years out of college, Tim coinvented a modern game classic, TriBond, a game of thought association that has sold over 3 million copies and has been translated into seven languages. (Will tournaments be forthcoming?)

Tim has touched the world of Monopoly by virtue of his superb compendium of twentieth-century toys and games entitled *The Playmakers: Amazing Origins of Timeless Toys*. An entrepreneur at heart, Tim (blessed with an understanding wife and daughters) self-published this $50 wonder from his home in Sarasota, Florida. Its success inspired Andrews-McMeel-Universal to license it and republish the book under the name *Timeless Toys*. Monopoly fills a key chapter in Tim's book. Among Tim's revelations is that Darrow's cousins suggested using charms as tokens. With the cooperation of Darrow's son, Bill, he also published photos of letters by Milton Bradley and Parker Brothers rejecting Monopoly. (My Buckwalter game print and Lizzie's King's Men game also came, via eBay, from Tim's collection.)

Tim's book has become a must-have reference among toy and game collectors, including Monopolyphiles. Among these, Marc Winters is arguably the king.

The California home of this successful financial adviser contains over 3,000 different worldwide, authorized editions. Marc originally housed his collection in his home office, but his wife insisted on finding a better place. She was worried about the floor-to-ceiling fire hazard. Marc temporarily moved his collection to shelving in his garage. His new game room addition permanently showcases his Monopoly collection—probably the world's largest.

Like many of us, Marc got hooked on Monopoly as a kid. He's been collecting for thirty of his forty-nine years. Monopoly taught him that investing in real estate and stocks could provide significant rewards and opportunity to build assets systematically. Marc is quick to note that he didn't learn these practical facts in school; few of us do.

At age sixteen, Marc found himself penniless and homeless in New York City. He scraped by, returned to California, and bought his first property—an apartment house in a low-income neighborhood. From this humble beginning, he plunged into the world of real estate, invested with a passion, and succeeded beyond measure. By age thirty-three, he decided to retire. Ten years later, when boredom set in, Marc reentered the investment world. Today Marc is immersed in the world of stocks and bonds and also controls the deeds to twenty-eight real estate properties (which happens to be the same number found in Monopoly).

Marc's collection brings him great satisfaction, but he has his favorites among those he owns and hopes to own: the two Darrow editions, the 1935 Parker trademark sets (number seven and number nine), the number twenty-five deluxe wood edition by Parker, along with the fine and gold editions of that same year (1936) and the Waddington Leeds limited edition. (Listings of Monopoly, Monopoly-related, and official U.S. affinity editions can be found in the appendix.)

While Marc may be the king of the hobby, Bill Boyd is its statesman. He's been at it for thirty-five years. His first exposure to the game occurred in California when he was three years old. He was fascinated with the touch and appearance of the game's components and couldn't wait to grow big enough to play. This childhood passion was set aside while he attended high school and served in the military. Nevertheless, after an honorable discharge, Bill returned to Monopoly, this time as a collector. His desire was influenced by his work redeveloping the aging downtown of Torrance, California. Today Bill serves as a municipal consultant (when he isn't tending his Monopoly collection).

Bill Boyd's number one goal is to own a copy of each edition published by Parker Brothers. Now in his fourth decade of collecting, Bill has found thirty-nine of the forty-one editions he seeks. At his home in Phoenix, Bill wrote an illustrated product history of Monopoly, which took two years to research. *Collector's Eye* magazine published it in 1999. Bill is a rarity in his own right because he has elected not to join the world of e-mail and eBay. Rather, he relies on professional dealers, including Paul Fink of the website gamesandpuzzles.com, to keep a sharp eye out for games he desires. (Fink, a charter member of AGPC, is an expert at restoring antique games.)

Many Americans have devoted much of their adult life to exploring aspects of Monopoly's past, be it researching the life of Elizabeth Magie Phillips, the intricacies of Robert Barton's acquisition of the game and its variants, or the game's many postwar developments. And the Monopoly game has sparked historical research by fans beyond American shores. In Sweden there's Dan Glimme; in Australia, Kade Hansson and Jeff Rosales; in Israel, Jehudith Inbar; in Italy, Spartaco Albaterelli; in France/Brazil, Hervé Théry; and in the United Kingdom, J. Matthew Horton. These thoughtful individuals have one other thing in common: they revere a man named Albert Veldhuis.

Albert is proud of the fact that he entered life the first year Parker Brothers published Monopoly. Now, as a septuagenarian, Albert bears a wonderful resemblance to Mr. Monopoly and on occasion even dresses like him, complete with top hat and tails, for forays into European gaming conventions.

Albert Veldhuis is the most accomplished and devoted historian of Monopoly editions published outside the United States. His website is a breathtaking journey through time and across the borders of many nations. Want to know about any set Waddington published in the United Kingdom? Go to Albert's site, flip to his country index, and click on Great Britain. You'll see pictures of them all, along with detailed information and the name of the contributor. Spain? Italy? Hungary? Germany? China? Australia? If a country has issued Monopoly or Monopoly-like games, Albert has tracked it down and brought it to his site.

Albert arrived in Holland at age eleven. He supplemented his command of Dutch with French, German, and English while he was a student in Senor Secondary School. (He has since learned Hungarian as well. His language skills enhanced the pace of his website's compilation.) He played Monopoly for the first time soon after arriving in Holland. The set was a prewar English edition. He and his friends played for the entire weekend.

Years passed before he would resume his passion. In 1985, while selling industrial glass, Albert was made aware of the game's Fiftieth Anniversary edition. He bought an English copy and traded it for cheese. Soon he felt a touch of remorse and purchased German, Swiss, and French editions on business trips. His collection grew steadily and then exploded after he discovered the Internet, e-mail, and eBay. He now has four hundred sets, his personal limit.

During the past two decades, Albert developed a deep knowledge of all the sets made around the world. While his interest in collecting appeared satisfied, he was burning with desire to do something meaningful with his collection and share the knowledge he had accumulated. Since no reference book existed that he could use to catalog or evaluate his collection, he decided to initiate a website to post his catalog of Monopoly sets. From the outset, Albert realized the advantage this offered: it could be updated and modified at will. And rather than consume space he no longer had at home, he could electronically acquire and post photos and descriptions of sets he didn't own.

Albert also recognizes the value to collectors of detailing comparisons on his site (such as the differences between the German and American Bible editions, or Dutch wine and Napa Valley wine sets). The breadth of his listings testifies to the reach of Monopoly and the extent of its association with cultural icons around the world.

Monopoly's conquest of the world is clearly visible on Albert Veldhuis's website, thanks to a map that he displays. It pinpoints the year Monopoly was first published in countries around the globe. Any potential conqueror would envy the game's steady outward expansion. As Albert says, "America's Game is the world's game too."

The game's remarkable journey from the mind of Elizabeth Magie Phillips, to its spread via Scott Nearing and his student evangelists, to its publication by Dan Layman and Charles Darrow, to the codifying of its rules by George Parker, to its growth through Parker Brothers, John Waddington Ltd., and Hasbro Corporation is now largely complete.

In the twenty-first century, Monopoly will continue to inspire and influence millions as an ambassador of success endorsed by millions. Monopoly can inspire hope in anyone who plays it. For many, Monopoly is the first economic teacher suggesting that a richer life is available if one is willing to reach for it.

For Chris Williamson, this message goes hand in hand with what he preaches. And for Chris, his family—and the growing world of Monopoly players, historians, and collectors—there exists hope of even better days to come.

16

MONOPOLY MONEY

I n 2005 Hasbro Games released a Seventieth Anniversary edition of
the Monopoly game to geat fanfare. In Berlin a 3,000-square-foot
game board was constructed on the turf of a major stadium to
mark the occasion. In Europe a successful Here & Now edition was
published based on a simple thesis: if Monopoly appeared for the first
time today, what would it look like, what would its values be, and
how would it play, given the passage of seventy years?

It had been seven decades since Charles Darrow sold Monopoly to
Parker Brothers. Add the prior thirty-two years of the Landlord's Game
existence, and ten decades—a century—has whizzed by.

Monopoly has become an enduring part of life, a close friend we continue to share, as the twenty-first century unfolds. It is a rite of passage
for children first contemplating adulthood. It is a means of measuring
mental and negotiating agilities among students and young adults. It is a
source of enjoyment adults gladly share with family and friends. Monopoly provides a stage to play out our fantasies and dreams, and on this
stage we are all gifted. We know the script by heart; only the ending remains open. The excitement of this unknown, the suspense experi-
enced as it unfolds—the decisiveness of it—draws us back to the stage,
time and again.

Monopoly Money

Mr. Monopoly as portrayed by Merwin Goldsmith

J. P. Morgan, the original Monopoly player

1852–Present

What would life be like if Monopoly had never come into existence? Chances are, a different money game would have arisen. But I'd lay odds this hypothetical game would lack the global appeal of Monopoly. Why? What are the odds of any other game having thirty years of underground play to achieve perfection before it is published? It hasn't happened since Monopoly. And given the aggressive coverage favored by today's media, no game like it could escape attention during its seminal years. Even if such a game could stay quiet this long, what are the odds it could pass from theorists, through educators, into the hands of students, and then receive the common person's touch?

I once asked a friend—a game lover—what he thought separated Monopoly from other modern classics like Scrabble, Pictionary, and Trivial Pursuit. His answer was down to earth. "It's the money," he replied. "All that Monopoly money."

Well, seventy-one years after Parker's publication, that statement is more accurate than ever. In 2006, the Here & Now edition crossed the pond along with its wildly inflated rents, property values, penalties, and rewards. How do you feel about paying $4 million instead of $400 for the game's most expensive property? Or collecting $2 million just for passing GO?

With this game's appearance, the long-standing principle of no inflation in Monopoly was cast aside. But why not? What's wrong with marrying the game's classic play with modern monetary reality? Why not handle bills with more zeros than most of us earn in a lifetime?

Here & Now doesn't stop with inflation. It rolls on like a bulldozer sweeping aside the entire neighborhood. Translation: all the streets from Atlantic City are vanquished from its board. In their place come avenues and landmarks from New York City, San Francisco, Las Vegas, and Honolulu. All twenty-two of these usurpers were decided by an Internet contest organized by Hasbro on its monopoly.com website.

Purists were understandably outraged by this departure from tradition. Folks in Atlantic City felt particularly hurt; they were no longer exclusive citizens of "Monopoly's city." The backlash resulted in a wave of complaints. Several politicians petitioned Hasbro to reconsider.

Lost in translation, however, was a more comforting fact: number nine—the game's tried-and-true standby—was not going away. Instead, it was momentarily stepping out of the limelight while Here & Now was introduced. In fact, plans are afoot to make number nine more exciting than ever.

Capitalism has many virtues, and one of the most notable is choice. For Monopoly and its maker, choice has become a passion. To wit, in 2006, consumers were also offered a "bigger, better" version of Monopoly that fully embraced the long-standing traditions of constant monetary values and Pitney's plan.

Its name—Monopoly: The Mega Edition.

This is the biggest Monopoly game ever published. Fifty-two spaces line the perimeter of its board, rather than forty. Among the added spaces—joining existing color groups—are eight more streets from Atlantic City (including California, Florida, Massachusetts, and Michigan Avenues). Also included are tall skyscraper buildings and charming railroad depots. The familiar scrip is bolstered by $1,000 bills. Combined, these additions make Monopoly and its association with Atlantic City more rewarding than ever.

You might think that the end result of these new features would be an exceedingly long game to play. Amazingly, thanks to two other additions, Monopoly: The Mega Edition takes only 60–70 minutes to play. How is this possible, you ask? First, a new deck of bus tickets selectively offers players the ability to plan moves. Second, and more importantly, the new speed die enhances the action on every turn. This shiny blue cube (rolled along with the regular dice) features icons of Mr. Monopoly on three of its sides. Whenever he appears, you'll either get a bus ticket or a bonus move to the next unowned property. Just as significantly, after all thirty-seven properties are owned, he compels you to move to the next rent you must pay. The tickets and die create a gaming experience filled with many high points, a few low ones, same basic rules of play, and less reliance on the whims of the dice. Monopoly: The Mega Edition is published under license by Winning Moves Inc. (Yes, this game's design bears my imprint.)

Thanks to Here & Now and the Mega Edition, Monopoly enters the twenty-first century with as much verve and edginess as when it first appeared on the scene. This assures that tons of Monopoly money will be printed in the future.

In the past seventy years, the printing presses have produced over $3 trillion worth of its colorful bills. During the era of Morgan's money, the U.S. Treasury needed only $100 million of his money to remain solvent. Even allowing for inflation (about 2,100 percent since then), that's a mere $2 billion today, not even 0.1 percent of this total. And since Monopoly money has experienced no inflation, the comparison would be more lopsided if it had.

It's not as silly as it may seem to equate Monopoly money with Morgan's money if you measure the effect of this multihued currency on the lives of so many, both at home and abroad. The success of Monopoly mirrors the success of capitalism. No other economic system ever produced so much wealth for its constituents.

Whereas 70 percent of workers in 1900 earned $1,000 a year or less ($21,000 today), the median household income today is about $45,000, so the average family earns more than twice as much real income per year, before taxes. Home ownership was difficult a century ago. Today it is a dream most can fulfill. Education? There are 75 million students in America today, many times more—especially on a percentage basis—than in 1900. In part, it is because Nearing's great cause—the elimination of child labor—was accomplished long ago.

Those who work for a living achieve far more in the same time than their ancestors did and in better working conditions, with greater benefits, and above a sturdier safety net. Productivity continues to soar in these early years of the twenty-first century, a testament to work skills and enhancers such as computers, cell phones, the Internet, and software programs. Inflation remains in check despite large increases in the number of workers employed (by comparison, throughout the twentieth century, similar rises in employment caused payrolls and inflation to rise in lockstep).

The great trusts of a hundred years ago no longer threaten economic disruption. A fitting epitaph was written, perhaps, when AT&T was absorbed in 2005 by one of its former Baby Bell regional phone companies—SBC Communications (which promptly changed its name to AT&T). The "mother" of all monopolies had not only been broken up, but it was acquired and replaced by one of its "children."

Despite its record of preventing economic concentration and its efforts to achieve fairness for all, capitalism retains nagging flaws. The U.S. national debt currently exceeds $6 trillion, and foreign capital accounts for nearly a half of total savings. The country's debt is twice as large as its gross domestic output. That's a lot of "Monopoly money" for future generations to shoulder. Despite progressive tax rates, the wealthy have done much better than the less well-off. Talent, opportunity, and drive explain much of this. But poverty still plagues our system. We continue to endure recessions, although the Fed (now led by Ben Bernanke) does a better job than ever at managing interest rates and the money supply (recall the miscues that led to financial panics and the Great Depression).

When the score is tallied, however, capitalism outdistances rivals of all stripes. Capitalism got us to this advanced state of grace thanks to the careful application of Morgan's money by several generations of entrepreneurs, businessman, and dedicated workers. Many continue in J.P.'s long shadow. They help our society take risks, recover from setbacks, fight wars to defend our beliefs and way of life, and help many more to apply their newfound knowledge. But bold experimentation and profiting from lessons learned have always characterized capitalism. All of us are capable of probing the borders of its frontiers. Collectively we can challenge the rules of capitalism to make them work better tomorrow. Systems that lack the ability to change and adapt either falter or die or, worse, threaten world peace.

In many ways, the Monopoly game reinforces the importance of taking risks. It teaches us that wise moves are often rewarded with gain, while ill-conceived moves nearly always lead to loss.

Of equal importance, Monopoly teaches that we cannot hope to be masters of our fate. We can only try. That's important. Reality is always present beyond the board, like it or not. Luck and nature can be more powerful than any system or any game. But Monopoly at least demonstrates that careful planning can minimize the role of luck.

Most of us do not think about the influence Monopoly has had on our lives. I think its broad-based impact would make for a worthy study. I am certain that the lessons imbued by its play run deeper than this book has plumbed. The next generation may well consider undertaking this quest.

Monopoly is replete with symbolism that has spilled into everyday life: phrases like "Go directly to Jail" or "Advance to Go, collect $200," and names like Boardwalk, Park Place, and Chance. A friend has suggested to me the possibility of classifying a player's personality based on choice of favorite token. Who among us does not identity (often passionately) with the race car, the Scotty, or the top hat—or even the humble thimble?

This affinity links the world. Think about it: Monopoly provides a common bond with people in countries you have never visited, perhaps never will. If four strangers from any of eighty nations could be teleported into your living room, the sight of your Monopoly set would brighten their eyes. This they would recognize. Forget language; Monopoly would provide the basis for your mutual understanding.

Beyond its breadth of appeal, its analysis, its historical study, its role in shaping our economy's leaders, and its rise along with capitalism during the twentieth century, Monopoly can be distilled down to one overriding attribute: it is a bountiful giver of enjoyment.

In the end, that's why it endures. Plus all that Monopoly money!

APPENDIXES

Appendixes I–V provide complete lists of published Monopoly and Monopoly-related games in the United States. They do not include one-of-a-kind games or the myriad of foreign editions not mentioned in the text. For the most complete listing of foreign editions, please visit Albert Veldhuis's website: www.muurkrant.nl/monopoly.

APPENDIX I
DARROW AND PARKER BROTHERS
MONOPOLY EDITIONS

Year Introduced	#	Version/Edition	Comments
1934		Darrow White Box (large)	2 print runs. White-backed boards initially
1935		Darrow Black Box (small)	Utensils box
		Darrow/Parker Hybrid	Darrow Black Box with Parker rules and label on back of Darrow board
	7	Parker Popular (small)	4 legal line changes
	9	Deluxe White Box (large)	3 legal changes
1936	6	Standard	Black or blue border. Some had "pencil sketch" cards
	8	Popular	Green or red border. Mr. Monopoly added to cards
	10	Fine	Grand hotels. Some copies were issued in late 1935
	12	Gold	Wood chips, Bakelite buildings, gold foil board, and package
	25	Deluxe wood	Metal coins, Bakelite buildings, brass tokens, framed wood board

continues

Year Introduced	#	Version/Edition	Comments
1937	6	Standard	"New Edition" or "A Parker Trading Game" headline. Black or blue border
	850	Library	Small box with tray, became #12 during WWII
1939	12	Gold revised	No chips, smaller tray
	25	Deluxe wood revised	Cheaper case, no frame on wood board
1942	6	"Junior" Wartime	Insert, no cello wrap
	11	Ivoroid	Formerly Gold edition
1946	8	Popular	Revised package
	9	White Box	Minor graphic additions
1949 or 1951	8	Deluxe	Large box, light or dark green border
	9		Minor graphic changes
1953	5	Deluxe	New package, French-made houses
1954	8	Popular	New package, green or red border
1957	9	From now on standard	Train cover (became #12)
	12	Better (larger box)	
1958	9		New cover
1959	6	Deluxe	Wood case
1961	12	Library	
1962	9		Graphic change to cover
1964	11	Deluxe	Large red cardboard box, Styrofoam tray
1965	12	Anniversary	Plastic case, French-made houses and hotels
1971	9		Minor graphic changes
1975	11	Anniversary	Dark blue cover, white border
	3	Deluxe	Leatherette case
1976	9		New cover
1985	7	Anniversary	Blue cover
	9		Mr. Monopoly joins logo
	1	Commemorative Fiftieth	Tin package
1991	7	Anniversary	White border

Year Introduced	#	Version/Edition	Comments
1992		Special Last Salem	Given to employees only
1995	11	Sixtieth Anniversary	Gold foil package
1995		Deluxe	Blue/silver foil design
1999	9		More compact box, quadfold board
	4080	Heirloom	Wood case, sold only at Toys R Us
2000		Millennium	
		Millennium	Avon exclusive
		Library	Bookcase, blue
		Nostalgia	Wood case; 1957 train graphic on sliding cover
2001	4150	Collectible tin	Packed in a large car-shaped tin
2003		Collector's train	Packed in a large tin featuring a train
2005	9		New cover graphics
		Vintage	Mr. M wood bookshelf edition
		Seventieth Anniversary	Deluxe wood version, sold only in Sam's Clubs
2006		Here & Now	Launched in Europe in 2005

APPENDIX II

MONOPOLY ACCESSORIES AND
PARKER BRAND EXTENSIONS

Year Introduced	#	Version/Edition	Comments
1935		Fortune	
1936	35	Money Pad	
		Stock Exchange	Capitol Novelty Co., then Parker Brothers
		Bulls & Bears	Darrow endorsed, 2 box styles, each with 2 graphic versions
		Finance	Parker edition, and also Finance Game Company edition
1937–		Finance and Fortune, then Finance again	Several cover changes in next few years
		Play Racks	
1941	55	Dig	
	56		Better edition
1946	30	Rich Uncle	
1972		Jigsaw puzzle	Parker edition
1982	3900	Playmaster	Electronic add-on
1985	14	Advance to Boardwalk	
1988	87	Free Parking	

continues

Year Introduced	#	Version/Edition	Comments
1989		Collector's Edition	Franklin Mint
1990	441	Monopoly Jr.	
1991	34	Don't Go to Jail	
	14	Advance to Boardwalk	White border
	87	Free Parking	White border
1993		Express Monopoly	Card game
1998		The Monopoly Calculator	Winning Moves, Inc., electronic accessory
		Monopoly Gift Pack	Winning Moves, Inc., the calculator and book
1999		Monopoly: The Card Game	Winning Moves, Inc.
2000		Deluxe Edition of Monopoly: The Card Game	Included 4 plastic trays
2001	1009	1935 #9 Reproduction	Winning Moves, Inc.
2002		America Monopoly	Properties named for American landmarks
2006		Monopoly: The Mega Edition	Winning Moves, Inc. Bigger, richer, faster to play

APPENDIX III
GAMES SIMILAR TO MONOPOLY

Year Introduced	Name	Comments
1906	Landlord's Game	Economic Game Company
1927	Reading Edition	Thun Brothers
1932	Landlord's Game	AdGame Company
	Finance	Electronic Laboratories
1933	Finance	Knapp Electric
1936	New York	Amesbury Game Company
	Big Business	Transogram, revised in 1937
	Easy Money	Milton Bradley. Six variations including legal line changes, Monopoly patent numbers, removal of deeds
	Inflation	Rudy Copeland
1936?	Mo-Nop	Appears to be of Minnesota origin
1937	Carnival	Based on EMP's 1904 game
1939	Landlord's Game	Parker Brothers edition
1973	Anti-Monopoly	
1977	Anti	Following Parker victory in first trial
1984	Anti-Monopoly II, then as Anti-Monopoly	Talicor
	Medical Monopoly	Withdrawn from market
	Gay Monopoly	Withdrawn from market
2005	Anti-Monopoly—new edition	University Games

APPENDIX IV
USAOPOLY OFFICIAL AFFINITY VERSIONS

USAopoly, Inc., is a leading specialty market board game developer based in Carlsbad, California. For more than ten years, USAopoly has marketed America's favorite game with a twist, combining its familiar game play with hot licenses and brands. These are authorized themed editions under official license from the Hasbro Properties Group.

Edition Title	Year	Type
American Express Funds	2000	Corporate
Ariel Capital Management	2005	Corporate
Avalon Communities	2001	Corporate
Bank of America Toy Bank	2004	Corporate
Bank of America Official Bank of MLB	2005	Corporate
Berkshire Hathaway	2005	Corporate
Best Buy	2002	Corporate
Boy Scouts of America	2004	Corporate
Chile Heads	2004	Corporate
Estes Express	2005	Corporate
FedEx	2004	Corporate
FedEx Kinkos	2005	Corporate

continues

Edition Title	Year	Type
Fisher Scientific Centennial	2002	Corporate
Future Electronics	2001	Corporate
Fox Cities	2003	Corporate
Grand Rapids, MI	2004	Corporate
City of Green Bay, WI	2000	Corporate
Hard Rock Café	2002	Corporate
HP Supply Chain	2005	Corporate
ING Direct	2005	Corporate
M&M's	2004	Corporate
Marshall Field's	1997	Corporate
City of Manitowoc, WI	2000	Corporate
MCI Classic Edition	1997	Corporate
Nummi	1994	Corporate
Option One	2000	Corporate
Pedigree Dog Lover's	2002	Corporate
Puerto Rico	2005	Corporate
QVC	1999	Corporate
Sheboygan County Road America	2001	Corporate
Snap On	2000	Corporate
Sunterra	2005	Corporate
United Way Boston	2005	Corporate
UPS	2005	Corporate
West Virginia State Parks & Forests	2004	Corporate
Astronomy	2001	Specialty/Licensed
Batman	2005	Specialty/Licensed
Batman & Robin	1997	Specialty/Licensed
Betty Boop	2002	Specialty/Licensed
Century of Flight Aviation	2003	Specialty/Licensed
Coca-Cola	1999	Specialty/Licensed
Coca-Cola Classic Ads	2005	Specialty/Licensed
Corvette	1998	Specialty/Licensed
Corvette 50th Anniversary	2002	Specialty/Licensed
Disney-Pixar	2005	Specialty/Licensed
The Dog Artist Collection	2003	Specialty/Licensed
Elvis 25th Anniversary	2002	Specialty/Licensed
Elvis	2002	Specialty/Licensed

Edition Title	Year	Type
Elvis (square box for Avon)	2003	Specialty/Licensed
Fantastic Four	2005	Specialty/Licensed
Ford 100th Anniversary	2003	Specialty/Licensed
Garfield 25th Anniversary	2003	Specialty/Licensed
Garfield	2003	Specialty/Licensed
Harley-Davidson Authorized	1997	Specialty/Licensed
Harley-Davidson 95th Anniversary	1998	Specialty/Licensed
Harley-Davidson Live To Ride	2000	Specialty/Licensed
I Love Lucy 50th Anniversary	2001	Specialty/Licensed
I Love Lucy	2001	Specialty/Licensed
I Love Lucy "California Here We Come"	2005	Specialty/Licensed
Jim Henson's Muppets	2003	Specialty/Licensed
John Deere	2005	Specialty/Licensed
Justice League of America	1999	Specialty/Licensed
Lionel—Postwar Era	2000	Specialty/Licensed
Looney Toons	2003	Specialty/Licensed
The Lord Of The Rings	2005	Specialty/Licensed
Marvel Comics	1999	Specialty/Licensed
Mickey Mouse 75th Anniversary	2004	Specialty/Licensed
Mickey Mouse 75th Anniversary (square box for Avon)	2004	Specialty/Licensed
Mustang	1999	Specialty/Licensed
Mustang 40th Anniversary	2003	Specialty/Licensed
National Geographic Mountaineering	2001	Specialty/Licensed
National Parks	1998	Specialty/Licensed
National Parks	2001	Specialty/Licensed
National Parks (America's)	2005	Specialty/Licensed
Night Sky	2004	Specialty/Licensed
Peanuts	2002	Specialty/Licensed
Rudolph the Red-Nosed Reindeer	2005	Specialty/Licensed
Scooby Doo Fright Fest	2000	Specialty/Licensed
Scooby Doo (square box for Avon)	2002	Specialty/Licensed
Sesame Street 35th Anniversary	2004	Specialty/Licensed
The Simpsons	2001	Specialty/Licensed
The Simpsons Treehouse of Horror	2005	Specialty/Licensed
Snoopy	2005	Specialty/Licensed

continues

Edition Title	Year	Type
Spider-Man	2002	Specialty/Licensed
Star Trek The Original Series Limited	2000	Specialty/Licensed
Star Trek The Next Generation	1998	Specialty/Licensed
Thunderbird 50th Anniversary	2005	Specialty/Licensed
U.S. Air Force	2003	Specialty/Licensed
U.S. Army	2002	Specialty/Licensed
U.S. Marines	2005	Specialty/Licensed
U.S. Navy	1998	Specialty/Licensed
United States Space Program	1998	Specialty/Licensed
Wizard of Oz	1998	Specialty/Licensed
X-Men	2000	Specialty/Licensed
Alaska Iditarod	1998	Sports
Bass Fishing	1998	Sports
Bass Fishing Lakes	2005	Sports
Boston Red Sox (MLB)	2000	Sports
Centennial Olympic Games	1996	Sports
Chicago Bears (NFL)	2005	Sports
Chicago Cubs (MLB)	2002	Sports
Chicago Cubs (MLB)	2005	Sports
Cleveland Browns (NFL)	1999	Sports
Dale Earnhardt	2000	Sports
Dale Earnhardt Legacy	2003	Sports
Dallas Cowboys (NFL)	2004	Sports
Dodgers (MLB)	2000	Sports
Dodgers (round box) (MLB)	2000	Sports
Golf	1996	Sports
Golf	1998	Sports
Golf	2000	Sports
Golf	2002	Sports
Golf Signature Lakes	2005	Sports
Major League Baseball (larger box)	1999	Sports
Major League Baseball	2003	Sports
Major League Baseball	2004	Sports
Major League Baseball	2005	Sports
Major League Baseball (square box for Avon)	2005	Sports
Miami Dolphins (NFL)	2004	Sports

Edition Title	Year	Type
Minnesota Vikings (NFL)	2005	Sports
NFL	2003	Sports
NFL	2004	Sports
NHL (bilingual/larger box for Canada)	1999	Sports
NHL	1999	Sports
NHL Original 6	2001	Sports
NASCAR Official	1997	Sports
NASCAR (Sam Bass)	2002	Sports
NASCAR 50th Anniversary	1998	Sports
NASCAR NEXTEL Cup	2005	Sports
NASCAR NEXTEL Cup (square box for Avon)	2005	Sports
New England Patriots (NFL)	2003	Sports
New England Patriots (NFL)	2004	Sports
New York Mets (MLB)	2001	Sports
New York Mets (MLB)	2005	Sports
New York Yankees (MLB)	2000	Sports
New York Yankees (MLB)	2001	Sports
New York Yankees Century's Team (MLB)	2004	Sports
New York Giants (NFL)	2003	Sports
New York Jets (NFL)	2005	Sports
Oakland Raiders (NFL)	2004	Sports
Green Bay Packers (NFL)	2000	Sports
Green Bay Packers (NFL)	2003	Sports
Philadelphia Eagles (NFL)	2003	Sports
Pittsburgh Steelers (NFL)	2004	Sports
Red Sox World Series Champions (MLB)	2004	Sports
St. Louis Cardinals (MLB)	2001	Sports
St. Louis Rams Super Bowl XXXIV Champions (NFL)	2000	Sports
San Francisco Giants (MLB)	2003	Sports
San Francisco Giants (MLB)	2004	Sports
Seattle Mariners 25th Anniversary (MLB)	2001	Sports
Seattle Mariners (MLB)	2001	Sports
Seattle Seahawks (NFL)	2005	Sports
Snowboarding	2004	Sports
Super Bowl XXXII Denver/Green Bay (NFL)	1998	Sports

continues

Edition Title	Year	Type
Surfing	2003	Sports
Washington Redskins (NFL)	2005	Sports
World Cup France '98	1998	Sports
Alaska	1997	State
Alaska	2003	State
Arizona	1998	State
Florida	1998	State
Hawaii	1996	State
Maine	1999	State
New England	2001	State/Region
Oregon	1998	State
Rhode Island	1998	State
Texas	1999	State
Texas (state shape)	1999	State
Utah	1998	State
Atlanta	1994	City
Atlanta	1995	City
Baltimore	1997	City
Boston	1994	City
Boston	1995	City
Boston	1996	City
Boston (Historic)	1998	City
Charlotte	1997	City
Chicago	1995	City
Chicago	1996	City
Chicago	2000	City
Cincinnati	1998	City
Cleveland	1996	City
Dallas	1995	City
Denver	1996	City
Detroit	1997	City
Hollywood	1997	City
Houston	1996	City
Indianapolis	1996	City
Kansas City	1997	City
La Jolla	1994	City
Las Vegas	1997	City

Edition Title	Year	Type
Las Vegas	2000	City
Las Vegas (square box for Avon)	2003	City
Los Angeles	1996	City
Napa Valley	1997	City/Region
New York City	1994	City
New York City	1995	City
New York City	1996	City
New York City	1998	City
New York City	2001	City
Orlando	1997	City
Philadelphia	1996	City
Pittsburg	1996	City
San Diego	1994	City
San Diego	1995	City
San Diego	1996	City
San Diego	2002	City
San Francisco	1994	City
San Francisco	1995	City
San Francisco (Historic)	1998	City
Seattle	1997	City
St. Louis	1997	City
Twin Cities	1997	City
USA Greatest Cities	2005	City
Washington, D.C.	1995	City
Florida State University	1998	University
Indiana University	1998	University
Kansas State University	1998	University
Longhorn (University of Texas)	1998	University
Ohio State University	1997	University
Penn State University	1998	University
University of Kansas	1998	University
University of Kentucky	1998	University
University of Michigan	1997	University
University of Nebraska	1997	University
University of Tennessee	1998	University
University of Washington	1998	University

Note: While USAopoly is the primary marketer of affinity editions of Monopoly, Parker Brothers has also issued several, including editions based on Times Square, Shrek, Theme Parks, Star Wars, Toy Story, Star Wars Trilogy, Nascar, Puff Girls, Star Wars Episodes I, II, and III, Puzz 3D, Looney Tunes, NFL '99, Jackpot, Dot Com, Dig'n Dinos (Jr.), Pokemon, Lord of the Rings, U.S. Air Force, Major League Baseball, Duel Masters, and Disney Princess (Jr.).

In Europe, Winning Moves International publishes another complete range of Affinity Monopoly editions based on European cities, regions, sports, and other topics.

APPENDIX V
FOREIGN EDITIONS
MENTIONED IN THE TEXT

Year Introduced	Version/Country	Comments
1913	Brer Fox—Scotland	Newbie Game Co.
1936	#1 Standard—UK	John Waddington Ltd.
	#2 Black Box—UK	John Waddington Ltd.
	#3 Gold Edition—UK	John Waddington Ltd.
	#4 Deluxe—UK (alligator skin paper)	John Waddington Ltd.
	Standard—French	Miro
	Gold—German	Franz Schmidt
	Business—Austria	Unknown maker
	Shanghai Real Estate—China	Unknown maker
	Zurich—Switzerland	Carlit
	Brussels—Belgium	Deska
	Standard—Australian	John Sands
	Metropoli—Chile	
	Monopoli—Italy	Editrici Gioci
1938	Monopol—Sweden	Alga
1942	Monopoly Jr.—Netherlands	Uitgave
1950	Danza de Milliones—Spain	

continues

Year Introduced	Version/Country	Comments
1961	"Safe"—Hungary	Communist wanna-be version
	Standard—German	Franz Schmidt
1966	Ultra—UK	John Waddington Ltd.
1986	Deluxe—UK	John Waddington Ltd.
1992	Standard—UK	John Waddington Ltd.

APPENDIX VI

GEORGE PARKER'S

1936 MONOPOLY RULES

George Parker of Parker Brothers standardized the rules for the Monopoly game in 1935 and improved them slightly in 1936. To this day, they accurately describe how the game of Monopoly is played.

Parker prided himself on composing clear, vivid rules. Darrow's Monopoly instructions lacked thoroughness and proper organization. Before Darrow, players typically learned at the feet of others, without reliance on written guidelines. But this technique could not be expected to work when Parker Brothers began distributing the game into vast regions of the country where the game was largely unknown. Parker's rules closed the gap.

MONOPOLY
(Source:
REG. IJ. S. PATENT OFFICE
A PARKER TRADING GAME
U.S. PATENT 2.026.082 COPYRIGHT 1936 BY PARKER BROTHERS, INC.)

BRIEF IDEA OF THE GAME
THE IDEA OF THE GAME is to BUY and RENT or SELL properties so profitably that one becomes the wealthiest player and eventual MONOPOLIST. Starting from "GO" move Tokens around the Board According to throw of Dice.

When a Player's Token lands on a space NOT already owned, he may Buy it of the BANK: otherwise it is Auctioned off to the Highest Bidder. The OBJECT of Owning property is to Collect Rents from Opponents stopping there. Rentals are greatly increased by the erection of Houses and Hotels, so it is wise to build them on some of your Lots. To raise more money Lots may be mortgaged to the Bank. Community Chest and Chance spaces give the draw of a Card, instructions on which must be followed. Sometimes players land in Jail. The game is one of shrewd and amusing trading and excitement.

RULES
For from Three to Seven Players

EQUIPMENT
MONOPOLY Equipment consists of the BOARD with spaces indicating Avenues, Railroads, Utilities, Rewards and Penalties over which the players' pieces are moved. There are Two DICE, PLAYING PIECES (sometimes called Tokens), thirty-two green HOUSES and Twelve red HOTELS and Two sets of Cards for CHANCE and COMMUNITY CHEST spaces. There are Title Deed Cards for every property and Scrip representing MONEY of various denominations.

PREPARATION
PLACE the Board on a good-sized table putting the Chance Cards and Community Chest cards face down on their allotted spaces on the board. Each player is provided with One PLAYING PIECE to represent him on his travels around the board. Each player is given $1500. All other equipment goes to the BANK. One of the players is elected BANKER. (See BANK and BANKER.)

MONEY EACH PLAYER is given $1500 divided as follows: One $500—Seven $100—Two $50—Five $20—Seven $10—Five $5—Five $1. All remaining money goes to the Bank.

TO START THE GAME
STARTING with the Banker each player in turn throws the dice. The Player with the highest total starts the play. He places his token on the corner marked "GO" throws the two dice and moves his TOKEN in the direction of the ARROW the number of spaces indicated by the Dice. After he has completed his play, the Turn to play passes to the Left. The TOKENS remain on the spaces occupied and proceed from that point on the Player's next turn. Two or more tokens may rest on the same space at the same time.

ACCORDING TO THE SPACE which his Token reaches, a Player may be entitled to buy Real Estate properties, or be obliged to pay Rent (If another owns the property), pay Taxes, draw a Chance or a Community Chest Card, "Go to Jail," etc.

IF A PLAYER THROWS DOUBLES he moves his Token as usual the sum of the two dice and the Space thus reached is effective (i.e. The Player is subject to any privileges or penalties, pertaining to that Space.) Retaining the dice he throws again and moves his Token as before and, again, the Space thus reached is effective. If, however, he throws three doubles in succession, he does not move his token on his third throw but Immediately "GOES TO JAIL" (See JAIL). In the course of the game, Players will encircle the board several times.

SALARY (THE "GO" SPACE)

Every time that a Player's Token either lands on or passes over "GO," while going in the direction of the Arrow, the Banker pays him $200 "Salary."

LANDING ON UNOWNED PROPERTY

When a Player lands on an unowned property (i.e., on a Property space for which no other player holds the title deed) whether by a throw of dice or by a move forced by the Draw of a Chance or Community Chest Card, the Player has the Option of Buying that property from the Bank at its printed price. If a Player elects to Buy, he pays the Bank for that property and receives the Title Deed Card showing Ownership, which he places face up in front of him. If the Player declines this option, the Banker immediately offers this property for sale at AUCTION and sells it to the highest Bidder, accepting Money in payment and giving the buyer the proper Title Deed Card as evidence of Ownership. Any Player, including the one who declined the option of buying at the printed price, may bid. Bidding may start at any price.

LANDING ON OWNED PROPERTY

When a player lands on owned property either by throw of Dice, or by a move forced by a Chance or Community Chest Card, the Owner collects RENT from him in accordance with the list printed on the Title Deed Card applying to it. Note: If the lot contains a House or houses, the rent is larger than it would be for an unimproved lot. If the lot is mortgaged, no rent can be collected. Mortgaged property is designated by turning face down the Title Deed representing that property. Note: If the owner fails to ask for his Rent before the second player following throws the dice, the Rent is not collectible.

ADVANTAGES FOR OWNERS

It is an advantage to hold Title Deeds to ALL of a complete Color Group (for example: Boardwalk and Park Place, or Connecticut, Vermont and Oriental Avenues) because the Owner may then charge Double Rent for unimproved Lots of that property. (This rule holds true even though another lot of that color-group be mortgaged.) The advantage of owning Houses and Hotels rather than unimproved property is that Rentals are very much Higher than for Unimproved Lots and profit the owner immensely.

LANDING ON "CHANCE" OR "COMMUNITY CHEST"

A player takes the top card from the pack indicated and after following the Instructions printed thereon, returns the card face down to the bottom of the pack. The "Get Out of Jail Free" card, however, is retained until used. After being used, it is returned to the bottom of the pack. This card may be Sold by a player to another player at a price agreeable to both.

LANDING ON TAX SPACES

Pay the bank. INCOME TAX is 100/0 of a player's total worth. It is figured on CASH ON HAND, Printed PRICE of properties (mortgaged or not) and Cost Price of any buildings he may own. A player may estimate his tax at $200 and pay the bank at once.

If he prefers, however, to pay the tax on his actual worth he can do so, but he must make his decision before he adds up his total worth.

BANKER

Select as BANKER a player who will also make a good Auctioneer. If, as is customary, the Banker also plays in the game, he must, of course, keep his personal funds separate from those of the Bank. When more than five persons play, the Banker sometimes elects to act only as Banker and Auctioneer.

THE BANK

The Bank holds, besides the Bank's Money, the Title Deed Cards and Houses and Hotels prior to purchase and use by the Players. The Bank pays Salaries and Bonuses and Sells Properties to the Players and delivers the proper Title Deed Cards; Auctions Lots; sells Houses and Hotels to the Players and loans money when required on Mortgages of property at the Mortgage Value which is one-half of the Price printed on the board. The Bank will at any time buy back Houses and Hotels from Building Lots at half price.

PAY TO THE BANK the price of all properties you buy from it, taxes, fines, money penalties, loans and interest.

THE BANK never "goes broke." If the Bank runs out of Money it may issue as much Money of its own as it may need by merely writing on any ordinary paper. This Bank Money is equal in value to the regular Monopoly Game Money.

JAIL

A PLAYER LANDS IN JAIL—(1) If his piece lands on space marked "GO TO JAIL"; (2) If he draws a card marked "GO TO JAIL"; (3) If he throws Doubles three times in succession.

NOTE: When a player is sent to Jail he cannot collect $200 salary in that move since, regardless of where his piece is or of the path of the board, he must move his piece DIRECTLY into Jail. A player's turn ends whenever sent to Jail.

VISITING JAIL. If a player is not "sent to Jail" but in the ordinary course of play reaches that space, he is "just visiting," incurs no penalty, and moves ahead in the usual manner on his next turn.

A PLAYER GETS OUT OF JAIL—(1) By throwing Doubles on any of his next three turns after landing in Jail. If he succeeds in doing this he immediately moves forward the number of spaces shown by his Doubles throw. (2) By purchasing a "GET OUT OF JAIL FREE" card from another player, at a price agreeable to both, (unless he already owns such a card, having on a previous turn drawn it from Chance or Community Chest). (3) By paying a $50 fine BEFORE he throws the dice for either his next turn or succeeding turn to play. (4) A player MUST NOT remain in Jail after his third turn (i.e., not longer than having three turns to play after being sent to Jail). Immediately AFTER throwing the dice for his third turn he must pay a $50 fine unless he throws Doubles. He then comes out and immediately moves *forward from the Jail the number of spaces shown by his throw.* A player may buy and erect a house, sell or buy property, and collect Rents, even though he is in Jail.

HOUSES

HOUSES can be bought only from the Bank and can only be erected on Lots of a COMPLETE COLOR-GROUP, which the Player owns. (Example: If one player succeeds in owning Connecticut, Vermont and Oriental Avenues, i.e. a complete Color-Group, he may at any period of his Ownership Buy a House or Houses from the Bank to erect thereon. If he Buys one House, he may put it only on one of these three lots. The next House he buys and erects must be put on one of the unoccupied lots of this or of any other complete Color-Group he may own. The Price he must pay the Bank for each House is shown on his Title Deed of the Lot. On the Unimproved lots of his complete Color-Group, he can collect Double Rental from an opponent landing thereon, etc. A Player may Buy and Erect, in accordance with the above rules, at any time, as many Houses as his judgment and financial standing will allow, but he must build EVENLY (i.e. you cannot erect more than one House on any one lot of any Color-Group until you have built one House on every Lot of that Group. You may then begin on the second row of Houses and so on up to a limit not exceeding Four Houses to a Lot. But, you cannot build, for example, three houses on one lot if you have only one house on another lot of that group.)

HOTELS

A Player must have Four Houses on each lot of a complete Color-Group before he can buy a Hotel building. He may then Buy a Hotel from the Bank to be erected on any lot of that Color-Group, delivering to the Bank therefore the Four Houses from that Lot together with the Money price shown on Title Deed. (It is very desirable to erect Hotels on account of the very large Rental that may be charged. Only one Hotel may be erected on any one Lot.)

BUILDING SHORTAGE

When the Bank has no Houses to sell, players wishing to build must wait for some player to turn back or to sell his houses to the Bank before building. If there are a limited number of Houses and Hotels available, and two or more players wish to buy more than the Bank has, the Houses or Hotels must be sold at auction to the' highest bidder.

SELLING PROPERTY

UNDEVELOPED LOTS, RAILROADS AND UTILITIES (but not buildings) may be sold to any Player as a private transaction for any amount that the Owner can get. No Lot, however, can be sold to another player if buildings are standing on any lots of that Color Group. Any Buildings so located must be sold back to the Bank before the owner can sell any Lot of that color group.

HOUSES AND HOTELS may be resold by Players to the Bank only, but this may be done at any time and the Bank will pay one-half the price paid for them. Hotels cost the price of Five Houses and the BANK will pay one-half that price for them.

MORTGAGES

MORTGAGING PROPERTIES can be done through the Bank only. The mortgage value is printed on each Title Deed. The rate of interest is 10 per cent, payable when the mortgage is lifted. If any property is transferred which is mortgaged, the new owner may lift the mortgage at once if he wishes, but must pay 10 per cent interest. If he fails to lift the mortgage he still pays 10 per cent interest and if he lifts the mortgage later on he pays an additional 10 per cent interest as well as the principal.

Houses or Hotels cannot be mortgaged. Only Lots may be mortgaged. Before a Lot can be mortgaged a player must sell back to the Bank all Buildings on that Lot and on any other lots of the same group. The Bank will pay half of what was paid for such buildings. No Rental can be collected on Mortgaged lots or utilities but rent can be collected on unmortgaged property in that same group.

In order to rebuild a house on mortgaged property the owner must pay the Bank the amount of the mortgage, plus the 10 per cent interest charge and buy the house back from the Bank at its FULL PRICE.

BANKRUPTCY

A player who is bankrupt, that is, one who owes more than he can pay, must turn over to his Creditor all that he has of value, and retire from the game. In making this settlement, however, if he owns Houses or Hotels, these are returned to the Bank in exchange for Money, to the extent of one-half the amount paid for them, and this cash is given to the Creditor. If a Bankrupt player turns over to his Creditor property that has been mortgaged, the new owner must at once pay the Bank the amount of the interest on the loan. At the same time he may at his option lift the mortgage by paying the principal.

When a Player cannot pay his Taxes, or penalties even by selling his Buildings and mortgaging property, the Bank takes over all his assets and sells by Auction everything so taken (except Buildings). The Player then retires from the game. The Last Player left in the game WINS.

MISCELLANEOUS

The Bank loans Money only on mortgage security.

Players may not borrow money or property from each other.

GOOD SHORT GAMES OF MONOPOLY

Copyright 1936 by PARKER BROTHERS, Inc.

There are two popular short-game-rules as follows:

TIME LIMIT GAME: Agree before starting upon a definite Hour of termination, Richest Player then winning. Before starting game Title Deed Cards are Shuffled and cut, and Banker deals TWO Title Deeds to each Player. Players immediately pay Bank price of property thus dealt to them.

SECOND BANKRUPTCY METHOD: Agree before starting that the game shall end as soon as the second Bankruptcy occurs, richest player winning.

APPENDIX VII

THE LANDLORD'S GAME
EXCERPT FROM 1904 PATENT

Be it known that I, LIZZIE J. MAGIE, a citizen of the United States, residing at Brentwood, in the county of Prince George and State of Maryland, have invented certain new and useful Improvements in Gameboards, of which the following is a specification.

My invention, which I have designated "The Landlord's Game," relates to gameboards, and more particularly to games of chance.

The object of the game is to obtain as much wealth or money as possible, the player having the greatest amount of wealth at the end of the game after a certain predetermined number of circuits of the board have been made being the winner.

In the drawings forming the part of this specification, and in which like symbols of reference represent corresponding parts in the several views, Figure 1 is a plan view of the board, showing the different spaces marked thereon. Figure 2 shows the various movable pieces used in the game; and Fig. 3 is a view of the boxes, the same being designated as the "bank."

The implements of the game consist of a board which is divided into a number of spaces or sections and four (4) spaces in the center indicating, respectively, "Bank," "Wages," "Public Treasury," and "Railroad." Within these four spaces are preferably placed four (4) boxes, one of which is shown in the drawings and represented by the numeral 24.

The movable pieces used in the game, only one piece of each set for convenience of illustration being shown in the drawings, are as follows: Four pairs of dice, four shaking boxes, four checkers to check the throws made, taxes representing, respectively, "Bank," "Wages," "Public Treasury," and "Railroad," and also various colored chips or tickets representing lots, money, deeds, notes, individual mortgages, bank mortgages, charters, legacies, and luxuries. These chips are not to be limited to any certain number or colors.

25 indicates lot tickets; 26, the dice; 27, shaking boxes; 28, deeds; 29, notes; 30, individual mortgages; 31, bank mortgages; 32, charters; 33, luxuries; 35, money; 36, checkers; and 34 legacies.

The game is played as follows: Each player is provided with five hundred dollars. The lot tickets, twenty-two (22) in number, are placed face downward upon the board, and each player draws one until twelve have been taken. The rest are put back in the wages box. Each player looks at the tickets he has drawn and may purchase the lot corresponding to his ticket if he can afford to or so chooses. If he does not purchase, he does not have to pay rent, but simply puts the ticket back into the wages box again. When these twelve lots have been bought or the privilege refused and the owner's deeds placed upon those purchased, the game begins.

The series of spaces upon the board are not colored to distinguish them; but of course other means of making them distinctive may be employed. The lot-spaces "1" to "22," which are preferably green, are for sale at the highest figure marked upon them or for rent at the lowest figure marked upon them. If a player chooses to buy a lot, he must pay into the "Public Treasury" the price of it and place his deed upon it. If he chooses to rent it, he must pay the rent to the "Public Treasury."

Absolute Necessities: These spaces, which are preferably blue, indicate absolute necessities—each as bread, coal, shelter, and clothing—and when a player stops upon any of these he must pay five dollars into the "Public Treasury." (This represents indirect taxation.)

No Trespassing: Spaces marked "No Trespassing" represent property held out of use, and when a player stops on one of these spaces he must go to jail and remain there until be throws a double or until he pays into the "Public Treasury" a fine of fifty dollars. When he comes out, he must count from the space immediately in front of the jail.

Railroad: "R.R." represents transportation, and when a player stops upon one of these spaces he must pay five dollars to the "R.R." If a player throws a double, he "Gets a pass" and has the privilege of jumping once from one railroad to another, provided he would in his ordinary moving pass a "R.R." If he stops upon it, however, he must pay five dollars.

Luxuries: These spaces, preferably purple, represent the luxuries of life, and if a player stops on a "Luxury" he pays fifty dollars to the "Public Treasury," receiving in return a luxury ticket, which counts him sixty dollars at the end of the game. The player may purchase the luxury or not, as he chooses or can afford; but if he does not purchase it he loses his move.

Franchises: These spaces, preferably yellow, indicate light franchise and water franchise and are public necessities. The first player who stops upon one of these franchises puts his charter upon it, and all through the game he has the privilege of taxing all the other players five dollars whenever they chance to stop upon it. It costs him nothing and counts him nothing at the end of the game.

Public Park: A player may stop in the "Public Park" without paying anything.

Legacy: If a player stops on the "Legacy," he gets one hundred dollars cash and a legacy-ticket.

Mother Earth: Each time a player goes around the board he is supposed to have performed so much labor upon Mother Earth, for which after passing the beginning-point he receives his wages, one hundred dollars, and is checked upon the tally-sheet as having been around once.

Poorhouse: If at stay time a player has no money with which to meet expenses and has no property upon which he can borrow, he must go to the poorhouse and remain there until he makes such throws as will enable him to finish the round.

Rent: When a player stops upon a lot owned by any of the players, he must pay the rent to the owner. If he stops upon one of his own lots, of course he pays nothing. If two players stop upon the same lot, the second must pay to the first one-half of the rent, (in case of an odd number giving to the first the benefit of the fraction.) If a third player's throw brings him on the same lot, he cannot occupy it, but must remain upon the space next to it, counting his throw one less. In case of lot 1 the player gets the whole rent.

Borrowing: A player may borrow from the "Bank" in amounts of one hundred dollars, and for every one hundred dollars borrowed the "Bank" takes a mortgage on one or more of the borrower's lots, the total value of which must be at least ten dollars more than is borrowed. For every one hundred dollars borrowed from the "Bank" a bank mortgage is placed upon the property on which the loan is made, and the player puts his note in the "Bank," paying upon each note five dollars (interest) every time he receives his wages. One player may borrow from another, giving a mortgage on any property he may own and making the best bargain he can as to interest, terms of payments, etc. The player loaning the money places his individual mortgage on the top of the borrower's deed to show that he has a mortgage on that property. Should a loan be repaid before passing the beginning-point, the borrower saves the interest.

Five times around: When a player has been around the board five times he may move in either direction, provided he is clear of debt, until each of the other players has been around five times; but having passed the beginning-point the required number of times he receives no more wages. The game is finished when the last player has passed the beginning-point the fifth time.

Counting up: As the deeds are removed from the lots each player is credited with the value of the lots owned by him. His cash on hand is counted, and the amount set down under the total value of the lots. Then the luxuries are counted, (remember that each one counts sixty) and the amount set down under cash. Add together these three amounts—lots, cash, and luxuries—and the player who has the largest sum-total is the winner.

Playing without the lot tickets: Some have found it more interesting to play the game without using the lot tickets at all, players simply purchasing lots as they come to them in the ordinary moving. In this case the player is provided with one hundred dollars to begin with. The number of times around the board may also be regulated by the will of the players.

Emergencies: Should any emergency arise which is not covered by the rules of the game, the players must settle the matter between themselves; but if any player absolutely refuses to obey the rules as above set forth he must go to jail and remain there until he throws a double or pays his fine, as explained in paragraph "No Trespassing."

Having now fully described my invention, what I claim as new, and desire to secure by Letters Patent, is—

1. A gameboard, having corner-spaces, one constituting the starting-point, and a series of intervening spaces indicating different denominations, some of the spaces of the different series corresponding, and distinguished by coloring or other marking, so that the corresponding divisions on the four spaces may be readily recognized.

2. A gameboard, provided with corner spaces, intervening spaces of different denominations, some of the spaces of the different series corresponding, and distinguished by coloring or other marking, so that the corresponding spaces in the different divisions may be recognized, and a series of movable pieces having reference to the different divisions upon the board.

3. A gameboard, having a series of divisions of different denominations upon its outer border, one constituting the starting-point, four divisions within said series for the reception of boxes, a series of movable pieces having reference to the spaces upon the board, and a chance device to control movement of the pieces.

4. A gameboard, provided with corner spaces, intervening spaces of different denominations, and distinguished by distinctive marking, so that the corresponding divisions on the different spaces may be recognized, movable pieces having reference to the spaces, a chance device to control the movement of the pieces, checkers, and tickets representing money, deeds, notes, mortgages, bank mortgages, legacies, and luxuries, adapted to be used in connection with the same.

In testimony whereof I affix my signature in presence of two witnesses.

LIZZIE J. MAGIE

APPENDIX VIII

BRER FOX AN' BRER RABBIT NEWBIE GAME:
EXCERPT FROM 1913 PATENT

Company Patent 1913, London, England

PART 1
BUYING THE LAND.

The players begin by buying up the vacant plots of land as numbered on the Board. Each player receives £3000 in money tickets of the following values—five of £500, three of £100, three of £50, three of £10, four of £5, the remainder of the money being placed in the Bank. The "SITE" cards are then shuffled and dealt round, each player having the right to buy any or all of the sites on the Board corresponding to the cards dealt to him. On buying a site each player must pay the CAPITAL LAND VALUE (sale price of land) into the "BANK," and place a "SOLD" ticket, of the colour allotted to him, on his site. It is advisable to keep from £250 to £300 in cash to pay current expenses when playing.

Each player takes a pawn of the colour allotted to him, places it on MOTHER EARTH, throws the dice, and moves his pawn forward over the numbered spaces according to his throw. If he throws a "double" he has the option of using the number on one or both of the dice.

When alighting on any plot of land the player must follow the instructions printed on the Board, paying Rent (ANNUAL LAND VALUE) to the owner of the site. Unbought sites are rent-free.

Any player alighting on the "Solway Fisheries" or "Lord Tomnoddy's Grouse Moor" must go to "Gaol," unless he can strike a private bargain with the owner to be let off.

Any player alighting on "Dottyville Lunatic Asylum" must wait there in accordance with instructions; and on "Lord Broadacres' Estate" must go to "Gaol" without alternative.

A player alighting on "Imperial Taxes" must pay "Breakfast-table Duties" or "Tobacco Duties" into the "Public Treasury." A player alighting on "Luxury" or "Chance" draws a "Luxury" or "Chance" card, as the case may be, follows the directions upon it and returns it to the pack, which should then be re-shuffled and placed face-downwards.

If a player should be unable to pay his debts he must sell his property for what it will fetch, borrowing by players being strictly prohibited under the rules of the game, though the Public Treasury may, if necessary, borrow from the Bank. If he has not sufficient money, and the other players refuse to buy his property at any price, he must go to the "Poorhouse" until his debts are paid.

Each player, on making a complete round of the Board, is entitled to his "Wages" which he collects from the Bank each time he passes "Mother-Earth." After making three complete rounds of the Board he is entitled to an "Old Age Pension" every time he passes "Mother Earth."

At the beginning of the game Wages are £200 and Old Age Pensions £30, but when all the "Site" cards are bought up, Wages are halved, and Rents and Taxes are doubled.

The game may be played by four, three, or two players, and is continued for a specified number of rounds, depending on the convenience of the players, and when, for example, one player has completed, say, five rounds of the Board, the amount of property in land and cash is reckoned up, and the player holding the most is the winner of the game.

NOTE: The above has been reduced to its simplest form for juvenile players, but advanced players should note that the "Undeveloped Sites" (numbered 10 and 19 on the Board) represent land which is being speculatively held up, and which may be purchased at the beginning of the game at ten per cent of its Capital Value. It should be further noticed that the values of the plots immediately in advance of the "Undeveloped Sites" are enhanced, because any player alighting on an "Undeveloped Site" is compelled to "MOVE ON" to the next space.

The "Undeveloped Sites" themselves yield no rent during Part 1 of the game, though they may be bought up cheap. In case of beginners, however, they may be treated similarly to the other sites. After play has begun the CAPITAL LAND VALUE (sale price of land) is regulated by the demand, and though no card may be bought from the pack for less than the original sale price, this may be bid up as high as the players please; while sites may be bought at a very low price from a bankrupt player who is compelled to release.

PART 2
IMPROVING THE LAND.

In this part of the game each player receives a further £3000 from the Bank. The "IMPROVEMENT" cards are exposed on the table, their numbers corresponding to the numbers on the "SITE" cards. Players begin to improve their land under the present land system, in accordance with the previous directions, and with the following additions:

A player must pay the "CAPITAL" (sale price of improvement) to the "Bank," place the card representing the improvement on the site he wishes to improve, and put his "Sold" ticket upon it. If he is unable to improve all his sites he must allow any other player, who so wishes, to improve them for him.

"Undeveloped Sites" are not improved till Part 3.

When a player alights on an improved site he follows the directions on the Board, paying the "Rent" (ANNUAL LAND VALUE) to the owner of the site, the "INTEREST" (rent of improvement) to the owner of the improvement, and the "RATES" to the Public Treasury. No Rates are payable on Religious Edifices (e.g. Westminster Abbey).

Whenever a player's property is all improved his Wages are raised to £300, but, as in Part 1, when all sites are bought up, Wages are halved, and Rents, Taxes and Rates are doubled.

PART 3
UNRATING IMPROVEMENTS AND TAXING LAND VALUES.

In this part of the game Industry and Enterprise are relieved of all Rates and Taxes, and a new standard of rating is put into operation–LAND VALUES. The players proceed as before, with the following modifications:

"RENT" (ANNUAL LAND VALUE) is still paid to the owner of the site, but, as Rates are now levied on Land Values, the owner must immediately restore the equivalent amount to the Public Treasury.

INTEREST (rent of Improvement) is still paid to the owner of the improvement, but no Rates are now payable on the improvement. It will now pay the players to improve their properties as fast as possible.

"Solway Fisheries" being now valued at £500 by the Inland Revenue Department, the owner is compelled to pay the ANNUAL VALUE of £20 to the Public Treasury. He now finds it no longer pays him to hold it, so he is glad to sell it to the Government at half its face value, which is paid out of the Public Treasury, and the Gaol Penalty is thereafter annulled.

"Lord Tomnoddy's Grouse Moor" is similarly assessed at £500, with Land Value Tax of £20, which causes him to let it for Small Holdings under conditions applying to other sites. The Gaol Penalty is thereafter annulled, and Lord Tomnoddy, being no longer able to send trespassers to Gaol, or levy blackmail from poachers, moreover having, like other landlords, to pay a Land Values Tax to the Government, finds the game up, and emigrates to Canada, leaving his steward to collect the rents, and pay them to the Public Treasury.

"Lord Broadacres' Estate" has now been turned into a Public Park, and the Gaol Penalty is annulled.

"Undeveloped Sites" are now assessed at full face value for Land Value Tax, and their owners have now an interest in improving them to the utmost.

"Breakfast-table Duties" and "Tobacco Duties" are abolished, being no longer necessary for revenue, and any player alighting on these spaces escapes payment.

Any player becoming BANKRUPT, and unable release his property need no longer go to the Poorhouse, as he can betake himself to the nearest "NATURAL OPPORTUNITY SPACE" on the Board, where land is free, without payment of rent, and where he can earn wages to pay his debts. At his next throw he receives £100 wages, and if he can then pay his debts, moves on, beginning at the corner space where he happens to be. If still unable to pay all his debts he must remain on the Free Land till he has accumulated sufficient cash to clear himself. He receives £100 wages at each throw.

"Natural Opportunities" being now freely available to Labour, WAGES are determined by the maximum which Labour can produce by working on free land.

WAGES is Part 3, therefore, rise to £500 on passing Mother Earth, whilst Poverty and Unemployment disappear forever.

APPENDIX IX
PATENT TEXT REVISED
LANDLORD'S GAME
SEPT. 23, 1924, #1,509,312

UNITED STATES PATENT OFFICE
Elizabeth Magie Phillips of Washington, District of Columbia
Gameboard
Application filed April 28,1923, Serial no. 635,246

To all whom it may concern:
Be it known that I, Elizabeth Magie Phillips, a citizen of the United States, residing at Washington in the District of Columbia, have invented certain new and useful improvements in Gameboards, of which the following is a specification.

My invention, which I call the "Landlord's Game." Relates to gameboards, and more particularly to games of skill and chance, designed also as educational in its nature, it comprises a board which is used in conjunction with dice, cubes, and the like, which indicate moves to be made by the players.

The object of the game is not only to afford amusement to the players, but to illustrate to them how under the present or prevailing system of land tenure, the landlord has an advantage over other enterprises and also how the single tax would discourage land speculation. The player who first accumulates ($3000) three thousand dollars, in cash, wins the game. The amount, or goal, may be raised, if desired.

In the drawings forming a part of this specification, and in which like symbols of reference represent corresponding parts in several views: —

Figure 1 is a plan view of the board, showing the various spaces on the same;

Figure 2 shows the various movable pieces used in the game; and,

Figure 3 is a view of three of the forty-two cards used.

THE IMPLEMENTS

The implements consist of a board, which is divided into a number of spaces; a pack of forty-two cards, forty Improvement tags; an assortment of money pieces representing ($6600) six-thousand six-hundred dollars; four 'No Trespassing' signs; one 'For Sale' sign; four checkers; one Chance cube; one pair of dice; and one dice box.

The series of spaces, for which there are twenty corresponding cards, representing land in present use, for which the players pay or receive rental according to ownership. The three yellow spaces representing real estate offices where land may be bought or sold for speculative purposes.

Railroads.—These are the three corner spaces, for which there are three corresponding cards, and represent transportation, for which players make or receive payment, according to ownership.

Public Utilities.—The three orange squares, for which there are three corresponding cards, represent public utilities, for which the players make or retrieve payment according to ownership.

Taxes.—The blue spaces represent places where taxes are paid by the players on various kinds of property.

Lord Blueblood's estate.—This space represents foreign ownership of American soil, and carries with it a jail penalty for trespassing.

Jail.—The jail represents the place of punishment for those who trespass on another's property.

LaSwelle Hotel.—The space represents the distinction made between classes, only money guests being accepted.

Wages.—This space represents the wages received for actual labor.

Land in use.—The twenty green cards represent title deeds, or ownership of the twenty corresponding board spaces representing land in actual use; and the orange cards represent the ownership of the three corresponding board spaces representing public utilities.

Idle Land.—The sixteen yellow cards represent land which is held out of use, and which is bought and sold for speculative purposes only. One of the yellow cards represents a gold mine.

Tags.—The small, variously colored tags represent improvements which may be made upon the land.

For Sale.—This sign is to be put on top of any cards that may be on the board for sale.

No Trespassing.—This sign indicates that no player except the owner may stop on the space on which it is placed.

Money denominations.—The money denominations are 8 red pieces, value $500 each, $4000; 17 green pieces, value $100 each, $1700; 13 yellow pieces, value $50 each, $650; 21 blue pieces, value $10 each, $210; and pink pieces, value $5 each, $40; making a total of $6,600.

In playing the game the cards are shuffled and dealt out one at a time to the four players until each player has received eight cards. The remainder of the cards are placed in the middle of the board, with the "For Sale" sign on top of the same. Players own the board spaces according to the cards they hold. Yellow cards have no corresponding board space.

After the cards are shuffled each player is provided with a checker, one Improvement tag, one No Trespassing tag, tags being same color as checker, and $500 in game money pieces. For convenience in making change take 3 $100 (green), $300; 3 $50 (yellow), $150; 4 $10 (blue), $40; and 2 $5 (pink), $10; making a total of $500.

In the drawings I have designated the cards by the numeral 2; Improvement tags 3; money pieces 4; No Trespassing signs 5; For Sale sign 6; checkers 7; Chance cube 8; dice 9; and dice box 10.

Each player puts his Improvement on any land space owned by himself; all players putting their checkers in the wages corner from which they begin to count. The dice are thrown to determine the first player, high winning. First player then throws his dice and moves along the board to the left, the number of spaces indicated by the dice. Count Jail space 1, Wayback 2, etc., the player following the rule applying to the space upon which he has stopped, the rules number being found in margin of board space.

The object of each player is to be the first to accumulate $3000 and thus win the game. The limit may be raised at the option of the players. The various ways in which the players obtain money are from rent (for land or improvement); railroad fares; public utilities; wages which they receive each time they make a complete round of the board; and from the sale of Idle land cards.

RULES

1. *Land in use.*—A player stopping on this space is supposed to be occupying and using the land, and pays to the owner thereon the amount of land rent indicated. If there is an "Improvement" on this land, he pays $100 in addition to the land rent. If a player is himself owner of the space, he takes from the board the amount of rent indicated. If the space is for sale, that is, if the corresponding card is still on the board, all the players bid for it, the highest bidder paying to the board the amount of his bid and taking the card into his hand. If there is a No trespassing sign on the space, a player cannot stop there at all, unless it is his own, but must go to jail, that is, put his checker on the Jail space. If at any time a player has no money, or an insufficient amount to meet his obligations, he must sell one of his cards to one of the other players, getting the best price he can for it. If the proceeds from the sale are still insufficient he must offer other cards for sale until he realizes enough to pay his debts. When a player has no money and no cards he is out of the game.

2. *Local public utility.*—A player on this space pays to the owner the amount indicated ($50). Or, if he himself holds the franchise card, he takes $50 from the board. If one player owns the three local public utilities Slambang Trolley, Soakum Lighting System, and Ting-a-Ling Telephone Company, he has a Monopoly. In case of a Monopoly the rates are raised to $100 each space.

3. *Railroad.*—A player on this space pays to the owner thereof the amount indicated ($100). Or, if he is himself the owner, he takes that amount from the board. If one player owns all three railroads, he has a Monopoly. In case of a Monopoly the railroad fare in each case is $200. After payment of the railroad fare a player may move to any space he pleases 8 or a less number of spaces either forward or backward.

4. *Real Estate Office.*—A player in this space may sell to the board any or all of the Idle land cards which he may hold, receiving therefore $200 each, except in the case of the Gold Mine card, for which he receives $500. Or, a player may buy one or more Idle land cards from the board, paying therefore $100 each. When buying such cards, if the Gold Mine card is among those on the board, the player must draw blindly, after the cards have been shuffled by another player. A player cannot buy and sell in the same turn.

5. *Taxes on personal property.*—A player on this space pays to the board $10 on each $100 in money that he has. If he has less than $100, he is exempt from such taxation.

6. *Taxes on land.*—A player on this space pays to the board $10 for every land card (green or yellow) that he holds.

7. *Taxes on improvements.*—A player on this space pays to the board $25 on every Improvement tag, every Railroad card (red), and every Public utility card (orange), in his possession.

8. *Lord Blueblood's estate.*—A player on this space is supposed to be trespassing and must go to jail, that is, put his checker on the Jail space.

9. *Jail.*—A player in jail must pay a fine of $50 and throw 6 or more before he may move out.

10. *LaSwelle Hotel.*—A player on this space pays to the board $25 if he has in his possession $2,000 or more in cash. If he has not such an amount, he throws his dice again and moves backwards.

11. *Wages.*—A player reaching this space stops on it, no matter how many more spots his dice show, and receives from the board $400 in wages. A player reaching this space by exact count of the dice receives $500 from the board as wages.

12. *Chance Cube.*—When a player throws a double, after moving and completing his transaction as he would on an ordinary throw, he then throws the dice again, including therewith the Chance cube. He moves, completes his transaction as usual, and then does one of the following things—according to the number shown on the uppermost side of the cube. (Note: These may be replaced by other gains or losses at the pleasure of the players. The cube runs from 5 to 30, increasing five points on each side. These indicate the penalty or reward agreed upon.) 5 Caught robbing a hen-roost—go to jail; 10 Caught robbing the public—take $200 from the board. The players will now call you Senator. 15 Draw a card from the cards (if any) left on the board. 20 Take an Improvement tag from the board. 25 Loss by fire. Return to the board your nearest Improvement tag. 30 a judgment against you. Pay $200 to the next player on your left.

SUGGESTIONS

A player may, in his turn, before throwing, buy from the board as many Improvements as he pleases, at the rate of $60 each, and place one each on any of his own (green) land spaces. For each Improvement so placed, he receives $100 rent in addition to the land rent. An Improvement once placed cannot be removed except to change its color according to change in ownership (that is, when sold to another player.)

A player may at any time in his turn put a No Trespassing sign on any (green) land space owned by himself, thus sending any trespassing player to jail. When there are at least four Improvements on any one side of the board, the land rent on that whole side of the board is doubled.

Players may buy from, sell to, or trade cards with each other at any time during the game. Preferably, all such transactions should be in the regular turn of one of the players. When a player has business transactions with the board, oftentimes it would avoid confusion, dispute, and playing too soon, if the player next to the left should act as clerk for one playing.

Having now fully explained my invention, what I claim are new, and desire to secure by Letters Patent, is:—

1. A gameboard, provided with corner spaces, intervening spaces of different denominations and values, some of the spaces of the different series corresponding and distinguished by coloring or other marking, so that the corresponding divisions may be recognized, a series of cards of changeable value, two or more of which are alike and relate to two or more certain spaces on the board, and a series of movable pieces to be used in conjunction with the spaces of the board and controlled by dice, so as to determine the play.

2. A gameboard, provided with corner spaces, intervening spaces of different denominations and values, some of the spaces having distinct markings, some of the intervening spaces corresponding with each other, movable and interchangeable pieces which may be used in combination with the board and with each other, dice, a cube to be used in combination with the dice and with the board, said cube having upon its faces symbols to indicate a condition or move.

3. A gameboard, provided with corner spaces, intervening spaces of different denominations and values and distinguished by suitable marking, dice, cards representing franchises, title to land in use and to land held out of use, Improvement tags, checkers, and a Chance cube to be used with the dice and with the board.

4. A gameboard, provided with corner spaces, intervening spaces having distinctive markings, some of them representing offices and buildings, railroad transportation, foreign ownership of American soil, wages, land in use and land held out of use, and a series of cards of changeable value, tags representing improvements on the land, money pieces, No Trespassing signs, For Sale sign, and a cube to be used in combination with the board, said cube having upon its face symbols to indicate a condition or a move.

5. A gameboard, provided with corner spaces, intervening spaces, some of the intervening spaces being identical in combination with a pack of cards, some

having changeable value and having relation to more than one board space, tags representing improvements, money pieces, No Trespassing signs, For Sale signs, checkers to indicate the action of different players, a pair of dice, and a Chance cube to be used with the dice and a board, said cube having symbols to indicate a condition or a move.

In testimony whereof I affix my signature.

ELIZABETH MAGIE PHILLIPS

APPENDIX X
RULES FOR FINANCE

PROCEDURE FOR BEGINNERS

Set up the FINANCE board. Shuffle the red cards and place them face down in the corner of the board marked Chance Cards. Place the green cards in the corner marked Community Chest Cards. Put poker chips and paper money in the middle of the board. This represents the Bank. Each player takes $1,000 in FINANCE money and a playing piece or "man."

Appoint one player to be Auctioneer. This in no way changes his capacity as a player. The Auctioneer takes custody of the large yellow cards, which are property leases. These he arranges in numbered order with No. 1 on top (number in lower right corner).

Roll the dice and high man moves first. He rolls the dice again and moves his man a corresponding number of spaces from the corner marked Start toward the corner marked Taxes. If he stops on the space marked Community Chest he cuts the green cards and pays into the Bank the amount stipulated on the card cut. If he stops on Chance he cuts the red cards and does as his card directs. If he stops on 10 percent Tariff he must pay 10 percent of all his cash only to the Bank. If he stops on Taxes $20, he pays the Bank $20. If any player stops on Luxury $75 (further around the board) he pays the Bank $75. In moving around the board, play on the inside corner spaces only.

If a man is moved onto any space with a proper name, the Auctioneer selects the corresponding card from his stack of leases (yellow cards) and offers the space, or "property," for sale. It is then sold to the highest bidder, who pays the amount of his final bid to the Bank. The Auctioneer gives the lease card to the purchaser. The owner may collect the amount of rent stipulated in the upper left corner of the lease from every player who stops on his property thereafter.

The players move in rotation, the Auctioneer watching each new property space as it is stopped on and offering it for sale if it has not been sold. This continues until all the properties have been sold.

EACH PLAYER COLLECTS FROM THE BANK AN INCOME OF $250 EVERY TIME HIS MAN TRAVELS COMPLETELY AROUND THE BOARD.

Certain properties have a cash value printed beside them on the board. On any of these spaces, owners may build houses and increase their rent income. But before any owner may erect a house he must own a complete series of properties.

A COMPLETE SERIES of properties consists of all the spaces having the same cash value. All properties in the same series are the same color. A printed list of the series groups appears inside the back cover of this rule book.

A player who owns a complete series of properties may erect a house at any time. The cost of a house is the same as the cash value of the property it is built on (printed on the board and on each lease).

A house owner collects higher rent according to his lease card. For example, on WAYBACK (lease No. 1) one house raises the ordinary $2 rent to $10, to be paid to the owner by all who subsequently stop on this space; two houses bring the owner $30; three houses bring $80; four houses bring $160; five houses bring $200. (See under "House Rents" on WAYBACK lease card.) Each property has corresponding increases as shown on its lease card.

No player can build more than five houses on one space. Each owner can have but one house more on one space than on any other in the same series.

A player may buy, sell or trade property with another at any time, provided his man is not in motion and his debts are settled.

A player is forced to withdraw from the game when he cannot raise sufficient funds to pay a legitimate rent. When a player is put out, all his property is withdrawn from the game. The leases go back to the Bank and cannot be sold again.

The last player to remain in the game is the winner.

Players should not try to learn too much from the rule book before playing. Very little need be remembered is order to play, and the learning comes quite easily from playing a single game. For beginners to play a satisfactory game, they need only refer to the following:

1. Each player take $1,000 at start.
2. Take $250 every time around the board.
3. Men line up in space marked Start and move clockwise according to players' dice.
4. At the corners play only on inside triangular spaces.
5. When man stops on Community Chest, cut green cards and pay Bank.
6. On Chance, cut a red card and do as directed.
7. Taxes—pay Bank $20. Luxury—pay Bank $75.
8. Auction spaces with proper names when stopped on for first time.
9. Owners build houses and collect higher rents.
10. When you cannot pay a rent, retire.

Properly speaking, there are few "rates" to Finance. Certain customs are given here which have been found to work well in playing, but players need not at first actually know and follow them all to play an interesting game.

OBSERVANCES FOR BEGINNERS

JAIL. When a player stops on the corner (or cuts the Chance card) which reads "Go to Jail," he moves his man back to the corner marked Jail. On his next turn he may pay $50 and come out, or if he rolls double dice he comes out free. He may stay in Jail for three turns, attempting to roll double dice. On the third turn he must come out whatever the number rolled.

MORTGAGES. Each property has a definite value (printed on the board and in upper right corner of lease). Any owner may borrow this amount from the Bank at any time. Simply turn the lease face down with a corner under the gameboard and take the cash value from the Bank. By returning to the Bank this cash value plus 10 percent interest, the mortgage may be redeemed.

HOUSES CANNOT BE BUILT NOR RENT COLLECTED ON MORT-GAGED PROPERTY.

HOUSES. Houses can be built only on a completed series, no property of which is mortgaged. The cost per house is the same as the printed value of the property. Houses once built may be "torn down" to raise money. An owner receives from the Bank half the purchase price of each house he tears down. Full price must be paid to rebuild.

RAILROADS. Railroads pay a straight income depending on the number owned by one player. A player having one lease gets $15 per ride; two leases bring $30; three leases bring $70; four leases bring $150. (These amounts appear on each Railroad lease.)

U. G. I. AND A. P. & L. These public utilities pay a variable income depending on the dice of the player who stops on them. One lease pays 4 times. Both leases pay 10 times. For example, if a player rolls a 5 on the dice which brings him to U. G. I., he pays the owner $5 x 4 or $20. He pays $5 x 10 or $50 if the owner also has A. P. & L.

PARTNERSHIPS. If two or more players own the Railroads, they may combine and share the full income according to their own arrangement. This may be done also with the power companies (U. G. I. and A. P. & L.). Two players cannot share income on any other properties.

TO THE AUCTIONEER

When any piece of property is put up for sale, the Auctioneer must announce whether it is the 1st, 2nd or 3rd piece in that series to be auctioned. No player may volunteer information concerning who has bought which properties.

When the bidding is in process, the Auctioneer should call each raise three times unless the price is again raised before he can do so. For instance, he should say, "Going once for $305. Going twice for $305. And sold for $305." The word "and" should be distinctly prolonged to allow for last-minute bidding.

Bids are always raised by a minimum of $5 because odd dollar raises simply prolong the process unnecessarily.

The Auctioneer may sell the last 3 or 4 properties without waiting for them to be stopped on if their non-sale delays the game. Do not sell all at one time. Sell the lowest number first.

SUGGESTIONS FOR EXPERIENCED PLAYERS

JAIL INSURANCE. Players may insure against going to Jail by paying $25 to the Bank on approaching the "Go to Jail" corner. The $25 must be paid before throwing the dice. If the player's man falls short of the corner, he must pay another $25 if he wishes to insure on his next turn. $5 insures against going to jail by a Chance card.

HOUSE OWNERS. A house owner cannot insure against Jail.

A player with 3 or more houses on one property cannot "languish" in Jail, but must come out on his first turn. He gets choice of three throws of the dice, all taken on the same turn. Each throw cancels opportunity to use the previous one.

A house owner cannot buy or take in trade property of which he does not already own at least one in the same series.

PAUPERS. A player cannot be put out of the game by a debt to the Bank. If all his property is mortgaged and he has less than $100 in cash, all payments resulting from Chance, Community Chest, Taxes, etc., are reversed in his favor.

FORGETTERS. If a player forgets to collect his $250 on the turn in which he completes the circuit of the board, he forfeits his right to collect it at all on that trip around.

If a player forgets to collect a rent or strike off a free ride, he forfeits the right to do so the moment the debtor moves his man away legitimately.

DOUBLE RENT. A player owning a complete series unmortgaged and without houses may collect double the regular rent.

SOMETIMES. Sometimes when a player is put out, only his completed series are withdrawn from the game. His odd property is auctioned again as before. This must be agreed to in advance.

UTILITY DEALS. If two or more players are splitting a full utility income, one player must actually hold all the leases. After the deal the leases cannot again change hands. The holding owner must guarantee his partner's income even if he mortgages his partner's leases. The latter forfeits his right to mortgage the leases handed over. If the holding owner is put out, all the leases go with him. If the partner is put out, the holding owner becomes full owner.

FREE RIDES. Property sellers often ask for "free rides" in compensation for less cash. A free ride is the privilege of stopping on a property without paying rent. Although a player may sell only one property in a series, his free rides are good on the entire series unless otherwise stated for special reasons.

Usually not more than 3 free rides are asked or given on any one series, and practically never more than 5.

Electronic Laboratories, Incorporated
INDIANAPOLIS, IND.
1932

BIBLIOGRAPHY

Monopoly: The World's Most Famous Game—And How It Got That Way is largely based on my personal archives, Monopoly collection, and personal experiences spanning nearly four decades. In the course of my research, I relied on numerous printed and electronic sources. The following is a list of the significant books, manuscripts, transcripts, magazine articles, and websites I consulted.

Ansoff, H. Igor. *Corporate Strategy*. New York: McGraw-Hill, 1965.

Anspach, Ralph. *The Billion Dollar Monopoly Swindle*. Palo Alto, CA: American, 1998.

Anti-Monopoly, Inc. v. General Mills Fun Group, Inc., C-74-0529, LAB, November 1976.

Brady, Maxine. *The Monopoly Book*. New York: David McKay, 1974.

Carruth, Gorton. *What Happened When*. New York: Signet, 1989.

Chernow, Ron. *Titan*. New York: Vintage, 1998.

Clay, John. *Culberton*. London: Weidenfeld & Nicolson, 1985.

Darzinskis, Kaz. *Winning Monopoly*. New York: Harper & Row, 1987.

DiBacco, Thomas. *Made in U.S.A.* New York: Harper & Row, 1987.

Gordon, John. *The Business of America*. New York: Walker, 2001.

Hixson, Walter. *Parting the Curtain*. New York: St. Martin's, 1997.

"Honey, They Shrunk the Fed." *Business Week,* November 7, 2005.

Morris, Edmund. *Theodore Rex*. New York: Random House, 2001.

Nearing, Scott. *The Good Life*. New York: Shocken, 1989.

_____. *The Making of a Radical*. White River Junction, VT: Chelsea Green, 2000.

Orbanes, Philip. *The Game Makers*. Cambridge: Harvard Business School Press, 2003.

_____. *The Monopoly Companion*. Boston: Adams Media, 1999.

Porter, Glenn. *The Rise of Big Business*. Arlington Heights, IL: Harlan Davison, 1992.

Ruoff, Henry. *Century Book of Facts*. Springfield, MA: King-Richardson, 1900.

Sackson, Sid. *A Gamut of Games*. New York: Random House, 1968.

Standiford, Lee. *Meet You in Hell*. New York: Crown, 2005.

Stryker, Roy, and Nancy Wood. *This Proud Land*. New York: Galahad, 1973.

Walsh, Tim. *Timeless Toys*. New York: Andrews McMeel-Universal, 2005.

WEBSITES

Wikipedia: The Free Encyclopedia: www.wikipedia.org.

The Association of Game and Puzzle Collectors: www.agpc.org.

The following are Monopoly-related sites:

Albert Veldhuis: www.muurkrant.nl/monopoly.

Anti-Monopoly: www.antimonopoly.com.

Dan Fernandez: www.sundown-farm-and-ranch.com.

Hasbro's Monopoly page: www.monopoly.com.

Michael Salvucci: www.monopolymuseum.com.

Paul Fink: www. gamesandpuzzles.com.

Thomas Forsyth: www.tt.tf.

Tim Walsh: www.theplaymakers.com.

USAopoly: www.usaopoly.com.

Winning Moves UK: www.winningmoves.co.uk.

World of Monopoly: www.worldofmonopoly.co.uk.

PHOTO CREDITS

The visual matter in this book is based on games and materials in the author's personal collection except for the following:

Photos of the 1906 Landlord's Game and the Arden Landlord's Game are © 2005 Thomas Forsyth. Used with permission.

Photos of the circular Darrow game, Todd board, and corresponding Darrow square oilcloth board are © 2005 Forbes Gallery. Used with permission.

Photo of Scott Nearing courtesy of The Good Life Center, Harborside, Maine, and the Thoreau Institute at Walden Woods, Lincoln, Massachusetts.

Photos of Victor Watson I and Norman Watson are courtesy of Victor Watson II.

Photos of Robert and Randolph Barton and George Parker are courtesy of Randolph Barton.

Photo of Merwin Goldsmith as Mr. Monopoly, the 2004 U.S. Championship game, and of Philip Orbanes being interviewed near the Monopoly Express are courtesy of Merwin Goldsmith.

Photo of Matt McNally is courtesy of Matt McNally.

Photo of Sid Sackson is courtesy of Sid Sackson.

Photo of the Sherk game board is courtesy of the Berks County Historical Society and Chris Williamson.

Photo of Chris Williamson is courtesy of Chris Williamson.

Photo of handmade Monopoly components is courtesy of Ken Koury.

Photo of Albert Veldhuis is courtesy of Albert Veldhuis.

Photos of Roy Stryker, Columbia, and Rexford Tugwell are courtesy of Charis Wilson.

INDEX

WITHDRAWN

CPSIA information can be obtained
at www.ICGtesting.com
Printed in the USA
LVHW04s1513220518
578093LV00002B/376/P